Children and violence

Report of the
Gulbenkian Foundation Commission

The UK branch of the Calouste Gulbenkian
Foundation has taken the UN Convention on the
Rights of the Child, 'protecting the dignity, equality
and human rights' of children, as a broad
framework within which to initiate and support
specific projects of benefit to children and young
people. Particular attention is given to strategic
national and regional proposals which reflect the
values contained in the Convention.

Published by Calouste Gulbenkian Foundation
London 1995

Distribution by Turnaround Distribution Ltd,
27 Horsell Road, London N5 1XL.
0171 609 7836

Published by Calouste Gulbenkian Foundation
98 Portland Place, London W1N 4ET. Telephone 0171 636 5313

Designed by Susan Clarke for Expression Printers Ltd
Cover design by Chris Hyde
Printed by Expression Printers Ltd, London N5 1JT

ISBN 0–903319–75–6

British Library Cataloguing-in-Publication data
A catalogue record for this book is available from the British Library.

Contents

Section 2
Reducing violence involving children –
discussion and recommendations   77

Introduction

The Commission on Children and Violence was conceived during a wave of media debate and apparent public concern at levels of violence involving children, and in particular at perceived levels of violence by children.

The Commission has no desire to add to unrealistic fears of violence to or by children; its aims have been to research and summarise available knowledge of the extent of violence involving children, and why children become violent, and then to make recommendations for reducing all forms of inter-personal violence involving children.

In comparison with the USA, levels of inter-personal violence in the UK are very modest, and there is recent evidence that in comparison with some European countries, levels of violence by children in the UK are low. In terms of trends it appears that children's involvement in some but not all crimes of violence in the UK has increased over the last decade. It remains true that only a very small proportion of children (three out of four of them male) get involved in committing violent offences.

There is increased knowledge of and sensitivity about violence to children, in particular sexual abuse, and bullying and other ill-treatment in institutions; it is not possible to tell whether the incidence of these and other forms of violence to children has increased or is simply more generally recognised, and there are obvious problems about building any accurate picture of the extent of violence to children within families.

In general, children are far more often victims of violence than perpetrators. Some age groups of children are disproportionately at risk of serious violence. One of the most disturbing social statistics is that babies aged under one are the age group most at risk of homicide; while the number of cases per year is small, the risk is four times as great as for any other age group.

It seems to the Commission that as individuals and as a society we are now faced with a crucial choice in relation to violence. No nation can afford to be complacent about any level of inter-personal violence. If we are to ensure that we do not follow the path of the USA, we have to commit ourselves to work towards a non-violent society. In America a child dies from gunshot wounds

1

every two hours; between 1979 and 1991 almost 50,000 American children were killed by firearms – equal to the number of US battle casualties in the Vietnam war; homicide is the 12th leading cause of death, and for black youths aged between 15 and 34 it is the leading cause of death. Bullet-proof vests, metal detectors and armed police are common in big-city schools.

Nobody, surely, wants a violent society. This is an issue on which we can expect and demand a consensus. A commitment to non-violence does not have to be pacifist, or non-competitive.

At the moment, our attitudes to violence, and in particular to violence involving children, are inconsistent. We do not consistently denounce violence. Macho male stereotypes are promoted and admired. Our appetite for very violent images appears to be on the increase. We still enthusiastically follow sports in which deliberately injuring opponents is the central aim. Politicians and other public figures still advocate violent punishments for children, despite the evidence that they will undoubtedly make the problem of violence worse. Physical punishment of children remains legally and largely socially acceptable – unique among forms of inter-personal violence.

Action to reduce and prevent violence is generally unco-ordinated (apart from child abuse protection, which only covers part of the full spectrum of violence to children). It is given no particular priority within crime prevention.

The Commission believes that the current context of heightened concern over violence involving children makes this the right moment to promote a formal and active commitment to non-violence. While the overall aim is the creation of a safe, non-violent society for all, our focus is on children because there is ample evidence to show that early intervention is vital to prevent the development of violent attitudes: that what happens in the early years, and in particular within the family and in schools, is most influential in determining attitudes to violence. We know more than enough of the factors that interact to cause violence to be able to promote detailed positive strategies, above all, strategies for positive parenting.

Our recommendations seek to make the commitment to non-violence, and the work required to build a non-violent policy, as comprehensive as possible. We believe the commitment should be perceived as having the same priority as a commitment to equal opportunities.

Of course much is already being done, consciously or unconsciously, to reduce or prevent violence involving children in the home, in schools and other institutions, and in community safety and child protection strategies locally and nationally. Existing programmes which help to prepare for parenthood, to support parenting and caring, and to provide positive opportunities for the optimal development of children and families are contributing to violence prevention. But reviewing all such programmes as we propose from a specifically anti-violence perspective goes further, focusing on what can be done within programmes and services to prevent and combat violence and replace it with positively non-violent attitudes, aspirations and behaviour.

We advocate comprehensive anti-violence policies because the other route, which may appear to some politically attractive, of attempting to identify high risk children, and to target resources on them, is full of dangers; it will wrongly identify some, miss many others, and create stigmatising services which may not be accepted, and which do little to emphasise every individual's responsibility for creating a non-violent society. Even more dangerous is the trend back towards more punitive responses to children, more custody for offenders; we are convinced that this will make the problem of violence worse.

The sort of policies and interventions which we propose from a violence prevention perspective will be of benefit to the whole community, since many of the factors implicated in the development of violent attitudes and actions are also linked to other forms of anti-social and criminal behaviour. Effective action to prevent or minimise violence can be expected to increase general levels of socialised behaviour.

The recommendations of the Commission arise not only from knowledge of the antecedents of violence, but also from the principles and standards of the United Nations Convention on the Rights of the Child. The Convention provides a framework for policy development for children, and one which the UK Government, through its ratification of the Convention, is committed to implementing. (Appendix 2, page 251, summarises relevant provisions of the Convention).

The Commission's aims and working definitions

Aims

The aims adopted by the Commission are to collect and disseminate through a report proposals aimed at reducing all forms of inter-personal violence involving children and young people in the UK.

In particular the Commission aims to:
(i) provide as accurate a picture as possible of the level of all kinds of violence to and by children and young people.
(ii) propose ways of challenging social and legal endorsement of any form of inter-personal violence and policies and practices which tend to increase violence involving children and young people.

Like other recent projects supported as part of the Gulbenkian Foundation's Social Welfare Programme, the Commission also aims overall to encourage a children's perspective in policy development, proper respect for the UN Convention on the Rights of the Child and a higher political priority for children and their development.

Definition of violence

Violence is defined as behaviour by people against people liable to cause physical or psychological harm.

Definition of child

'Child' is defined as in the UN Convention as everyone from birth to their eighteenth birthday.

Acknowledgements

The Commission members record their appreciation of the role of the Gulbenkian Foundation, which conceived the idea, convened the Commission, and hosted our meetings in agreeable surroundings.

The Foundation circulated relevant organisations and individuals about the Commission and its aims in 1993. In response it received a remarkable volume of material. Many other organisations and individuals were approached during the course of the Commission's work for further information. Libraries of government departments and major non-governmental organisations also provided much assistance for which we are grateful.

In addition, the Commission, within its limited resources, wished to hear the views of children and young people. A small number of the individuals and organisations which were initially circulated agreed that they could discuss the issues with children and young people with whom they were working. A questionnaire was drafted and circulated (see Appendix 5, page 286). The replies, from a range of schools and youth projects, have informed the Commission's work, and individual quotations have been included in the text.

Without this vast range of help and advice freely given, the Commission would have been unable to attempt the very large task it set itself. It recognises that it has not done justice to much of the material sent to it, but most sincerely thanks all those who have supported its work. Appendix 6 (page 292) lists many of those who have assisted the Commission.

In particular, the Commission thanks the staff of the National Society for the Prevention of Cruelty to Children, who have provided particular assistance with information gathering.

The Commission also extends very warm thanks to Miranda Horobin, its Research Assistant.

The Commission

The Commission on Children and Violence was convened in November 1993 by the Gulbenkian Foundation, which appointed Sir William Utting as chairman, and Peter Newell as Research Co-ordinator. The Commission invited written submissions from a variety of individuals and organisations (see Appendix 6, page 292). It held seven meetings between March 1994 and May 1995.

Members' biographies

Sir William Utting, Chairman: from 1970 to 1976 he was Director of Social Services for the Royal Borough of Kensington and Chelsea. In 1976 he became Chief Social Work Officer at the DHSS, and retired from the public service in 1991 as Chief Inspector of Social Services at the Department of Health. Throughout this time he was chief professional adviser on social services and social work to the Secretary of State. He is a member of the Committee on Standards of Conduct in Public Life.

Christopher Brown was Director of the National Society for the Prevention of Cruelty to Children from 1989 to 1995, following a career in social work and the probation service. Before joining the NSPCC he was Chief Probation Officer for Oxfordshire and then for Essex. He served on the Parole Board for England and Wales from 1985 to 1987, and has played a prominent role in social policy issues at national level.

Sheri Chamberlain is the Northern Ireland Divisional Director of Save the Children's UK and European Programmes Department having joined Save the Children as a Project Leader in 1985. In addition Sheri is a former Vice chair of the Northern Ireland Council for Voluntary Action and a founder member of the Children's Rights Alliance and the Northern Ireland Child Support Lobby Group.

Anne Crowley is a consultant on children's rights and children's advocacy. She was until 1994 Principal Advocacy Officer with the Children's Society. Based in Wales her work includes policy development around the management of youth crime, institutional care and the provision of advocacy services for young people. Before taking up this post in 1989 she worked with young offenders in Mid Glamorgan.

Paul Curno is Deputy Director of the Calouste Gulbenkian Foundation, UK Branch. He worked as a residential worker before qualifying as a Child Care Officer in the mid 1960s. He was Director of the Albany Centre in Deptford, south east London for seven years, before joining the Central Council for Education and Training in Social Work as a Social Work Education Adviser between 1972 and 1978.

Luke Daniels works at the Everyman Centre in south London, providing counselling for men who have been violent and wish to give violence up. Trained in co-counselling he has attended and led workshops on counselling for children and young people, both in the UK and US, including direct work with children in the play service. He has also worked with Exploring Parenthood, leading workshops on parenting.

Philip Graham is Chair of the National Children's Bureau and part-time Professor of Child Psychiatry at the University of Oslo. From 1975 to 1994 he was Walker Professor of Child Psychiatry, Institute of Child Health, London and Honorary Consultant Psychiatrist, Hospital for Sick Children, Great Ormond Street, London. He is also Chair of the Royal College of Physicians/ British Paediatric Association Working Party on Alcohol and the Young.

Rachel Hodgkin is Principal Policy Officer of the National Children's Bureau. She worked at the Children's Legal Centre from its inception in 1979 until 1992, and has been involved in a range of policy development work including care, education, special education, and health. She was a member of the Health Advisory Service team which reported on services for disturbed adolescents in 1986.

Penelope Leach is author of several books including *Baby & Child*; she received her PhD in psychology from the London School of Economics. A Fellow of the British Psychological Society and Chair of the Child Development Society, she works in various capacities for parents' organisations and sat on the Commission on Social Justice. Her most recent book *Children First: what our society must do – and is not doing – for our children today* was published in April 1994.

Allan Levy QC is a barrister specialising in child law and medical law who has appeared in many leading cases in these fields and is the author of four books on child law. He chaired the recent Pindown Inquiry in Staffordshire, is honorary legal adviser to the National Children's Bureau, chairman of the Intercountry Adoption Lawyers' Association, a member of the Councils of Justice and the Medico-Legal Society and a Fellow of the Royal Society of Medicine.

Kathleen Marshall was Director of the Scottish Child Law Centre from 1989 to 1994 and had previously worked as a solicitor in local government. She is currently Visiting Professor to the School of Social Work at Glasgow Caledonian University and Gulbenkian Fellow in Children's Rights at Glasgow University's Centre for the Study of the Child & Society.

Peter Newell has been co-ordinator of EPOCH – End Physical Punishment of Children – since 1989. He chairs the Council of the Children's Rights Development Unit, and is a member of the Council for Disabled Children. He is the author of *The UN Convention and Children's Rights in the UK*, 1992; and co-author of *Taking Children Seriously: a proposal for a Children's Rights Commissioner*, 1991.

Claire Rayner trained as a nurse and is the author of over ninety books, including a broad range of medical subjects from sex education for children and adults through to home nursing, as well as fiction. She is a leading 'Agony Aunt' whose page in the *Sunday Mirror* attracted fifty thousand letters annually. Among her many other commitments she is a member of the Royal College of Nursing Committee on Ethics, a member of the Video Consultative Committee of the British Board of Film Classification, President of Gingerbread, and non-executive director of Northwick Park and St Mark's NHS Hospital Trust.

Philippa Russell is Director of the Council for Disabled Children. She is an honorary member of the British Paediatric Association and of the Council of the NSPCC and Honorary Fellow of the University of Central Lancashire. She is Chair of the Mental Health Foundation's Committee on Children with Challenging Behaviour and Learning Difficulties, and has written a range of books and articles on various aspects of disability and special educational needs.

Norman Tutt trained as a clinical psychologist working with mentally ill adults and adolescents. His past positions include Principal Social Work Service Officer at the Department of Health with responsibility for advising on policy on juvenile crime, and Director of Leeds Social Services Department. He is currently Executive Director of Social Information Systems Limited, an independent research and monitoring consultancy.

Donald West is Emeritus Fellow of Darwin College, Cambridge; Emeritus Professor of Clinical Criminology, Cambridge; Mental Health Act Commissioner and Member of the Government Advisory Committee on Mentally Disordered Offenders; Vice-president of the British Society of Criminology and Member of the Council of the Howard League for Penal Reform. He has published numerous papers and reviews in journals of criminology, psychiatry and parapsychology and books on criminology.

Peter Wilson is Director of Young Minds, the National Association for Child and Family Mental Health, a newly established organisation committed to raising awareness of the mental health needs of children, young people and their families. Trained as a child psychotherapist, he has worked in a variety of child and adolescent mental health services in the UK and the USA and was a consultant psychotherapist at Peper Harow Therapeutic Community for 11 years until its closure.

Executive summary

Background

The Commission on Children and Violence was appointed by the Calouste Gulbenkian Foundation (UK Branch) to review what we know about the extent of violence involving children – violence to and by children; about why children become violent and to make recommendations for reducing and preventing all forms of inter-personal violence involving children. The Commission was chaired by Sir William Utting. Its members are listed on page 6. The Commission uses the principles and standards of the UN Convention on the Rights of the Child as a framework on which to base recommendations (see Appendix 2, page 251).

('Child' is defined as everyone from birth to their eighteenth birthday; violence is defined as 'behaviour by people against people liable to cause physical or psychological harm').

Levels of violence involving children

Children are far more often victims of violence than perpetrators of violence, and certain groups of children, including disabled children and some ethnic groups, are particularly at risk. One of the most disturbing social statistics is that the risk of homicide for babies under the age of one is four times as great as for any other age group. There is increasing knowledge of and sensitivity to violence to children, in particular to sexual abuse and to bullying and other violence in institutions; it is not possible to tell whether the incidence of these forms of violence has increased or become more visible. There are problems about building any accurate picture of violence to children within families, but the most recent UK research shows that a substantial minority of children suffer severe physical punishment; most children are hit by their parents, up to a third of younger children more than once a week.

Only a very small proportion of children – mostly male – get involved in committing violent offences. Very roughly, four per 1,000 young people aged between 10 and 18 are cautioned or convicted for offences involving violence against the person.

In terms of trends it appears that children's involvement in some but not all crimes of violence in the UK has increased over the last decade (for younger age groups and for girls and young women it may have increased quite substantially). But in comparison with the USA, overall levels of inter-personal violence in the UK are very low, and there is recent evidence that in comparison with some European countries, levels of self-reported violence by children in the UK are also low.

Why children become violent

If we want to reduce violence involving children, we need to know as much as possible about the development of violent attitudes in children and what triggers their involvement in violent actions. The Commission reviewed international research and commentaries which are summarised in the report (Section 1, page 31).

In particular, available research on child development disproves the theory – still popular in some quarters – of the original 'badness' of children.

Research into antecedents of violence cannot identify its causes beyond doubt, but it can identify risk factors, and make judgments about the relative significance of these factors. Many factors are involved and their interaction is complex. The most potent of the risk factors are clearly sited in childhood and within the family, and are amenable to change. The best predictor of violence in adulthood is violent behaviour in childhood. But that an individual child becomes violent is never inevitable; families can and often do provide the security and love necessary to protect children – even high-risk children – from becoming violent.

Violence is overwhelmingly a male problem, and the roots for this appear to be primarily social rather than biological, highlighting the inadequacies of current socialisation of male children, and the promotion of macho male attitudes and models in society.

There is no good evidence of specific genetic causation of violence by children, but one factor in a predisposition to violence may be an individual's temperament. Certain conditions affecting brain function may result in an increased risk of violent behaviour, but the numbers involved are very small, and even with such children, positive parenting can ameliorate the potential for violence. Genetic and social influences are inextricably intertwined. From the earliest age, how a child behaves will determine its relationships with others and how it is treated, by parents and other adults, by siblings and other children, and by teachers.

Most of the risk factors for violence are the same as for delinquency. Very substantial research evidence highlights negative, violent and humiliating forms of discipline as significant in the development of violent attitudes and actions from a very early age. Effects of family structure and break-up are indirect, and can be mediated through the quality of the parenting process. Inadequate monitoring and supervision of children can be crucial in the realisation of a potential for violence.

The extent to which a society condones violence influences the values of individuals within it. In the UK today there are ambivalent attitudes to violence, and in particular to violence towards children. Physical punishment and deliberate humiliation remains common and legally and socially acceptable. There is ambivalence too towards violence in sport, and adults and children show an appetite – possibly an increased appetite – for violent images, which some commercial interests do not hesitate to feed and exploit.

Economic and environmental deprivation are powerful stress factors which make it more difficult to be an effective parent: in the UK there has been a massive increase in the numbers and proportion of children living in poverty. Prejudice and discrimination can exacerbate economic inequality and poverty and increase stress. Levels of violence tend to be highest in countries with the sharpest inequalities.

School experiences undoubtedly influence children's behaviour, but it is difficult to determine their significance and whether they can be separated from factors operating in the family. Thus while much bullying occurs in schools, the principal identified factors contributing to the development of bullying are found in the child and family. But school organisation and ethos can also be significant.

The connection between mental illness and violence is also complex. A small proportion – perhaps five to 10 per cent – of adults and children involved in serious acts of violence will be classified as showing some form of mental disorder; a further significant proportion will have personality disorders.

Alcohol and substance abuse and violence may result from common factors. A high proportion of young people and adults who are victims and perpetrators of violence have been drinking alcohol. But again the connection is complex rather than direct. The illegal drug trade is related to violence largely through violent crimes committed in the course of distribution and purchase.

The extent of violent images in the media is a reflection and a part of a violent culture; that a heavy diet of violent images does nothing positive for child development is agreed, though the evidence that many children in the UK have such a diet is disputed. There is a weighty body of psychological opinion internationally which believes that higher levels of viewing violent images are correlated with increased acceptance of aggressive attitudes and increased aggressive behaviour, and may de-sensitise society, and children in particular, to violence. But these beliefs are strongly challenged by others who suggest that the analysis and attempts to isolate such effects are flawed. Other commissions on violence have suggested that media images play a minor role in producing violence. As with other factors, it is clear that the context in which a child views violent images, and the presence or absence of a critical commentary not approving of violence, is likely to influence whether or how the child is affected.

Working towards a non-violent society

In making recommendations, the Commission relied not only on its review of why children become violent, but also on the principles and standards of the UN Convention on the Rights of the Child. It is most important not to contribute to unrealistic fears of violence, and to recognise that the levels of inter-personal violence in the UK remain comparatively low. But no country can afford to be complacent about any level of inter-personal violence. The Commission believes that both as individuals and as a society, we are faced with a crucial choice in relation to violence.

A commitment to non-violence

Nobody, surely, wants a violent society: this is an issue on which we can expect and demand a consensus. But we cannot leave it to chance: building a non-violent society means turning the consensus into an overt and stated commitment to non-violence. The Commission emphasises the need to encourage and promote non-violent values in a comprehensive and consistent way. Its priority recommendations are on pages 18 – 27; these and other recommendations are expanded in Section 2, page 77.

The Commission recommends that a commitment to non-violence – which does not have to be pacifist or non-competitive – should be adopted by individuals, communities, and government at all levels; it should be of similar standing to existing commitments to equal opportunities.

The aims of the commitment are to work towards a society in which individuals, communities and government share non-violent values and resolve conflict by non-violent means. The very considerable knowledge that has accumulated about the roots of violence (see Section 1, page 31) shows that building such a society involves above all reducing and preventing violence to children, by developing:
• understanding of the factors which interact to increase the potential

for violence involving children, and those which prevent children from becoming violent
- action to prevent violence in all services which work with families and children
- consistent disavowal of all forms of inter-personal violence, in particular by opinion-leaders.

The Commission wishes to see the consensus against violence and the commitment translated into consistent action. It therefore proposes that a series of *Checklists for working towards a non-violent society* should be prepared and disseminated for parents and for all those working with or for families and children, in conjunction with appropriate working groups of practitioners. The Commission has started the process by drafting the first generic checklist on parenting (see Appendix 1, page 241).

The Commission sees positive parenting as the foundation of a non-violent society. It minimises the chances of children experiencing violence and, consequently, minimises the likelihood that they in turn will behave violently. Furthermore, the effect should be self-perpetuating, as such children are likely to grow not only into non-violent adults, but also into positive parents in their turn.

The Commission commends the following key principles to be applied to all relationships involving the care and education of children:
1 Expectations of, and demands made on, children should realistically reflect their maturity and development
2 All discipline should be positive, and children should be taught pro-social values and behaviour, including in particular non-violent conflict resolution
3 Non-violence should be clearly and consistently preferred and promoted
4 Adults should take responsibility not only for protecting children from violence done to them but also for preventing violence done by them.

The Commission recognises that any programme which contributes to timely and realistic preparation for parenthood, to practical and emotional support for parents and carers and to opportunities for optimal health and development for all children, is relevant to prevention of violence. Taken as a whole, such programmes may produce a social context which is generally unsympathetic to violence.

More specifically, the Commission believes that programmes, and the services which produce them, must be reviewed from a specifically anti-violence perspective, focusing on what is being done or could be done within the programme to prevent and combat violence by applying non-violent attitudes, aspirations and behaviour. It is this process of review at every level of practice that the proposed checklists are intended to facilitate. While parents and parent-figures are the first and arguably the most compelling influence on their children, they are not the only influence and do not act in isolation. A commitment to non-violence and a violence-prevention perspective is important in all services that can influence and impact on children and families – most obviously for those in health services, daycare, education and youth services.

Co-ordinating a UK-wide strategy against violence

The Commission sets out detailed proposals for co-ordination; working towards a non-violent society should become the first priority of community safety strategies at all levels of government, led by an inter-departmental ministerial group and reflected in regional and local co-ordination. There should be a government-sponsored media campaign to promote non-violent values and encourage work towards a non-violent society. At a broader level, the Commission commends the proposal for a statutory Children's Rights Commissioner, to promote respect for children's rights across government.

The formation and implementation of community safety strategies should become a statutory duty for local authorities. A key segment of such strategies should be to reduce and prevent violence involving children. Authorities should also be obliged to prepare and monitor implementation of children's services plans, which should include proposals for assessing and reducing and preventing violence involving children.

Appropriate voluntary organisations should come together to review existing voluntary initiatives here and abroad which aim to reduce and prevent violence involving children. They should consider how best to encourage the development of voluntary and volunteer neighbourhood initiatives, including initiatives involving children, within the framework of community safety strategies.

The Commission emphasises that all initiatives aiming to reduce and prevent violence should:
1 encourage children's active participation, and take their views seriously: this and other principles in the UN Convention on the Rights of the Child should be used as a framework for policy development
2 challenge discrimination: the violent victimisation of particular groups in society should be recognised, and protection from violence and prevention of violence should be sought without discrimination. Information and materials for violence prevention should be available in appropriate forms and languages for all communities.

Legal reforms

The Commission proposes a series of legal reforms which aim primarily to remove acceptance of violence, and to ensure that responses to violent behaviour contribute to the solution rather than the problem: these reforms include prohibiting physical punishment and humiliation of children, reviewing the criminal justice system for young offenders to ensure that its sole aims are rehabilitation and necessary protection of the public from serious harm, providing consistent obligations to act against bullying in all institutions and reviewing and simplifying the law on possession and use of firearms and other offensive weapons.

Support and services for children and families

Inequality, discrimination and lack of appropriate support and services for children and families all increase the potential for violence. So the Commission adds the compelling perspective of violence prevention to the case for urgent and concerted action to challenge the extent and growth of child poverty, and to an agenda of supportive reforms for children and families, including the following:

- reviewing arrangements for supporting working parents to establish adequate rights to child-related leave
- integrated local support services for families, made flexibly available, and comprehensive information and advice services on community resources
- good quality daycare for all who seek it, and a rapid expansion in pre-schooling
- central and local co-ordination of policy on play and leisure and adequate funding
- comprehensive health visiting and school nursing services
- comprehensive tiered mental health services, collaborating with other services and organisations to provide a comprehensive community-based treatment service
- assessment with consent and adequate rehabilitative treatment for all child victims of violence.

Other issues

The Commission reviews other issues – both particular manifestations of violence to children, and factors implicated in violence – and makes recommendations or in some cases refers to more detailed recent studies.

The following are examples of many issues related to violence prevention raised in the report:

The Commission proposes that prices of alcohol should be increased through higher taxation to provide a real disincentive to children.

It proposes that the government should set up a UK-wide review of law, policy and practice relating to child deaths (from birth to 14), to make recommendations for law, policy and practice designed to promote a better analysis and understanding of the causes of child deaths, and thus to prevent them.

It makes a series of recommendations on violent images, among them:
- that all media accessible to children should seek to realise the huge potential of the media for promoting pro-social behaviour and non-violent conflict resolution
- there should be careful monitoring of the effectiveness of classification schemes for films, videos etc. to inform debate on any further controls
- the evening watershed on television should be rigorously observed on all channels and clearly explained to viewers
- accurate information should be available about all programmes, and be displayed on the packaging of videos and other materials, to enable children, parents and other carers to exercise informed control over viewing/listening
- further codes should be developed for coverage of violent events in news reports and documentaries
- teachers and schools should seek increased critical understanding by pupils of the new communications technologies.

Information and research

The Commission proposes that government should commission a comprehensive review of available information on levels of violence to and by children in the UK, to provide recommendations for the consistent collection of data on violence and children which will both inform the public including children, and be useful for developing preventive strategies.

There should be an attempt to cost the direct and indirect, short and long-term effects of violence involving children.

Current research on the antecedents of violence involving children should be reviewed to consider how to make the best use of studies to inform prevention. Local projects aiming at violence prevention and community safety should be systematically evaluated, analysing wherever possible both short and long-term effects.

The following sets out the Commission's priority recommendations; these and other recommendations are expanded in more detail in Section 2 of the report (page 77), which specifies which people or bodies have responsibility for implementation.

1 Making a commitment to non-violence

Individuals, communities and government at all levels, should adopt a 'Commitment to non-violence', of similar standing to existing commitments to equal opportunities.

The aims of the commitment are to work towards a society in which individuals, communities and government share non-violent values and resolve conflict by non-violent means. Building such a society involves in particular reducing and preventing violence involving children, by developing:

• understanding of the factors which interact to increase the potential for violence involving children, and those which prevent children from becoming violent
• action to prevent violence in all services and work with families and children
• consistent disavowal of all forms of inter-personal violence – in particular by opinion-leaders.

(see page 80)

Translating the commitment into action: checklists for working towards a non-violent society

A series of Checklists for Working Towards a Non-violent Society, *following the framework developed in the Commission's report, should be prepared and disseminated for parents and for all those working with or for families and children, in conjunction with appropriate working groups of practitioners (see page 82).*

Principles for care and education of children which underpin a commitment to non-violence

The Commission commends the application of the following basic principles to all relationships involving the care and education of children:

1 Expectations of, and demands made on, children should realistically reflect their maturity and development

2 All discipline should be positive, and children should be taught pro-social values and behaviour, including in particular non-violent conflict resolution

3 Non-violence should be clearly and consistently preferred and promoted

4 Adults should take responsibility not only for protecting children from violence done to them but also for preventing violence done by them.

These principles should be taught to, and observed by, anyone who is involved in any capacity with children of any age. The principles are equally relevant to parents, childcare workers and teachers, and to infants, pre-school and older children.

Help and advice on reducing and preventing violence should be available to all involved in care and education of children, and should be sought if violence threatens to escalate.

(The Gulbenkian Foundation has agreed to consider co-ordinating development of further materials, and a partnership of major organisations is being formed to help. The Commission has started this process by drafting the first generic checklist on parenting – see Appendix 1, page 241).

A UK-wide media campaign to promote non-violent values and attitudes
The Department of Health and other appropriate government departments should plan and implement a media campaign aimed at developing individual and community responsibility for achieving a non-violent society, and in particular reducing and preventing violence involving children (see page 87).

Co-ordinating a UK-wide strategy against violence
Working towards a non-violent society should become the first priority of community safety strategies at all levels of government, led by an inter-departmental ministerial group and reflected in regional and local co-ordination. A key segment of such strategies should be to reduce and prevent violence involving children.

Central co-ordination
An inter-departmental Ministerial Group, covering the whole of the UK and reporting to a Cabinet Committee, should agree and oversee implementation of an ongoing UK-wide community safety strategy whose first commitment should be working

towards a non-violent society. A key segment of its work should be to reduce and prevent violence involving children.

Regional co-ordination

The Ministerial Committee for Regeneration should ensure that action to reduce violence involving children is a specific priority within its responsibility for community safety, and within the objectives of the Single Regeneration Budget.

Local co-ordination

Community safety strategies

The government should introduce legislation to make the formation and implementation of a community safety strategy a statutory duty of local authorities, setting out the duty in such a way as to encourage an inter-agency, community-based approach. The legislation should be sensitive to the structure of local government in all jurisdictions, and should ensure participation of all authorities and the voluntary and private sectors.

Working towards a non-violent society should be a key aim for local community safety strategies, focusing particularly on the reduction and prevention of violence involving children. Local strategies should set out ways of ensuring co-ordination of relevant preventive work including:
- *local planning (see page 100)*
- *child protection (see page 101)*
- *prevention of family violence (see page 106)*
- *suicide prevention (see page 189)*
- *accident prevention (see page 155)*
- *prevention of sport violence (see page 218)*
- *victim support and rehabilitation (see page 215).*

National and local media and regulatory bodies for the media should be appropriately represented in the development of community safety strategies to reduce and prevent violence involving children.

Children's services plans

The Commission welcomes the decision of the Department of Health to require local authorities to prepare and publish plans for their children's services and to monitor their implementation. These plans should be comprehensive, rather than limited to children in need, and should include proposals for assessing, reducing and preventing violence involving children (see page 104).

Voluntary neighbourhood schemes

Appropriate voluntary organisations should come together to review any existing voluntary initiatives in the UK or other countries which aim to reduce and prevent violence involving children, and to consider how best to encourage the development of voluntary and volunteer neighbourhood initiatives, including initiatives involving children, within the overall framework of community safety strategies.

Principles for implementation

The Commission emphasises that all initiatives aiming to reduce and prevent violence should:

* encourage children's active participation: children's views should be sought and given careful consideration, and their active participation should be promoted. This and other principles in the UN Convention on the Rights of the Child should be used as a framework for policy development (see Appendix 2, page 251)
* challenge discrimination: the violent victimisation of particular groups in society should be recognised, and protection from violence and prevention of violence should be sought without discrimination. Information and materials for violence prevention should be available in appropriate forms and languages for all communities.

Promoting respect for children's rights

At a broader level, the Commission strongly supports the proposal for an independent statutory office of Children's Rights Commissioner, to promote children's rights and interests at government level and to encourage co-ordination of policies affecting children. Giving children a higher priority in policy-making is crucial from many perspectives, including that of violence prevention.

2 Legal reforms

The Commission makes various recommendations for legal reform, designed in particular to remove legal tolerance for any level of violence to children, and to ensure that responses to violent behaviour contribute to violence prevention, rather than to the problem of violence.

Physical punishment and deliberate humiliation of children

The current common law defence of 'reasonable chastisement' in so far as it justifies physical punishment or other humiliating treatment or punishment should be removed for the purposes of both criminal and civil proceedings. The Commission favours removing the concept of 'reasonable chastisement' altogether and replacing it with parental duties to guide and safeguard their children according to their evolving capacities, in conformity with the UN Convention (see page 133).

Parental responsibility for children

Laws concerning the upbringing of children in all jurisdictions should provide a definition of parental responsibility, and of parental rights necessary to exercise *responsibility, based on the principles of the UN Convention on the Rights of the Child (see page 117).*

The criminal justice system

The criminal justice system for under-18 year olds should be reviewed to ensure full compliance with the UN Convention and relevant UN instruments. The age of criminal responsibility should be reviewed and raised to at least 14 throughout the UK. Rehabilitation, and necessary protection of the public from serious harm, should be the sole aims of the system. Diversion should be promoted through legislation, guidance and financial incentives (see page 172).

The Government should review the criteria for detaining children in conditions of security in the penal and all other systems, and the provision and management of all secure places, in order to ensure that children are locked up only as a last resort and for the shortest possible time compatible with defined considerations of public safety, in line with the UN Convention and other UN instruments (see page 177).

The proposals concerning child witnesses in the Pigot Report should be implemented in full (see page 168).

Bullying

Responsible government departments should require all institutional settings for children and young people, both day and boarding, in the state, voluntary and private sectors to implement policies for preventing bullying and protecting children from bullying (see page 143).

Guns and weapons

The law on possession and use of firearms including air guns by children should be reviewed and simplified, with a bar on any possession or unsupervised use below the age of 14, and strict and consistent controls on possession and use under 18. Information about the simplified law should be adequately disseminated to children and parents (see page 224).

Pornography, children and violence

The Government should support European and international moves to harmonise legislation and promote measures to reduce the involvement of children in pornography (see page 211).

Boxing

The Commission supports the international and national campaigns for the eventual abolition of boxing and any other sporting activities in which causing a degree of injury to opponents is an aim. As a matter of urgency and a prelude to abolition, the involvement of children in boxing should be strongly discouraged (see page 220).

3 Support and services for children and families

Inequality, discrimination and lack of appropriate support and services for children and families all increase the potential for violence. The Commission therefore adds the perspective of violence prevention to the case for the following reforms:

Challenging inequality and poverty

The Commission recommends urgent and concerted government action to challenge the extent and growth of child poverty in the UK. Economic and taxation policies should seek to reduce inequality and ensure that basic benefit levels for those dependent on benefit match the actual costs of children. 16 and 17 year olds should be entitled to income support if they are unemployed and are not offered an appropriate training place. Benefit levels for those under 25 living independently should be the same as those for over 25-year olds (see page 112).

Family support

The Government should review arrangements for supporting working parents in order to establish rights to:
* *paid parental leave for either parent following maternity leave*
* *paid paternity leave and job re-instatement following birth or adoption*
* *paid family leave for illness and other emergencies*
* *grants or loans for new parents for appropriate equipment to prevent home accidents.*
(see pages 120-122).

Local authorities should be encouraged to develop integrated support services for families and bring them together in centres so that the full range is flexibly available to all children and carers, with an emphasis on suiting individual families' life-styles and preferences. In addition every local authority should offer a comprehensive information and advice service on community resources (statutory, voluntary and private) (see pages 122-128).

Early years care and education

The daycare review duty placed on local authorities should ensure that all authorities develop costed action plans for the provision of good quality daycare for all who seek it (see page 125).

The Commission adds the violence prevention perspective to the case for rapidly expanding pre-school education, welcomes the Government's current (1995) commitment to some expansion, and endorses the target of the National Commission on Education that by the year 2005 pre-school education places should be provided for 85 per cent of three year olds and 95 per cent of four year olds (see page 137).

Schools and education service

Education services and schools should adopt the commitment to non-violence and adapt and supply the checklists; non-violence should be recognised as a priority within the curriculum.

Children's opportunities for play and leisure

There should be central and local co-ordination of policy on play and leisure opportunities for children, and adequate funding to take account of the special needs of children and the proportion of the overall population which they form. Local authorities' corporate strategies must include planning of adequate play and leisure opportunities for children, and must be linked with community safety strategies; both must see re-asserting children's appropriate freedom of movement, through reduction of violence and unrealistic fear of violence, as an essential aim (see page 147).

Health services

The Department of Health should recognise that violence is a serious public health problem, and mount a new programme of prevention, based on research. The crucial surveillance and education role of health visitors should be protected and made available throughout the UK. Similarly, the school nursing service should be expanded appropriately to cover all schools (see page 151).

Mental health services

Within a comprehensive mental health service, primary care professionals should receive consultation, training and support in the identification and first line management of children with violent behavioural problems. If children have not responded to primary care management, facilities for assessment and treatment at the secondary level should be available within six weeks for all children showing significant violent behaviour, especially those with conduct disorders. Parents and teachers should have the opportunity to consult secondary care professional staff, even if the children themselves do not wish to be seen.

Mental health services should develop collaborative work with other organisations in the community to provide a comprehensive community-based treatment service (see page 158).

Victims of violence

All child victims of violence should be offered appropriate assessment to determine what measures are needed to promote recovery and social integration. Sufficient resources must be available for necessary rehabilitation. Compensation should be available to child victims of violence, taking full account of physical and psychological harm. Awards of compensation should not be dependent on prosecution of perpetrators (see page 215).

'Domestic' or family violence

All organisations concerned with violence within close relationships should consider the safety and welfare of children at all times, including episodes in which violence occurs only between adults (see page 162).

4 Other issues

Alcohol and substance abuse

Prices of alcohol should be increased through higher taxation to provide a real disincentive for children. Those involved in alcohol production, distribution, marketing and sales should be encouraged to adopt the commitment to non-violence, and to develop clear guidelines and voluntary controls to prevent alcohol abuse by children, as well as cooperating fully to ensure that legislative controls are rigorously enforced (see page 195).

Community-based sources of help for substance addiction should be adequately resourced.

Child death inquiries

As a matter of urgency, the government should set up a UK-wide review of law, policy and practice relating to child deaths (birth to 14), with appropriate inter-departmental observers. The review should cover:
* the law on child homicide including the various relevant offences, and policy and practice over prosecution
* law, policy and practice on recording and investigation of all child deaths, by coroners, medical personnel, social services and so on
* collection and interpretation of statistics relating to child deaths.

Its terms of reference should enable it to make recommendations for law, policy and practice designed to promote a better analysis and understanding of the causes of child deaths, and to prevent child deaths (see page 184).

Suicide and self-harm

The Government's Health Target relating to suicide should be amended to include a particular focus on reducing suicide and attempted suicide among young people.

The Department of Health should prepare information materials and ensure their wide circulation to appropriate professionals, voluntary agencies, parents and young people on identification of risk of suicide and self-harm (including eating disorders), and prevention. This should include clear information on when and how to seek specialist help and counselling, lists of relevant statutory and voluntary agencies; all those involved in developing programmes in schools and communities should be particular targets for information and training (see page 189).

Children and the violent conflict in Northern Ireland

On the basis of expert advice, the Government should develop a comprehensive strategy and make available appropriate resources to enable individuals and communities within Northern Ireland to address the effects of the violent conflict on children (see page 198).

Violent images and violence involving children

All media accessible to children should seek to realise the huge potential of the media for promoting pro-social behaviour and non-violent conflict resolution and discouraging inter-personal violence.

All those involved in the production, distribution and sale of media which may include violent images should be aware of the state of current knowledge of the potential effect on children who may have access to them.

The Commission recommends careful monitoring by regulatory bodies of the effectiveness of the classification schemes for films, videos etc., including recent changes in the Criminal Justice and Public Order Act 1994, to inform debate on any further controls.

On television, the evening watershed should be rigorously observed on all channels and clearly explained to viewers in all programme guides. A code should be developed for the coverage of violent events by news and documentary programmes which emphasises the importance of accurate reporting, avoiding exaggeration, not dwelling on the detail of violence, and providing careful warnings to viewers. Similarly, there should be explicit guidance to counter any encouragement of violence in sport.

All relevant bodies should ensure accurate information is available on programmes, and on the packaging of videos and other materials, which indicate clearly the content, and enable children, parents and other carers to exercise informed control over viewing/listening.

All teachers and schools should seek increased critical understanding by pupils of the new communications technologies: the importance of this should be reflected in arrangements for the curriculum throughout the UK. Public education and participation in media policies should be encouraged through public forums organised by the industry and regulators (see page 205).

The Commission believes that in relation to toy manufacture and marketing, a combination of safety regulations, voluntary controls on 'aggressive' toys, and accessible advice to parents and other carers is required (see page 213).

5 Information and research on violence involving children

Statistics and other information

Appropriate government departments should commission a review of available information on levels of violence to and by children in the UK, undertaking in a more comprehensive way the exercise attempted by the Commission and reported in Appendix 3 (page 256). The review should provide recommendations for the consistent and accurate collection of data on violence involving children which will both inform the public including children and provide information useful for the development of preventive strategies.

There should be an attempt to 'cost' the direct and indirect short- and long-term effects of violence involving children.

Research

Relevant research bodies, and in particular the Economic and Social Research Council, Department of Health and Home Office should jointly review current research on the antecedents of violence in children, and how to make the best use of longitudinal studies to give information on risk factors for violence.

Statutory and voluntary bodies responsible for funding local projects aimed at violence prevention and community safety should insist on arrangements to ensure systematic evaluation, wherever possible, both short- and long-term (see page 230).

Section 1
Why children become violent

Introduction

Reading most newspapers at the end of the trial of
James Bulger's two 10 year old murderers, one
might have thought that little or nothing was
known of the reasons why children become violent.
The conduct of the case had certainly not encouraged
any overt investigation into why these two small
boys had acted so savagely. The judge described the
boys' action as 'an act of unparalleled evil and

> Quotes boxed in the text are
> from children and young
> people who took part in
> discussions based on a
> questionnaire circulated by
> the Commission – see
> Appendix 5, page 286.

barbarity'. It was hard to comprehend, Judge Moreland told the court, 'how it
came about that two mentally normal boys, aged 10, and of average
intelligence, committed this crime'. It was not for him to pass judgment on
their upbringing, 'but I suspect that exposure to violent video films may in
part be an explanation'.

While no-one would wish to under-state the horror of what happened to
James, the tragedy for his family, friends and community, it was not
unparalleled. The risk of being a victim of murder is greatest in the first few
years of life. Usually it is their parents who murder babies and children in
horrible ways, but there has also been a very small but steady succession of
cases in which children have murdered children.[1] The high-profile
highlighting of one possible 'explanation' did nothing to increase overall
understanding: in fact the police investigating the case have stated that there
was no evidence that either boy had seen the particular video implicated –
Child's Play Three. Bearing in mind the information now available about the
boys' backgrounds, it is surprising none of it surfaced at the trial.

But the judge's suspicion had given the tabloids something to bite on. Their
headlines took us straight back to original sin: the
boys were 'Freaks of nature: the faces of normal
boys but they have hearts of unparalleled evil' ...
'Two evil freaks' ... 'Judge blames violent videos.'[2]

> 'Perhaps it's the way they
> are treated at home or the
> sort of school they go to. You
> can get hard against what
> life throws at you and hard to
> what happens at home.'

If we want to reduce violence involving children,
violence to them and violence by them, we need to
know as much as possible about the development of

violent attitudes and involvement in violent actions. This section of the report seeks to summarise briefly our current knowledge, which is considerable, as a prelude to drafting recommendations for action which by influencing one or more of the identified contributory factors, may help to reduce all forms of inter-personal violence involving children.

Violence by children is inextricably linked to violence to them. Available research disproves the still-popular theory of the original badness of children. Scapegoating of children for the development of violence when most of the identified determinant factors are controlled by adults is to do children a gross injustice, and moves us away from rather than towards solutions. And it is important to emphasise that only a very small proportion of children get involved in violence, as the review in Appendix 3 (page 256) shows.

A recent review of the backgrounds of a large sample of children who have killed or committed other grave (usually violent) crimes – section 53 offenders – found that 72 per cent had experienced abuse, and 57 per cent significant loss (death or loss of contact with someone important). 35 per cent had experienced both phenomena and a total of 91 per cent had experienced one or both. The report of the research emphasises that

> 'Not all children who experience these phenomena become violent offenders, and not all violent offenders have suffered these traumata. However the frequency is sufficiently high to make the pattern worthy of some attention and to ask how it can be avoided.'[3]

In considering violence and how to reduce it, a concentration on moral judgments is unlikely to be helpful, acting as a distraction from issues amenable to change. For example, while the rate of homicide in the USA is very much greater than in the UK, it is not helpful to think that there are many times more evil people in the USA than in the UK. Instead, those concerned with the problem should be looking at such issues as relative social deprivation, discrimination and access to firearms.

The Commission did not have the resources to support original research (although it does identify areas where further research is needed – see page 230). It has sought the views of a very wide range of organisations and individuals including young people (see Appendices 5 and 6, pages 286 and 292). It has consulted specialists and specialist libraries. In particular it has reviewed the conclusions of commissions and commentaries with related terms of reference in other countries, including the US, Australia, South Africa and Germany: they show very substantial agreement in their attempts to answer the question 'Why do people become violent?'

Research into the antecedents of violent behaviour cannot identify 'causes' beyond doubt. But investigations, and in particular longitudinal studies, can identify risk factors which appear, more or less consistently, to be present when a child or adult acts violently, and the relative significance of these factors can to some extent be judged. Knowledge comes from different sources: some studies have involved detailed investigation of large cohorts followed through up to three generations. Others have investigated the background of identified violent offenders. Then there are the subjective experiences and perceptions of people working with violent children and with those who are violent to children. But it cannot be emphasised too strongly that the multiplicity of potential risk factors, and their likely interaction, makes it difficult to predict accurately which individuals will become violent.

Much of the research on the development of violence identifies factors common to the development of other antisocial tendencies. This means, of course, that proposals to reduce violence that are linked effectively to our knowledge of the risk factors are likely to reduce other criminal and anti-social behaviour as well.

Commissions in other countries which have sifted the research evidence on the antecedents of violence over the last few years have come to broadly similar conclusions. Thus the report of the Australian National Committee on Violence concludes in summary:

'Violent behaviour defies simplistic explanation, and generally results from a variety of factors interacting with one another ... Essentially, it is the Committee's view that the experiences of childhood and the influence of the family are paramount in determining whether or not an individual becomes violent in his or her behaviour. We acknowledge that biological and personality factors may predispose individuals to violence, but strong evidence exists to suggest that in almost every case a loving and secure environment can overcome such predispositions. Likewise, although alcohol, the media, peers and school may all exert their influence, what children observe and learn in their homes – what they come to recognise as norms of behaviour – will largely determine their reaction to these influences.

'Of course, each child lives within a larger culture where factors such as economic and gender inequality may be realities they have to cope with on an individual basis as adults, and which may be sources of disillusion and frustration. Nevertheless, what is learned in the process of socialisation within the family can be both protection and a source of strength in coming to terms with or even altering these realities'[4]

Similarly, the American Psychological Association's (APA's) Commission on Violence and Youth (1993) states:

'Although no definitive answer yet exists that would make it possible to predict exactly which individuals will become violent, many factors have been identified as contributing to a child's risk profile. Biological factors, childrearing conditions, ineffective parenting, emotional and cognitive development, gender differences, sex role socialisation, relations to peers, cultural milieu, social factors such as economic inequality and lack of opportunity, and media influences, among others, all are thought to be factors that contribute to violent behaviour ...'[5]

The APA Commission found that

'... youth at risk of becoming extremely aggressive and violent tend to share common experiences that appear to place them on a 'trajectory toward violence'. These youth tend to have experienced weak bonding to caretakers in infancy and ineffective parenting techniques, including lack of supervision, inconsistent discipline, highly punitive or abusive treatment, and failure to reinforce positive, prosocial behaviour. These developmental deficits, in turn, appear to lead to poor peer relations and high levels of aggressiveness.

'Additionally, these youth have learned attitudes accepting aggressive behaviour as normative and as an effective way to solve interpersonal problems. Aggressive children tend to be rejected by their more conforming peers and do poorly at school, including a history of problems such as poor school attendance and numerous suspensions. These children often band together with others like themselves, forming deviant peer groups that reinforce anti-social behaviours. The more such children are exposed to violence in their homes, in their neighbourhoods, and in the media, the greater their risk for aggressive and violent behaviours.'[6]

The US National Academy of Sciences recently created a 'Panel on the Understanding and Control of Violent Behaviour'; the Panel's major report, *Understanding and preventing violence*, published in 1993, included a review of the most important findings and theories on why individuals develop a potential for violence. It again underlines the multi-factor approach:

'The likelihood of someone committing a violent act depends on many different factors. Biological, individual, family, peer, school, and community factors may influence the development of an individual potential for violence. Whether the potential becomes manifest as a violent act depends on the interaction between this violence potential and immediate situational factors, such as the consumption of alcohol and the presence of a victim.'[7]

The report emphasises in particular that

'... it is clear that aggressive children tend to become violent teenagers and violent adults. In other words there is significant continuity over time between childhood aggression and adult violence.'

It quotes research showing that adult violent offenders tend to have shown certain personality features as children:

> 'They are high on hyperactivity, impulsivity and attention deficit, tend to be restless and lacking in concentration, take risks, show a poor ability to defer gratification, and have low empathy. They also tend to have particularly low IQ scores. Other predictors in children, their families and surroundings include abnormally frequent viewing of violence on television, bullying in the early school years, harsh and erratic discipline, abuse or neglect, lack of parental nurturance, low income in large families, criminal behaviour by family members, early grade school failure, peer rejection, poor housing and growing up in a high-crime neighbourhood.'[8]

But again it is important to emphasise that there is no inevitability that violent children will become violent adults. The report also identifies 'protective factors' which appear to reduce the chance of childhood aggressive behaviour in what would appear to be high risk homes and neighbourhoods: '... a shy temperament, high IQ, being first-born, and a small, stable family characterized by low discord.'[9] The American Psychological Association's Commission also identified particular 'positive interactions with parents and other adults which can act as protective factors for children who are at risk for violence.'[10] In Norway, researchers have coined the term 'dandelion children' to describe those resilient children who appear to thrive in very unpromising environments. Research which can identify factors which prevent high-risk children from becoming violent is clearly as crucial as research into the risks.

A follow-up of several hundred boys from New York state found that peer-related aggression at age eight significantly predicted self-reported aggression in males at age 32.[11] In a book published in 1991, David Farrington, Professor of Psychological Criminology and Acting Director of the Institute of Criminology, University of Cambridge, reviewed this and other longitudinal studies which have provided a great deal of useful and generally consistent information on factors predisposing individuals to violence.[12] The Cambridge Study in Delinquent Development, for example, found that children rated by teachers and peers as 'most troublesome' at ages eight to 10 accounted for 22 per cent of the sample, but comprised 70 per cent of the future chronic offenders. With specific reference to violent offenders, an important early precursor was the harsh attitude and discipline of a boy's parents when he was aged eight.[13]

In a summary of 'influences on violence', *Understanding and preventing violence* continues:

> '... no one influence in isolation is likely to account for the development of a potential for violence, except perhaps in some special cases. It is possible, for

example, that to produce a violent adult, one needs, at a minimum, a child born with a particular temperamental profile, living in a particular family constellation, in a disadvantaged neighbourhood, exposed to models of aggression and patterns of reinforcement of aggressive behaviour, having a particular school experience, having a particular set of peer relations, and also experiencing certain chance events that permit the actualization of violent behaviour.'[14]

> **'It is all to do with the way they are brought up as a child. Once they are grown-ups you can't change their childhood. If they are brought up being hit all the time, they will naturally think it's OK.'**

Some generalisations can be made concerning distinctions between youthful violence and violence by adults. Youthful violence tends to be mostly a matter of lack of restraint and readiness to resort to violence habitually without much pressure or provocation to act aggressively. Violence by adults is more complex. 'Instrumental' violence in cold blood by a hired killer or disciplined soldier, for example, or the unexpected outburst of a normally restrained individual such as a chronically abused wife or extremely provoked husband.

Finally, it is important to acknowledge the potential of some kinds of interventions to exacerbate delinquent, anti-social and violent behaviour – for example the re-offending rates of incarcerated young offenders, and in particular research which suggests that periods in custody increase the likelihood of non-violent offenders becoming violent. In its *Mental Health Handbook for Young People* the Children's Legal Centre refers to the 'spiral effect', in which a child moves rapidly down a spiral of increasingly restrictive interventions, reacting at each stage with disturbance and/or violence provoked by the placement, which in turn is used to justify more restriction.[15] Thus a child excluded for relatively minor reasons from an ordinary school may move rapidly through special school, residential special school and then children's home into secure accommodation or a secure psychiatric unit.

Conclusion

Seeking to understand the reasons for violent behaviour involving children is a necessary step towards effective prevention.

There is considerable knowledge about the risk factors for violent behaviour. It is clear that very many factors are involved, and that their interaction is complex. The most potent of the identified risk factors are clearly sited in childhood and within the family, and are amenable to change. Most of the risk factors for violent behaviour are the same as for general delinquency. But punitive child-rearing involving physical punishment and deliberate humiliation appears particularly identified with the development of violent attitudes and actions. Violence is predominantly a male problem, highlighting the inadequacies of current socialisation of male children, and the promotion of macho, male attitudes and models in society.

That an individual child becomes violent is never inevitable. Families can and often do provide the security and love necessary to 'protect' children, even 'high risk' children, from becoming violent.

The following analysis does not pretend to be a comprehensive review of relevant research. We have been able to summarise the findings of other commissions with related terms of reference and considerably larger resources, which have sifted the research evidence. We have also sought out papers and reports that have attempted to draw together the conclusions from longitudinal and other studies. We can do no more than highlight areas of agreement, and in some cases, like the relative significance of any effects on children of viewing violent media images, passionate disagreement.

> 'It's just what you see everywhere, boys and men like to be macho. Attitudes should be changed by the family but it tends to be too late.'

> 'Some teenagers think that fighting resolves everything and think that people will look up to them if they are the so-called 'hard guy' so basically they are showing off, also the influence of alcohol is usually involved, some people may be doing it because they have problems at home and want attention.'

This is a necessary prelude to making recommendations aimed at reducing violence involving children, since these must be based on available knowledge, and on respect for children and their rights as people.

The Commission emphasises that the order of the following sections does not indicate an order of significance or priority. It starts with consideration of the child's innate condition and broadens to consider the effects of biological, environmental and other influences.

Genetic factors

The possibility that inheritance plays a significant part in causing violent behaviour has to be considered. First, many hold a deep-rooted belief that there is such a thing as 'bad blood' passed from generation to generation. Second, there is no doubt that there is often a familial pattern to violence, that if a parent is violent, there is an increased chance that their child will show violent behaviour (see page 46). One possible explanation, or part-explanation, is that there is a genetic mechanism operating.

There are understandable reasons for the widespread reluctance to look carefully for genetic causes. First, there is concern that if it were discovered that genetic factors are indeed important, it might lead politicians in the future to pursue eugenic policies. Second, there is a widespread belief that it is much more difficult to do something about genetically caused problems than those that are socially caused. These are important considerations, but they can be answered. As far as objectionable eugenic policies are concerned, their pursuit does not depend on a belief in genetic causes. Official discouragement of poor people from having children is a policy that has been pursued regardless of beliefs about the cause of poverty. So called 'ethnic cleansing' currently undertaken in Central Europe does not pretend to have a genetic rationale. The 'untreatability' of genetic disorder is another myth. In paediatric practice, some genetic disorders are relatively easy to prevent or treat, some are much more difficult. The same is true of socially-determined problems. Of course, violence is not a 'disorder' in the same sense as a genetic disease, but the same logic applies in considering its prevention.

Genetic predispositions can be turned to good or bad ends according to social circumstances. There are genetic influences in all kinds of behaviour, including youthful characteristics such as risk-taking, and the greater propensity for physical violence in males. What is the evidence for genetic factors operating in the production of violence? First, there is no clear evidence for genetic determination of racial differences in predisposition to violence. For example, homicide is the most common cause of death in young black men aged 15 to 24 years in the United States. But it is obvious from comparison of the crime figures in this group in different social settings that explanations for this horrifying statistic lie in discrimination, social deprivation and access to firearms.

Apart from genetic differences across racial groups, there is however also the possibility that predisposition to violence varies between individuals depending on their genetic make-up. The fact that there is no evidence for relevant between-group differences in genetic predisposition to violence does not rule out the possibility of genetically-caused within-group differences. There are findings from a number of studies of twins and adopted children which are relevant to considering this possibility.

Twin studies suggest that environmental factors are most significant in determining antisocial behaviour in the young but that there may be some genetic contribution.[16] However, violent behaviour is only one aspect of anti-social behaviour. Evidence for or against specific genetic causation of violence by children is lacking, but the indications are that it is of minor direct importance. The indirect influence of genetic factors may be more important. For example, it now seems likely from a number of studies that one of the very few psychiatric disorders of childhood to which there is an important genetic contribution is the so-called hyperkinetic syndrome (attention-deficit disorder). Both twin and other family studies support this conclusion.[17] Children with the hyperkinetic syndrome, as well as being unusually active also show poor concentration, distractibility and short attention span. They get about more and tend to flit from one activity to another much more than other children. As they get older, they also have an increased tendency to develop antisocial and sometimes violent behaviour, though this is the case for only a proportion of the children with the condition. The reasons for their increased predisposition to antisocial behaviour are unclear. However it is not difficult to imagine that if a young child is unusually active and exploratory, its behaviour may be seen by some parents as 'naughty'. Frequent use of punishment, sometimes violent punishment may follow; such treatment is associated with the development of violent behaviour in children. A child born into the same family but without a tendency to overactivity might not follow the same pattern: is the cause of the hyperactive child's behaviour genetically or socially determined? Obviously both mechanisms are involved.

Various personality traits have been associated with violent behaviour: in particular lack of empathy or regard for the feelings of others, and impulsiveness – an inability to defer gratification. The American Psychological Association Commission suggests that:

'Children who show a fearless, impulsive temperament very early in life may have a predisposition for aggressive and violent behaviour.'[18]

But the extent to which the temperament is innate, and the extent to which it develops in response to the environment and in particular the relationship with parents or carers, is impossible to judge. A baby's moods or behaviour can trigger rejection or inappropriate treatment by parents which can in turn increase any potential for violence.

The Australian National Committee noted that personality traits 'can be muted or amplified by family, peer group or cultural influences.'[19]

The US report *Understanding and preventing violence* suggested that:

'Violent offenders tend to have certain personality features as children. In particular they are high on hyperactivity-impulsivity-attention deficit, tend to be restless and lacking in concentration, take risks, show a poor ability to defer gratification, and have low empathy.'[20]

From the perspective of prevention, it is most important to note that while genetic factors may be significant here, the violent behaviour could most probably be prevented by different parent management strategies.

> 'Nothing could stop it. It's useless blaming it on videos etc because too many things contribute to it. It's human nature.'

It is likely that genetic factors have indirect influences in other connections too. For example all parents with more than one child know that from the first few weeks of life, children vary in their temperamental characteristics. It is quite likely, and indeed there is some reasonably strong evidence to suggest, that different children's temperaments will elicit quite different responses in parents, some of which might be more likely to involve violence than others. One strong implication of these findings is that parent management strategies need, to some degree, to be geared to a child's personality.

It is now generally agreed, and the above discussion hopefully makes clear, that genetic and social influences are inextricably intertwined, and that their relative importance will vary from child to child and from family to family.

Finally, it should be noted that this discussion of genetic influences on violence has focused entirely on children's violence. The issue of genetic influences on violent behaviour by adults and more particularly by parents is also relevant. However, insofar as the best predictor of violence in adulthood is violent behaviour in childhood, we can assume that the most important causal contributions to adult violence have already been made by the time adolescence is reached. We need to add however that it is possible that genetic as well as social factors are important in determining the continuity of violent behaviour. This possibility needs more research.

Biological factors

Gender

It would be reasonable to think that the strong male preponderance in both children and adults in acts of violence is partly biologically determined. For example, the male: female ratio for convictions for violent offences in 1991 was about 7:1.[21] Men are responsible for 92 per cent of convicted cases of violence against the person. From an evolutionary point of view, the greater physical strength of the male was clearly an advantage in hunter societies. The male sex hormone, testosterone, when injected into a wide range of animal species, increases their tendency to violent behaviour, but it would be dangerous to draw strong conclusions from that in relation to human behaviour. Some studies have suggested that gender differences in aggressiveness are found very early in life, before any differential reinforcement of aggression could take place for boys and girls.[22] Others have suggested that the tendency for men to behave more aggressively than women was more pronounced for aggression that produces pain or physical injury than for aggression that produces psychological or social harm, and that differences in aggression are a function of perceived consequences of violence that are learned as aspects of gender and other social roles.[23]

It is certainly true that most acts of aggression to children, women and men which result in injury or death (and fear of these) are carried out by males, and in particular young males. Men commit the bulk of the serious cases of physical violence towards women and children, and of course are largely responsible for sexual aggression. If we add to this the much higher rate of within-gender violence by males than females, it more than justifies singling out male violence. This is confirmed in studies of homicide and violent crime statistics, accounts of violent acts in public, major acts of violence in a domestic

'Men are bigger and lose their temper quicker and maybe they were hit more as kids than women.'

'Men are tougher and think they're big and hard because they beat their wives up.'

'Men want to rule things and women, it should change.'

'Blokes have got something to prove. They have to show off. They might pick a fight to show they are hard. I've known it happen with girls.'

context, and the use of violence by organised groups, whether the police, army or politically-motivated groups outside the law.[24] Careful analysis of homicide rates within marriage in the US found that while almost as many husbands are killed by wives as vice versa, practically all the killings by wives were motivated by self-defence, following years of physical violence from the husband. Men's reasons, on the contrary, often related directly or indirectly to a 'proprietary' attitude, and to jealousy based on real, possible or imaginary infidelity.[25]

There are good reasons to think that the gender differences in violent behaviour in our society are largely determined by social influences, and not by physical factors. The evidence for this view comes from a variety of sources. First one can point to admittedly unusual societies in which the biologically normal females have shown a greater tendency to violence than the biologically normal males. Secondly, we know that boys brought up in non-violent households with parents providing good quality care and living in non-violent neighbourhoods, show levels of violence that are very little different from girls brought up in the same circumstances. Thirdly, there is evidence that the levels of testosterone in young violent males are no different from those in non-violent young males.[26] Finally, it was noted about 20 years ago that males with an abnormal chromosome pattern (XYY instead of the normal XY) were over-represented in institutions for mentally ill offenders. Subsequent work has shown that most males with an XYY constitution are not violent, and although there is indeed a small over-representation of such individuals in institutions for mentally-ill offenders, the contribution these individuals make to the total picture of male violence is tiny. Further, it has been concluded that the link between XYY individuals and violence is really of no relevance to the issue of chromosomally normal male-female differences in predisposition to violence.

In considering strategies for reducing violence, there clearly needs to be a sharp focus on the social conditioning which appears responsible for the vast over-representation of males in all forms of violent behaviour.

Conditions affecting brain function

A small number of physical conditions, affecting both males and females, are accompanied by an increased risk of violent behaviour. These are all conditions affecting brain function, and it is thought their effects are mainly caused by interference with the normal mechanisms for inhibiting such behaviour. Epilepsy affecting the temporal area of the brain is the most important example, together with certain degenerative brain diseases, brain injuries (see page 44) and tumours. However, to keep this problem in perspective, it should be remembered that temporal lobe epilepsy affects about 2 per 1,000 of the adolescent population, and of these only about a quarter will have an increased tendency to violent behaviour.

As the Australian National Committee on Violence emphasises after reviewing biological factors:

'Although it appears that a disproportionate number of violent offenders may suffer some sort of brain dysfunction ... such an association is likely to be indirect rather than direct: for example, brain dysfunction may adversely affect a person's intelligence, learning ability, impulse control, one's perception of the world, or ability to cope with frustrating events. It seems probable that the association between neurological dysfunction and aggressive behaviour is mediated by psychological processes and environmental factors. These provide the link between neurological and social explanations.'[27]

Environmental or acquired biological factors

Violence is never a biological inevitability. As indicated above (page 38), some factors associated with violent behaviour may be genetically transmitted from parent to child. But from the earliest stage, how the child behaves and how they and their behaviour are perceived, will determine their relationships with others and how they are treated, by parents and other adults, by siblings and other children, and by teachers. The American Psychological Association's Commission concludes:

'Children's inherited biological characteristics, such as temperament, activity levels and hormonal levels may help shape their social environments as well as their patterns of behaviour. Acquired biological deficits, such as the effects of low birthweight and other pre-natal and perinatal complications, exposure to lead and other neuro-toxins, head injury, and other trauma, may also influence both children's social environment and their behaviour patterns. Whatever the balance between the contributions of nature and nurture, it is likely that a model stressing the interaction of these factors will most accurately describe the development and continuity of aggressive and violent behaviour patterns.'[28]

Brain injury

Some surveys have suggested that complications in pregnancy and at birth are risk factors for involvement in violence, and that this could be because they result in damage to brain mechanisms which act to inhibit violent behaviour. Alternatively, violence may be a by-product: brain injury is a risk factor for behaviour problems and impulsivity, hyperactivity and low IQ, factors which can operate cumulatively and interactively with other factors in the family, with peers and the wider community, in school and elsewhere, to increase the risk of violence. Such injuries can also of course occur after birth and during childhood.[29]

The violence prevention perspective provides one of many obvious justifications for seeking to reduce the incidence of brain injury before and after birth through various strategies including teenage pregnancy prevention, improved pre-natal care and accident prevention.

Chronic exposure to lead has been found to be associated with low IQ scores and behaviour problems. There is also some evidence that pre-natal exposure to alcohol and some drugs is a risk factor for behaviour problems (see page 67), even after taking account of the high-risk environment into which such children are born.[30]

Nutrition

There has been considerable interest in the possibility of a link between diet and violent behaviour. Hyperactivity has been related in some studies to the presence of various additives and other substances in the diet, but other studies have not confirmed the claims. Parents and others often report the effectiveness of additive-free diets, but this could be due partly or wholly to the degree and type of parental involvement required to control a child's diet.

Influence of the family and parenting

As the Australian Committee on Violence concluded, there is common agreement that 'the experiences of childhood and the influence of the family are paramount in determining whether or not an individual becomes violent in his or her behaviour.'[31]

Undoubtedly for many children, the family, whatever its particular structure, is a force for good. For children living in violent neighbourhoods under the stress of poverty, discrimination, poor housing and environmental bleakness, the family can and often does provide the love and security to protect children from such risk factors. The American Psychological Association, for example, emphasises that

'People have to be brought up without violence and be taught right from the start how bad it is to use violence, especially on someone smaller and weaker than yourself. If the message is put through as a child you will learn.'

'If parents start beating the children they in turn will turn violence onto other people. Children follow a lot of their parents' examples.'

'Most of the time they've had an awful time at home – parents hitting them etc.'

'Positive interactions with parents and other adults may act as protective factors for children who are at risk for violence. Among these protective factors are appropriate parental supervision, alternate adult caretakers in the family (such as grandparents, aunts and uncles) and a supportive same-sex model who provides structure.'[32]

Certain characteristics of parents make it more likely that they will have delinquent and/or violent children: David Farrington reports:

'Criminal, anti-social, and alcoholic parents tend to have delinquent sons ... Having convicted mothers, fathers and brothers by a boy's tenth birthday significantly predicted his own later convictions, including convictions for violence.'

David Farrington suggests that this may be explained by specific identified risk factors in parenting, but could also reflect genetic influences.[33]

There is substantial research, summarised below (page 50) which indicates that harsh physical punishment and deliberate humiliation of children is significantly linked with the development of violent attitudes and actions in childhood and later life. Unfortunately, this knowledge seems to be counter-intuitive. While there is a strong and growing professional consensus against such negative forms of discipline, they remain very common and socially and legally accepted in the UK, representing a particular indication of confused attitudes to inter-personal violence.

Family structure and break-up

There has been much debate on the effects of family structure and break-up, single parenthood, divorce and child separation from parents. But studies suggest that the effects are indirect, and mediated through the quality of the parenting process.[34]

There have been a number of studies considering whether divorce and separation, and lone parenthood are related to crime and delinquency. They are summarised in the recent report published by the Family Policy Studies Centre, *Crime and the family*. They tend to show that any associations are weakest in relation to serious and violent crime. The report concludes:

'Nothing, at this stage, shakes a continuing view that the influence of family structure – be it a dual earner household, working mother, lone parent or step family – is relatively weak. Like the stronger correlations that exist between later delinquency and low income and deprivation, their influence appears to be transmitted to children indirectly through their relationship with one or both parents ...'[35]

The Australian National Committee on Violence reports:

'Because of the acknowledged importance of family experiences in children's development, it is often assumed that the rupture of the family may easily result in delinquency in general and aggression in particular. However, the evidence is inconclusive. Even a traumatic break-up of the family may be no more damaging than its cause: a miserable prevailing atmosphere in the home may affect the child more than parental separation. A comparison of children in stressed, non-divorced families and low-conflict divorced families found that at two years of age boys from conflict-ridden nuclear families manifested more aggressive behaviour, and less pro-social behaviour, than boys in low-conflict, divorced families. The report acknowledges that mothers can compensate for absent fathers, 'but this entails even greater parenting effort. Inevitably, not all single parents can manage the extra burden.'[36]

A recent review of the backgrounds of section 53 offenders (children sentenced for grave – usually violent – crimes) found that a high proportion had experienced the death or loss of contact with someone important to them. 57 per cent of the sample had suffered such loss – 10 per cent experiencing the death of a parent, and 39 per cent loss of contact with a parent. The report of the research suggests that loss of this kind

> 'is an experience which, in common with acts of abuse, constitutes a major source of childhood trauma which, depending on how it is handled, may later contribute to disordered behaviour, including aggression and violence.'[37]

Recent UK research on variables associated with high use of physical punishment found that while single parent status did not significantly increase the risk, poor marital relationships did (see below, page 51).

Parenting styles

Very substantial research evidence, and in particular longitudinal studies, highlight certain styles of parenting, or parenting deficits, which appear to be very significant factors in the development of a potential for violence in children. All such factors may themselves be strongly influenced by stress related to poverty and inequality, discrimination and family conflict.

In the Cambridge Study in Delinquent Development,

> 'it was found that harsh or erratic parental discipline, cruel, passive or neglecting parental attitude, poor supervision and parental conflict, all measured at the age of eight, all predicted both convictions in general and convictions for violence in particular.'[38]

The biggest difference between the violent offenders and non-violent frequent offenders was in parental authoritarianism, with the violent offenders having more authoritarian parents.[39] Similar characteristics have been found in the parenting of school bullies.[40]

The learning of aggression in the family happens very early, a number of studies have confirmed.[41] Dan Olweus found that the mother's tolerance of child aggression and parental use of physical punishment and threat, in addition to child temperament and maternal rejection, helped to explain the development of aggression. His review of many longitudinal studies found that

> 'marked differences in habitual aggression levels manifest themselves early in life (certainly by age three) and may show a high or very high degree of stability for periods of at least one and a half years at this developmental level (in nursery school settings). Data from one study ... suggested that ratings of aggression in relation to the period from birth to three years may

have some predictive value of aggression variables assessed as long as 20 years later.'[42]

Detailed studies of parenting and interventions with parents at the Oregon Social Learning Centre in the US have shown that

'... parents of anti-social children are deficient in their methods of child-rearing. The parents do not tell the children how they expect them to behave, fail to monitor the behaviour to ensure it is desirable, and fail to enforce rules promptly and clearly with appropriate positive and negative reinforcement. The reinforcement for aggression in these anti-social children is provided directly in the parenting process.'[43]

Gerald Patterson (of the Oregon Centre) and James Snyder provide a compelling description of anti-social, including violent, behaviour as a failure of socialization, concluding that 'the anti-social child is a product and an architect of his environment':

'Disruption in the socialization can be thought to occur in two stages ... The first stage occurs during childhood and primarily occurs in the home setting. Inept family socialization practices like poor discipline result in high frequencies of relatively trivial antisocial behaviours by the child, like non-compliance, fighting, temper tantrums, petty theft and lying. These inept practices may also result in poor inter-personal and work skills. Given that the child is anti-social and lacks skills, he is likely to move into the second stage of anti-social training. He is placed at risk for rejection by peers and adults, and for academic and work failure ... The child's coercive and clumsy style 'puts people off'. This reduces the child's opportunities to develop skilled behaviour. The rejected child is also likely to associate with other unskilled, coercive children, thereby increasing his opportunities to acquire, perform and hone anti-social behaviour ... As the child continues to develop in a family environment with poor socialization practices and to associate with deviant peers, his performance of anti-social behaviour becomes increasingly frequent, varied, serious and successful. Although much of the second-stage training takes place outside of the home, the family continues to be important. Via supervision and ongoing disciplinary practices, parents can influence the peers with whom the child interacts and the activities in which he engages ... During both stages, parent-child and peer-child influences are reciprocal.'[44]

> 'Parents should set a good example and perhaps spend more time with their children.'
>
> 'Adults shouldn't be seen to be fighting or hitting each other as it is a bad example and can upset children.'

Monitoring/supervision of children

The degree to which parents are aware of and monitor their children's activities appears to be a fairly obvious important factor in determining whether a potential for anti-social and violent behaviour is realised. Parents of delinquent youths have limited awareness of where their children are, who they are spending time with and what they are doing.[45] Chance and opportunism are important factors in determining whether a child gets involved in violence, so inadequate supervision can be crucial in realising a potential for violence.

Discipline and punishment

The various commissions on violence that have recently reviewed the available research have all identified physical punishment and other inappropriate discipline as contributory factors. The American Psychological Association:

'Physical punishment may produce obedience in the short-term, but continued over time it tends to increase the probability of aggressive and violent behaviour during childhood and adulthood, both inside and outside the family.'[46]

The Australian National Committee on Violence reviewed a body of research suggesting that physical punishments make misconduct more rather than less likely:

'... in other words the child observes and perhaps copies the parent's aggressive actions, rather than absorbing the message of disapproval... The circumstances in which physical punishment is used against children contribute to a learning process. Children learn to associate love with physical punishment. The child is struck by those human beings to whom he or she is closest. As physical punishment is most typically employed as a means of redress for misbehaviour on the part of the child, the child may come to accept it as morally justifiable to use violence against a wrongdoer ...

'In a very real sense, families constitute the training ground for aggression. If families do not instil non-violent values in their children, those children are more likely to develop violent behaviours as they become adults.'[47]

One longitudinal study over three generations in New York State concluded:

'Our data ... indicate that aggression, as characteristic behaviour, is transmitted from parent to child. In the original study, there was a significant relation between how aggressive the children were rated by their peers in schools, and how severely they were punished for aggression at home. When the group were 19, they were asked how they would respond to aggression if they had an eight year-old child, and in 1981, those subjects who actually had children aged between six and 12 were asked the same question: there were highly significant correlations between their own peer-nominated aggression and their attitude to their own hypothetical or real children, and also between their parents' response to aggression and their own response 20 years later.'[48]

Leonard Eron reports the findings of a three-year longitudinal study of about 600 children in Chicago, replicated in Finland, Poland, Holland, Australia and Israel: when results for the USA, Finland and Poland were analysed, he concluded 'physical punishment by parents relates significantly to aggression of both boys and girls.'[49]

The most recent research into levels of physical violence to children in their homes in the UK, a major study sponsored by the Department of Health, found that children who were frequently aggressive with their siblings were four times as likely as those who were rarely aggressive with their sibling, to have been 'severely' punished at some time.[50] This study (see page 133 for further details) found that high rates of physical punishment persist in UK families: almost one in six children had received 'severe' physical punishment from their mothers, defined as involving the 'intention or potential to cause injury or psychological damage, use of implements, repeated actions or over a long period of time'. The research looked at variables associated with high levels of physical punishment. It found that overcrowding, low income and single parent status did not significantly increase the risks. But a third of children living with parents who had a poor marital relationship had experienced severe physical punishment, compared with seven per cent of those whose marriage was good. Similarly, mothers who said they were often irritable for reasons other than the child were more likely to inflict severe punishments.

> **'Hitting someone will not discipline them. They will just build anger up inside and take it out on someone else.'**
>
> **'Hitting children and old people is the lowest of the low.'**
>
> **'Some young children can be extremely naughty. I don't mean you bash them in, a smack on the bottom should do it.'**

John and Elizabeth Newson's long-term Nottingham research on child-rearing found a 'very clear association' between the frequency of physical punishment at 11 and the child's perceived delinquency. They comment:

'This poses a question: are these children delinquent because they are smacked, or are they smacked because they are delinquent? The question cannot be answered; what we can say however is that smacking and beating mothers do not succeed in producing non-delinquent children, and the dictum of "spare the rod and spoil the child" can't be upheld by these findings.'

The Newsons also looked at possible associations between various child-rearing variables at the age of seven and 11, and an eventual criminal record:

'Those which are of particular importance are those which still "shine through" as having significance even when we set aside the effects of class, sex and family size; those which do shine through can be fairly assumed to be causative in their association. The measures which stand out as being most predictive of criminal record before the age of 20 are having been smacked or beaten once a week or more at 11, and having had a mother with a high degree of commitment to formal corporal punishment at that age.'

They also point out that father's non-punitive involvement with the child at 11 stands out as protecting the child from acquiring a criminal record in adolescence.[51]

The review of the background of a sample of section 53 offenders referred to above found that 40 per cent had experienced physical abuse – the highest figure in the four abuse categories:

'Physical abuse, in this sample, included beatings, kickings and a variety of other forms of physical harm or torture. Almost all the reported incidents formed part of a regular pattern rather than a one-off act.'[52]

The British Psychological Society, in a 1991 submission to the Scottish Law Commission, stated:

> **'People should realise that it is not OK for anyone to be physically violent. No person has the right to abuse another living being.'**

'As a broad general principle, punishment, including corporal punishment, is seen as an inefficient method of modifying behaviour, being situation-specific and of short-term effect, and with a possibility of providing undesirable side-effects of both fear and learned imitative behaviour. More socially desirable attitudes would be encouraged by alternative methods of managing behaviour, such as withdrawal of privileges and the rewarding of more desirable alternatives.'[53]

In a new and very detailed study of available research, published in 1994, Murray A Straus concludes:

'Research over the past 40 years has been remarkably consistent in showing that hitting children increases the chances of a child becoming physically aggressive, delinquent, or both. The research in this book shows that corporal punishment leaves invisible scars that affect many other aspects of life.'[54]

Society's attitudes and norms of behaviour

The extent to which a society condones violence will influence the values of individuals within it. In the UK today there are ambivalent attitudes to violence, and in particular towards violence to children. Physical punishment and deliberate humiliation of children remains common and socially and legally accepted despite its implication as a particular factor in the development of a potential for violence.

Other than self-defence, or restraint of another's violence, physical punishment is the only form of inter-personal violence that remains legal, following the criminalisation of marital rape. While some recent opinion polls have suggested low levels of public support for the use of implements to beat children, courts continue to uphold parents' rights to use them: during 1993 parents who had admitted using belts, and canes causing heavy bruising were acquitted of assault and cruelty.[55] Our language has special words to describe violence when directed at children – 'smacking', 'spanking', etc, and phrases like 'a good hiding', 'six of the best', 'a healthy smack' indicate the unique approval expressed by many for this particular form of inter-personal violence.

The Government, while accepting Parliament's decision (by a majority of one vote) to end corporal punishment in state-supported education in 1986, has continued to defend the right of parents to pay to have their children educated at private schools which retain corporal punishment, and some private schools still advertise its use.[56]

During 1995, MPs and Peers have tabled amendments to criminal justice legislation seeking to re-introduce judicial corporal punishment.

> 'I think as it has been said that often people that are violent have been victims of violence either at home or been bullied at school so consider it to be all right. I don't really think that much can be done apart from drumming into people at every possible incident that violence is wrong.'

While there is no longer any acceptance in UK law of violence to women, there remains an ambivalence in male attitudes, again reflected in some sections of the media, in the extent and effectiveness of interventions, and in the level of resources made available for prevention programmes and refuges. As noted elsewhere in the report, men's violence to women is very often inextricably linked to violence involving children.

Adults and children have an appetite for violent images (see page 69). While modern technology has dramatically increased potential access to extremely violent images, the appetite was previously demonstrated in the crowds thronging to public executions, the circulation figures of horror comics and so on. War toys are aggressively advertised through television and widely bought.

There are also ambivalent attitudes to violence in sport. Some young spectators of sport, particularly football, use it as an opportunity for engaging in acts of violence. Certain sports including in particular boxing, have as their primary aim harming the opponent to some degree. In October 1983 the World Medical Association issued the following statement:

> 'Boxing is a dangerous sport. Unlike other sports, the basic intent of boxing is to produce bodily harm in the opponent. Boxing can result in death and produces an alarming incidence of chronic brain injury. For this reason the World Medical Association recommends that boxing be banned.'[57]

Commissions in other countries have underlined the importance of attitudes in the wider society: in America, the APA Commission found:

> 'Violence is woven into the cultural fabric of American society. Americans long have had an ambivalent relationship with violence. Though most Americans abhor violence in their communities, homes, and schools, this country has the highest rate of interpersonal violence of any industrialised society. Our folk heroes and media images – from the cowboy of the old west, to John Wayne, Clint Eastwood, and Arnold Schwarzenegger – often glorify interpersonal violence on an individual and personal level. Violent films are widely attended. American news media present image after image reflecting the violence in society, and in some cases may exploit or contribute to it. Football, one of the most violent of team sports, is an American creation. A plethora of guns and war toys are marketed and are coveted and possessed by small children. Although few Americans would claim to enjoy violence, many, at the very minimum, passively condone aggression and violence through acceptance of current film and television productions.'[58]

Similarly, in Australia the National Committee on Violence reported:

> 'Violence is not universally condemned in Australian society. Most parents accept the use of physical punishment in disciplining children. One in two advocate capital punishment for murder. Violence on the sporting field, in the home and in schools is tolerated by many Australians.'

It reports a 1988 survey which found that one in five people considered the use of physical force by a man against his wife is acceptable under some circumstances, though 'only' six per cent think that there can be justification for extreme forms of violence such as threatening or using a weapon on one's wife.[59]

In America, there is no doubt that the easy availability of guns makes youth violence more lethal. The APA Commission found 'considerable evidence' that the alarming rise in youth homicides is related to the availability of firearms; it indicated that

> 'students carry an estimated 270,000 guns to school every day ... In some cases the carrying of a weapon may be part of a youth's bonding to a gang or to a drug dealer's organisation. Some youth say they carry guns because they are afraid of others who have guns. Not much is known about the factors that motivate the decision to obtain and carry a gun.'

It also found that when young people who are already predisposed to violence have easy access to guns, they may be more likely to become violent.[60] In Britain, access to firearms is less easy (see page 224), and there is no evidence of widespread child or youth ownership of guns or other dangerous weapons. But there have been isolated cases. Any increase in availability could become a significant factor in relation to the translation of a potential for violence into serious violence.

Inequality and discrimination

International comparisons have found violence to be more common in societies characterised by widespread inequality. A survey of 31 nations found those with high income inequality to have the highest homicide rates. A review of 63 studies of the relationship between unemployment and crime (mostly in the US) found that rates of violent crime tended to be higher where there was greater unemployment, and that violent crime tends to increase during periods of economic decline.[61]

Low socio-economic status has been shown to be clearly related to delinquency and violence in many UK studies. Both victims of violence and violent offenders are predominantly drawn from the most disadvantaged socio-economic groups. In the Cambridge Delinquency Study, low social class, low income and large family size all predicted convictions for violence.[62] Another study found that convictions for serious offences and especially violent offences were most common among sons of the least skilled and educated manual workers.[63]

Again, it is important to emphasise that none of these factors 'causes' violence. They increase the risk of violence through their inter-relation with other risk factors. For example, the relationship of family size to violence may reflect child-rearing factors, since for example less attention can be given to each child. Stress caused by poverty can affect disciplinary strategies in the home, in turn affecting the child's development (see page 133). The Oregon Youth Study in the US found that the statistical connection between socio-economic status and the children's early delinquency was mediated by family management practices: social pressures affected the behaviour of parents which in turn affected the behaviour of children. The behaviour of children affects the type of peer group willing to accept them and the likelihood of rejection by school authorities.[64]

> 'Give the poor people more money for their kids. They only throw stones at poor people's homes, not the rich.'

Reviewing the effects of social status and income on crime, a report on *Crime and the family* published by the Family Policy Studies Centre in 1993 concluded:

'Family deprivation in the context of delinquency can be viewed as a cluster of adverse circumstances which include inadequate housing and a poor local environment as well as matters of hard cash. The mechanism by which these external pressures on a family translate into aggression or dishonesty among children cannot be a direct one. There is, however, a prima facie case for regarding economic and environmental deprivation as powerful stress factors which conspire to make it more difficult to be an effective parent.'[65]

'Some children are more violent due to different upbringing in the family, but also sometimes the area where children live. If it's not a nice area children tend to have to be rougher and be prepared to stand up for themselves. There are more gangs in rougher areas.'

The APA Commission on Youth and Violence emphasises that beyond mere income level, it is

'the socio-economic inequality of the poor – their sense of relative deprivation and their lack of opportunity to ameliorate their life circumstances – that facilitates higher rates of violence.'[66]

In the UK over the last 15 years there has been a massive increase in numbers of children living in poverty, using the definition of poverty accepted across Europe – those living on less than half the average income. By 1993 there were 4.3 million children living in poverty. This compares with 1.4 million in 1979. Perhaps particularly significant in relation to violence, inequalities have increased, with the poorest 10 per cent becoming poorer while 'average' income has increased and the incomes of the 'top' 10 per cent have increased very substantially.[67]

A very recent detailed review of possible links between socio-economic and familial origins of the rise in violence against the person in the UK highlights the effects of inequality. It reviews studies suggesting that inequality is the single most important factor in predicting variations in the amount of violence within and between nations across time and cultures:

'Since 1979 inequalities of all kinds have increased dramatically in Britain. These have impacted on the violence-against-the-person statistics since 1987 in two principal ways, indirectly and directly;
The increase in the number of boys being raised in low-income families has led to a substantial increase in the number of 10–16 year-olds cautioned or found guilty of violence against the person.
The direct effect of increased inequality on young men, particularly the 21-and-over age group'.

The book reviews the evidence that

'the difference between violent and non-violent men in technologically-developed nations is the way in which they were treated as children. In particular, severe and frequent physical punishment amounting to abuse, parental disharmony and irritability (especially in mothers) were identified as key variables'.

It goes on to show that these factors are significantly more common in families where the income is low, strongly suggesting 'that low income is a principal cause of violence-inducing parents'; other factors such as single mothering, low IQ or underclass culture play only a small part.

The book concludes that government economic and social policies during the 1980s:

> 'caused the increase in low-income families which created the rise in juvenile violence after 1987. They also created a winner-loser culture which may well have been influential in encouraging young men to interpret and express the new inequality in a violent manner.'[68]

Feelings of alienation can lead to violence by reducing inhibitions against such behaviour. Discrimination against children and young people, and against particular groups of children are rife in the UK. There is a great deal of evidence to show that some children suffer discrimination in schooling, in training and employment opportunities, and in access to leisure facilities, on grounds of the socio-economic status of their families, or of disability, ethnic background and sexuality. Prejudice and discrimination in themselves encourage economic inequality and poverty, and increase stress and can thus be implicated in other risk factors for violence. As the APA Commission states:

> 'Discrimination against ethnic minority groups, against women, gays, lesbians and persons with disabilities continues to operate through social policies and structural opportunities in society. It is also enacted in countless acts of inter-personal behaviour each day. Such discrimination fosters vast differences in economic status among the various ethnic minority groups and non-minority Americans. It also damages the self-confidence and self-esteem of those discriminated against and lays a foundation for anger, discontent and violence.'[69]

Studies of violent offenders and victims have found disproportionate numbers from some ethnic groups. The range of factors, many of them linked to discrimination, that may lead to the disproportion, and their potential interaction with each other, makes it wrong to highlight ethnicity as necessarily a factor in itself.

Recent studies have suggested that disabled children, and in particular those with learning difficulties, are at particular risk of abuse, including sexual abuse, both at home and in institutional settings.

The influence of school and peers

Almost all children spend a great deal of their childhood in schools – more than 14,000 hours during the period of compulsory schooling from 5 to 16. School experiences, including in particular relationships with adults and other children, the overt and 'hidden' curricula, will inevitably have some influence on children's attitudes to and involvement in violence. Only two decades ago, 80 per cent of 16 year-olds were in schools which still used corporal punishment.[70] In 1995, the Government continues to defend the right of parents to choose private schools which advertise their use of corporal punishment. Over the last few years there has been growing knowledge, in the UK and other countries, of the extent to which children suffer violence in the form of bullying, from other children in school.

There can be no doubt that school experiences influence children's behaviour, but it is probably impossible to determine the significance of the influence, and the extent to which it can be separated from other factors, including in particular those operating within the family.

The Australian National Committee on Violence concluded that there were two possible ways in which schools might affect the likelihood of an individual student becoming delinquent:

'First, they provide a social setting in which individuals with similar inclinations can meet and reinforce each other's behaviour. Second, they may operate in such a way as to label or stigmatise certain students so as to influence them towards delinquency. There is much research evidence to suggest that young people with low achievement levels at school and poor behaviour are much more likely than other children to be delinquent and become criminals.'

The Committee's overall conclusion was that:

'School experience and friends, it seems, are largely incidental to the more important factors of

> 'I reckon some kids might bully because their parents are violent and shouting at each other. I also think they do it for fun. A kid by ours got bullied and hung himself in the woods.'
>
> '... because they are bullied at home. They are very insecure and because they are weak inside they have to appear strong on the outside.'

personal traits and family experience in determining criminality in general, and violent behaviour in particular.'[71]

But that does not of course mean that schools could not have a significant positive effect, in particular if they did more to try to integrate 'troublesome' pupils rather than neglecting, rejecting or expelling them.

Early experiences in the family, inter-related with biological and genetic factors, can lead to children entering school with low self-esteem, poor inter-personal and work skills, and high levels of aggression. There is then the risk of rejection by other students and teachers, low achievement and stigmatisation in schools. Some researchers have suggested that aggressiveness is the single most important reason for a child to be rejected by peers, finding that 30-40 per cent of socially rejected children were highly aggressive.[72] While much bullying occurs in schools, simply because of the concentration of children in them, the major identified factors contributing to the development of bullying behaviour are found not in the school but in the child and family: lack of warmth and involvement of the primary caretaker; permissiveness regarding child's aggressive behaviour by primary caretaker; the use of physical punishments and violent emotional outbursts as childrearing methods; and an 'active and hot-headed' temperamental predisposition of the child.[73]

Various factors involving the organisation and ethos of schools have been associated with high or low bullying rates in some studies, but not consistently. For example, one recent UK study comparing six high-bullying schools with six low-bullying schools found that head teachers in the low-bullying schools tended to express articulate, considered views on bullying and attached importance to controlling and preventing it.[74]

Some American research has identified environmental or spatial factors that can influence the incidence of bullying: relatively high number of individuals in limited spaces; a reduced capacity to avoid confrontations; imposition of behavioural routines and conformity which can lead to feelings of anger, resentment and rejection; and poor design features which can facilitate the commission of violent acts.[75]

In a recent research review David Farrington concluded:

'While it is plausible to assume that bullying incidents arise from the interaction between potential bullies and potential victims in environments that provide opportunities for bullying, and while a great deal is known about characteristics of bullies, victims and environments, no comprehensive theory of bullying that connects the disparate results has yet been developed. Researchers should attempt to develop such an all-embracing theory to guide future research and prevention efforts.'[76]

The Cambridge Delinquency Study found that low school achievement at age eight to 10 was one of the four most important predictors for chronic offending, but of course the reasons for low achievement can lie outside the school.[77] The Study found huge differences in offending rates between secondary schools (one school reporting 20.9 court appearances per 100 boys per year, to another where the corresponding figure was 0.3). But it showed that the children rated as 'most troublesome' in their primary schools tended to go to the high-delinquency-rate schools. Most of the difference in delinquency rates, the Study concluded, could be explained by differences in intake, with the schools in the survey themselves having only a small effect on the rate of boys' offending.[78]

The detailed study of the effects of schooling on delinquency carried out by Michael Rutter and others in the 1970s found that differences in delinquency rates could not be entirely explained by differences in the intake, measured in terms of social class and verbal reasoning scores: variable factors in the school process appeared to be having an effect. Schools which appeared to be influencing students away from offending tended to have teachers who were committed to educational values, set and marked homework consistently and concentrated on rewarding good behaviour rather than punishing bad.[79]

The 1989 Government-commissioned Elton Inquiry into *Discipline in schools* reviewed recent studies and concluded that schools can make a difference:

> 'Most researchers now agree that some schools are much more effective than others in promoting good work and behaviour. This does not mean that schools can eliminate the effects of social differences between pupils... Research evidence suggests that pupils' behaviour can be influenced by all the major features and processes of a school. These include the quality of its leadership, classroom management, behaviour policy, curriculum, pastoral care, buildings and physical environment, organisation and timetable and relationships with parents.'

In particular, the inquiry concluded that schools which put too much faith in punishment to deter bad behaviour were likely to be disappointed: punitive regimes (and in particular the use of corporal punishment) tended to be associated with worse rather than better standards of behaviour.

> 'The message seems to be that in order to create a positive atmosphere, schools need to establish a healthy balance between punishments and rewards.'

The report recommended avoiding punishments which humiliate pupils. In relation to violence within schools — bullying and racial and sexual harassment, the report recommended that headteachers and staff should be alert to any signs of it, should 'deal firmly' with such behaviour and take action.

'based on clear rules which are backed by appropriate sanctions and systems to protect and support victims.'[80]

It seems clear that schools, at best, can help to reduce the risk of children becoming violent; at worst, they can reinforce the development of aggression, and can increase the child's experience of violence.

The peer group which children meet in school more often than not determines their friendship patterns. Some types of violent offending tend to be group activities, and peer pressure may be a significant factor in encouraging some forms of violent behaviour. Also, as indicated above, peer rejection and stigmatisation may encourage it.

Violent gangs and mob violence

Child involvement in violent gangs and in mob violence is still relatively rare in the UK. In America, while the APA Commission states that

'Only a small percentage of youth join delinquent gangs, and the absolute amount of violent behaviour by gang members is small',

it also reports that things were changing from the 1980s onwards:

'Delinquent gangs no longer are confined to certain states and to the inner city, and their membership encompasses a wider age range, with members as young as nine and as old as 30. The new roles for younger and older gang members reflect the increase of gang involvement in drugs.'[81]

Gang activity and gang violence are overwhelmingly male phenomena, and almost 90 per cent of members are from ethnic minorities.

The Commission also describes mob violence involving young people in America, suggesting it can occur under a variety of conditions:

'when rising expectations are unfulfilled, when people perceive their life circumstances are worsening, or when injustice is perceived. Often a specific event precipitates the violence.'

The inadequate available data suggests that males are the most frequent participants in mob violence, many of them with no delinquent history. Violence can escalate quickly, through a process of 'contagion'. In the UK, there has been mob violence on occasions at sporting events, and there have been isolated occasions in which young people have participated in or led localised riots – focusing violence generally on the police; some young offender institutions have also experienced mob violence, directed at prison officers and buildings.

Mental illness and violence

Although mental distress is common and is itself a powerful explanatory factor in violence to children, psychotic mental illness is much less usual and explains rather little. It is important to dispel inaccurate general connections in the public mind between mental illness and violence, which can lead to discrimination.

As the Australian National Committee on Violence noted:

'The concepts of mental illness and violence have frequently been linked in the public imagination. This is no doubt partly due to media publicity given to particularly heinous crimes of violence committed from time to time by deranged offenders, and partly due to a tendency to the ascription of madness as the only feasible explanation for some especially horrific acts. As a result, it is commonly held that by virtue of being mentally ill a person is more likely to engage in violent behaviour.'[82]

The relationship between mental illness and violence involving children is complicated by issues of definition. As one example, the Commission was told that when mothers responsible for Munchausen Syndrome by Proxy were referred to psychiatrists for a diagnostic opinion, it was not at all unusual for them to be deemed not to be suffering from mental disorder. In such cases, mothers systematically poison, suffocate or

> **'I don't think you can stop some people from being violent as they are sick!'**

otherwise impair the physical health of their children in order to gain attention for their children and themselves. How can such women not be regarded as at least mentally disordered?

In order to assist understanding of the categories used by psychiatrists, refer to the current official International Classification of Diseases.[83] The following observations are intended to clarify this system and its helpfulness or otherwise in considering links between violence on the one hand, and mental illness and so-called personality disorder on the other:

1 Violence is not being perceived by psychiatrists as in itself evidence of either illness or personality disorder. In coming to a judgment about whether violent behaviour was indeed associated with mental illness or personality

disorder, psychiatrists would take into account the nature and context of the behaviour and other features of the mental state of the person concerned. Repeated, serious violence and violence that appeared irrational would be much more likely to be seen as evidence of mental abnormality.

2 The delineation of psychiatric disorders as separate entities involves an effort to group together conditions that have similar presenting characteristics, and, as far as possible, a similar set of causes and a similar response to treatment. The advantages of being able to delineate disorders in this way are obvious, but there are disadvantages. In particular, an individual adult or child can present with serious problems that just do not fit into any of the pre-determined categories. Textbooks of psychiatry deal almost entirely with well-delineated conditions. Consequently, psychiatrists are sometimes at a loss how to classify the disorders of individuals who have not, so to speak 'read the books'.

3 Those who frame psychiatric classifications are anxious to ensure that people who commit crimes, including violent crimes, are not automatically assumed to be suffering from psychiatric disorders. Psychiatrists are likely to believe in a penal system that has strong therapeutic and rehabilitative elements. But like many others, they are also likely to subscribe to the view that a penal system needs to have deterrent and punitive components. Justification of the two latter components of the penal system would not be valid if everyone who committed a violent crime was automatically assumed to be showing a mental disorder.

4 While the above considerations will lead to the exclusion of individuals from categorisation of mental disorder, it is also true to say that those who frame the diagnostic systems are also anxious that individuals who might respond to psychiatric treatment are categorised as showing some form of mental abnormality so that they are more likely to receive such treatment. Now there are many areas of practice in which psychiatrists, no matter what their orientation, agree very well on what constitutes appropriate treatment. However, in general, conditions involving violence do not fall into this category. Especially in relation to adult personality disorder involving violent behaviour and conduct disorder in childhood, there is a wide set of beliefs among general and child psychiatrists, ranging from reasonable optimism to profound pessimism about the likely effectiveness of psychological treatments. Clearly the way forward here lies in the more systematic evaluation of existing treatments and the development of new and better forms of treatment, but in the meantime there is likely to be disagreement among psychiatrists, depending on their therapeutic attitudes, as to whether particular individuals do show mental illness or personality disorder.

The issues of whether someone is or is not suffering from mental disorder and of whether such a person might or might not benefit from psychological help are often needlessly, and illogically, confounded. It is more than possible that individuals not suffering from mental illness or personality disorder might benefit from counselling and other forms of psychological help, and indeed this is well recognised in the provision, for example, of marriage and divorce counselling. No one believes that individuals who receive such counselling are showing mental abnormalities. The line of argument is not, however acceptable in relation to physical methods of treatment. There is for example reasonably good evidence that some forms of medication can be helpful in reducing levels of aggression in some seriously violent children and adolescents. The use of such medication would not generally be regarded as acceptable unless the individual concerned had been diagnosed as showing definite mental illness or personality disorder.

Bearing these limitations and complexities of our existing psychiatric classification in mind, there are nevertheless a number of reasonably clear-cut statements that can be made about links between violence, mental illness and personality disorder:

1 Most parents who seriously abuse their children are not showing signs of mental illness as currently defined. However, a small proportion, perhaps 5-10 per cent, do suffer from schizophrenia or severe, sometimes psychotic, depressive disorders. Of the remainder most, but by no means all, are young, immature people, living in stressful social circumstances. A significant proportion, perhaps in the region of 50 per cent, might reasonably be regarded as showing some form of personality disorder, usually of 'emotionally unstable type'. One would not expect a high level of agreement between psychiatrists as to which parents were or were not showing personality disorders except in that 10 per cent or so showing unmistakable signs of such an illness.

2 Parents and others who sexually abuse children are likely to display unusually strong sexual arousal towards children, a condition known as 'paedophilia'. Child molesters include men who retain a preference for adult sexual partners but abuse children because of easy access. There may be considerable differences between parental child sex abusers and others. A high proportion, perhaps 50 per cent, of men involved in such behaviour would be classified as showing some form of personality disorder on the basis of other aspects of their mental state and social functioning. A small further additional number, perhaps 5-10 per cent, will show signs of mental disorder, especially depressive and anxiety states, though the presence of these will not necessarily be linked causally to their sexual behaviour. A majority of sexual abusers of children, although they may be doing a lot of harm, are not physically violent.

3 The great majority of children showing seriously violent behaviour would, if seen by psychiatrists, be regarded as showing conduct disorders, or would be thought not to be showing any form of psychiatric disorder. It is known, for example, that most children involved in bullying at school do not show signs of psychiatric disorder. In urban areas, about 5-10 per cent of children show conduct disorders (about half this rate for children living in rural or semi-rural areas). However it is not known in what proportion of these violent behaviour forms one component.

Thus about 5-10 per cent of individuals, both adults and children, involved in serious acts of repeated violence will be classified as showing some form of mental disorder. Of the remaining 90-95 per cent, most will not be showing mental disorder, but a significant and not well-determined proportion will be showing personality disorders, commonly of the 'emotionally unstable' type. The remainder will not be showing signs of either mental illness or personality disorder. It is important to note that the above discussion only involves violence that is both serious (in the sense of causing physical injury) and repeated. Most violence in our society does not fall into this category, for example most physical punishment by parents and most bullying by children. Such violence is often socially approved or at least socially acceptable. And there is no question of the individuals concerned showing either mental illness or personality disorder.

Substance abuse

Alcohol in particular, and other forms of substance abuse, is associated in various ways with violence. In relation to children's potential for violence, both their parents' and their own alcohol and substance abuse are risk factors.

Alcohol

About five per cent of men and two per cent of women in the UK are 'problem' drinkers. Alcohol consumption almost always begins in childhood and adolescence, and problem drinking among young people appears to be increasing. Changes in alcohol consumption in the young are thought to generally reflect changes in adult alcohol consumption. Alcohol consumption increased in the total UK population between 1970 and 1990 from 5.3 litres to 7.6 litres of alcohol yearly – a rise of 43 per cent.[84] More than one in five 13 year old boys and more than one in eight 13 year old girls report having been 'very drunk' once or more in the previous year. Further, violent behaviour among young teenagers when drunk is common. Around one in three 15 year old boys and one in five 15 year old girls have got reportedly into arguments or fights after drinking.[85] A league table of youth drinking in European countries suggests that the UK has an unsatisfactorily high position.[86]

> 'People should stop getting drunk and try and get stress out of their lives. And turn over a new leaf.'
>
> 'Men and boys when they have had a drink seem to think they are hard and able to beat anyone up.'

Studies in Australia and the US show that at least half of all homicides involve alcohol use by either offender, victim or both. The APA reports:

> 'In about 65 per cent of all homicides, perpetrators, victims or both had been drinking, and alcohol is a factor in at least 55 per cent of all fights and assaults in the home. Among both youth and adults, violence frequently occurs in places in which alcohol is consumed.'[87]

But the association is not simple. As the Australian National Committee on Violence states:

'The suggestion that drugs cause violence is a gross over-simplification. The effect of a drug on an individual's behaviour is the product of a range of drug and non-drug factors which include the pharmacological properties of the substance in question, the individual's neurological foundation, personality and temperament, his or her expectations of the drug's effects, and the social setting in which the individual is located.

'Drug use and violent behaviour may result from a common cause – the inability to control one's impulses. Beyond this, drug use may compound the impairment of impulse control in an otherwise aggressive person.'

Problem drinking may be only one of a number of personality disorders in the alcoholic, and some of these in combination may be systematically associated with alcohol-related violence.[88]

Abuse of alcohol (and other drugs) by parents is a risk factor for physical and sexual abuse of children, and for neglect which may expose children to greater risk of abuse by others. This has also been identified as a risk factor for their children developing violent behaviour. In addition, an American review points to the

'unknown amount of violence (that) occurs, especially in families, in disputes over expenditure, time spent away from home, and other indirect consequences of drug and alcohol use.'[89]

A useful modern survey of links between alcohol and violence was published in the USA in 1991.[90]

Violence while in states of intoxication is more likely to occur where the intoxicant is alcohol or amphetamine than cannabis or opiate; thus the effect appears to be a result both of the pharmacological properties and of a product of co-existing psychological, social and cultural factors.

Illegal drugs

Reviews of research find little evidence of a direct association between the pharmacological properties of most illegal drugs and violence. Illegal drugs are related to violence largely through violent crimes committed in the course of distribution and purchase, and young people are often implicated in this illegal trade. Users of addictive drugs commit crimes involving violence to support their addiction. In America, the National Institute on Drug Abuse estimated that at least 10 per cent of homicides occur during drug sales.

Effects of violent images

In considering why children become violent, a topic that has tended to dominate public debate over three or four decades has been the effect of media violence, of violent images seen on film, television, videos, with a resurgence of concern and activity alongside developing technology (the most recent being computer-generated images). In fact concern over children's access to violent images is a recurrent one, pre-dating modern technology. As a group of researchers and writers in the field of media studies wrote recently:

'For more than 100 years, each time our society has found itself in confusion or crisis, there have been attempts to shift the blame for social breakdown onto the media: penny dreadfuls, music hall, film, rock music, horror comics, television and now video games have each in turn played the role of the "witch-essence" which must be causing street crime, cruelty to children, attacks on horses etc. etc. Again and again, it has been shown that attacks on the "influence of the media" act as masks for other kinds of social concern. Each attack claims that "This time it is different, this time there are special dangers". There are many things that should worry us about these panics, but it must be a matter for serious concern that much that calls itself "research" has been distorted by an inability to see beyond the vague categories and embodied fears of moral campaigners.'[91]

Since the advent of television, there have been many research studies and reviews of research. Debate on interpretation of the research has often become extremely heated; it is a debate which this Commission has approached with some trepidation.

> 'I don't think TV makes people violent, but it can make violence look good.'
>
> 'Television can have an effect sometimes, but it depends on the person, if a person is violent anyway, violent films can make them worse.'

The extent of violent images in the media is undoubtedly a reflection and a part of a violent culture. There is a broad consensus (and a very strong 'public' gut feeling suggested by coverage of the debate in the media) that a heavy or continuous diet of violent images does nothing positive for child development, though the evidence that many children have such a diet in the UK is strongly disputed. There is an authoritative body of psychological opinion internationally which believes that higher levels of viewing violent images are correlated with increased acceptance of aggressive attitudes and increased aggressive behaviour; that it may help to develop or reinforce a potential for violence, and may de-sensitise children, and society generally, to violence. But these views are challenged by others who seek to show that the analysis of the images and their context, and attempts to measure the effects are inadequate or flawed. It is clear at least that the context in which the child views violent images, and the presence or absence of a critical commentary not approving of violence, is likely to influence whether or how the child is affected.

But any consensus seems to break down when considering the relative significance of viewing violent images in comparison with other factors that may contribute to the development of violent attitudes, and considering what should be done.

Looking first at the views of commissions in other countries, one finds some reflection of the passion and confusion of the debate, but a clear concern at the extent of children's exposure to violent images.

The Australian National Committee on Violence concluded hesitantly that while no direct causal link has been established between viewing violent images and violent behaviour, television, video and film viewing may be associated with subsequent aggression in some viewers. The relationship appears to be bi-directional – violence viewing gives rise to aggression and aggression engenders violence viewing. The Committee suggests that the consensus of opinion is that it is unlikely that violence on television plays more than a minor role in producing violence and violent crime directly when compared with many other social factors:

'At the same time, it is generally conceded that the viewing of television violence may produce attitude change, provide justification for violence and suggest that problems can be solved through aggressive behaviour'.

The Committee drew attention to research suggesting that heavy violence viewing by parents was correlated with aggressive behaviour in children – and that parents' viewing habits are a better predictor of children's aggressiveness than the habits of the children themselves.

The Australian Committee received more submissions expressing concern at effects of television violence on children than on any other issue. In summarising the feelings expressed, it quotes the lead singer of the rock group Midnight Oil:

'There may be continued debate about the direct relationship between television violence and real violence, but it is hard to believe that the constant vicarious, relentless portrayal of violence of all levels at all times of the day on the most popular medium for young people does not in some way shape perception and reflect social and cultural values ...'[92]

The American Psychological Association (APA) Commission on Youth and Violence reflected what appears to be the majority opinion of psychologists involved in the debate – although it is by no means an unanimous view – that:

'There is absolutely no doubt that high levels of viewing violence on television are correlated with increased acceptance of aggressive attitudes and increased aggressive behaviour ...

'In addition to increasing violent behaviours towards others, viewing violence on television changes attitudes and behaviours towards violence in significant ways:

'• Viewing violence increases fear of becoming a victim of violence, with a resultant increase in self-protective behaviours and increased mistrust of others

'• Viewing violence increases desensitisation to violence, resulting in callused attitudes towards violence directed at others and a decreased likelihood to take action on behalf of the victim when violence occurs ... and

'• Viewing violence increases viewers' appetites for becoming involved with violence or exposing themselves to violence.'[93]

The Commission also found that film and television portrayals of women in victim roles, and ethnic minorities in aggressive and violent roles, exacerbated the violence experienced by women and ethnic minorities. In explicit depictions of sexual violence, 'it is the message about violence, more than the sexual nature of the materials, that appears to affect the attitudes of adolescents about rape and violence toward women.'[94] The Commission goes on to emphasise that effects of viewing violence on television can be mitigated, for example through teaching children 'critical viewing skills' at home and school, and also that 'television can be an effective and persuasive teacher of pro-social attitudes and has the potential to make a major contribution towards reducing violence'.

With regard to sexual violence, there is special concern about sadistic pornography, because it may have the effect of reinforcing dangerous tendencies in some criminally disposed individuals or of encouraging deviant sexual interest in young viewers. Any depiction of children in sexual situations is generally regarded as dangerous and the possession of such material is a criminal offence in the UK. Against this it has been argued, with some supportive evidence from Denmark, that the availability of deviant pornography may act as a safety valve that reduces some real-life crimes.[95]

Another very recent American review of available research (covering 188 studies and 1,126 comparisons carried out between 1957 and 1990) concluded:

'Overall, the vast majority of studies, whatever their methodology, showed that exposure to television violence resulted in increased aggressive behaviour, both contemporaneously and over time.'[96]

On the other side of the debate, a prominent UK commentator on the issue, Dr Guy Cumberbatch, Director of the Communications Research Group at Aston University, suggests that the majority of mass communications researchers agree first that in normal circumstances mass communication has

'a very limited effect on its audience. Moreover, the supposed evidence of a link between television violence and violence in real life is based on studies which are, for the most part, individually fatally flawed and collectively self-contradictory. Social policy decisions are simply not possible without far more robust evidence than we have had to date.'[97]

Guy Cumberbatch points in particular to the inadequate analysis of the context of violence in television and video, and the lack of acknowledgement that very often pro-social, anti-violence messages prevail. He also challenges the suggestion that children are particularly vulnerable, perhaps because they lack understanding of the real world and hence may confuse fantasy with reality; studies which have explored children's media literacy dispute this.[98]

Professor Elizabeth Newson created a new intensity of debate over the effect of violent videos when in March 1994 she circulated a paper on 'Video violence and the protection of children' which had been endorsed by 25 professionals involved with children. It asked what could be seen as the 'different' factor that has entered the lives of countless children and adolescents in recent years, and answered:

'This has to be recognised as the easy availability to children of gross images of violence on video.'[99]

While it quoted majority psychological opinion in support of a link with aggressive behaviour, it made insufficient reference to criticisms of the methodology of the research. It did emphasise the need for systematic research, 'in order to keep pace with both the growth of violence in children and the growth of violent visual material available to them'. That, at least, is likely to be a point of agreement among all parties to the debate, although the agreement will probably fall apart when research methodology begins to be discussed.

References

1 *The sleep of reason, The James Bulger Case*, David James Smith, (Century, London, 1994) p. 2 *et seq.*
2 *Daily Mirror*, 25 November 1993.
3 *Violent victims, the prevalence of abuse and loss in the lives of section 53 offenders*, Dr Gwyneth Boswell, (The Prince's Trust, London, 1995) p. 34.
4 *Violence - directions for Australia, National Committee on Violence*, (Australian Institute of Criminology, Canberra, 1990) p. xxiv.
5 *Violence and youth: psychology's response, vol. 1, Summary Report of the American Psychological Association Commission on Violence and Youth*, (American Psychological Association, Washington DC, 1993) p. 17.
6 *Ibid*, p. 21.
7 'Appendix A, The development of an individual potential for violence', *Understanding and preventing violence*, A J Reiss and J A Roth (eds.), (National Academy Press, Washington DC, 1993) p. 357 *et seq.*
8 *Ibid*.
9 *Ibid*, summary, pp. 7 and 8.
10 See note 5, p. 19.
11 'Stability of aggression over time and generations', Huesmann, Eron, Lefkowitz and Walder, *Development Psychology*, vol. 20, (1984) p. 1120.
12 'Childhood aggression and adult violence: early precursors and later-life outcomes, David P Farrington, in *The development and treatment of childhood aggression*, Debra J Pepler and Kenneth H Rubin (eds.), (Lawrence Erlbaum Associates, Hillsdale, New Jersey, 1991).
13 *Ibid*, p. 6.
14 See note 7, p. 363.
15 *Mental Health Handbook: Young people, mental health and the law - a handbook for parents and advisers*, The Children's Legal Centre, (The Children's Legal Centre, 1991).
16 'A preliminary study of criminality among twins', K O Christiansen, in *Biosocial bases of criminal behaviour*, S A Mednick and K O Christiansen (eds.), (Gardner Press, New York, 1977).
17 'A twin study of hyperactivity II. The aetiological role of genes, family relationship and perinatal adversity', R Goodman and J Stevenson, *Journal of Child Psychology and Psychiatry* 30, (1989) pp. 691-709.
18 See note 5, p. 18.
19 See note 4, p. 72.
20 See note 7, p. 366
21 *Criminal and Custodial careers of those born in 1953, 1958 and 1963, Home Office Statistical Bulletin 1989b*, (Home Office, London) referred to in note 33, p. 180.
22 *The psychology of sex differences*, E E Maccoby and C N Jacklin, (Stanford University Press, California, 1994) referred to in note 33, p. 180.

23 See note 4, p. 67.

24 'Introduction: male violence in perspective', John Archer, in *Male Violence,* John Archer (ed.), (Routledge, 1994) pp. 3-6.

25 *Ibid*, p. 5.

26 'Testosterone and aggression in children', J N Constantino, D Grosz, P Saenger *et al*, *Journal of the American Academy of Child and Adolescent Psychiatry* 32, (1993) pp. 1217-22.

27 See note 4, p. 65.

28 See note 5, p. 18.

29 For review of studies see *Prevention of violence: back to basics*, Frederick P Rivara and David Farrington, (unpublished) p. 7, later published in revised form as *Prevention of Violence: role of the pediatrician*, see note 43.

30 *Ibid*, p. 9.

31 See note 4.

32 See note 5, p. 19.

33 'The causes and prevention of offending, with special reference to violence', David Farrington, in *Coping with violence: a practical handbook for health-care workers,* Jonathan Shepherd (ed.), (Oxford University Press, 1994) ch. 9, pp. 150-182.

34 'Family factors related to the persistence of psychopathology in childhood and adolescence', P Cohen and J Brook, *Psychiatry,* vol. 50, (1987) pp. 332-45, reported in note 43, pp. 421-29.

35 *Crime and the family: improving child-rearing and preventing delinquency,* David Utting, Jon Bright and Clem Henricson, (Family Policy Studies Centre, 1993) p. 22.

36 See note 4, p. 79.

37 See note 3, p. 21.

38 See note 33, p. 163.

39 See note 12, p. 19.

40 'Understanding and preventing bullying', David P Farrington, *Crime and Justice, a review of research*, ed. Michael Tonry, vol. 17 (The University of Chicago Press, 1991) p. 399.

41 See note 12, pp.169–88.

42 'Environmental and biological factors in the development of aggressive behaviour', Dan Olweus, in *Explaining criminal behaviour*, W Buikhuisen and S A Mednick (eds.), (E J Brill, Leiden, 1988) pp. 90-120.

43 'Prevention of Violence: role of the pediatrician', Frederick P Rivara and David P Farrington, *Archives of Pediatrics and Adolescent Medicine*, vol. 149, (April 1995) pp. 421-29.

44 'Family interaction and delinquent behaviour', James Snyder and Gerald Patterson, in *Handbook of juvenile delinquency*, Herbert C Quay (ed.), (John Wiley, New York, 1987) ch. 8, pp. 218-43.

45 'The development of offending and anti-social behaviour from childhood: key findings from the Cambridge Study in Delinquent Development', *Journal of Child Psychology and Psychiatry*, vol.36 (1995) pp. 929–64, and also 'Parental Supervision: a neglected aspect of delinquency', H Wilson, *British Journal of Criminology,* vol. 20, (1980) pp. 203–35.

46 See note 5, p. 19.

47 See note 4, p. 78.

48 *Aggression and its correlates over 22 years*, Leonard B Eron, L Rowell Huesmann, Eric Dubow, Richard Romanoff and Patty W Yarmel, (University of Illinois, Chicago, 1983).

49 'Parent-child interaction, television violence and aggression of children', Leonard B Eron, *American Psychologist,* vol. 37 no. 4, (July 1974) p. 197.

50 *A community study of physical violence to children in the home, and associated variables*, Marjorie Smith, Thomas Coram Research Unit, poster paper presented at International Society for the Prevention of Child Abuse and Neglect Fifth European Conference on Child Abuse and

Neglect, Oslo, Norway, May 1995.

51 *The extent of parental physical punishment in the UK*, John and Elizabeth Newson, APPROACH Ltd, London, 1990 and paper prepared for Children's Legal Centre seminar on *Protecting children from parental physical punishment*, John and Elizabeth Newson, University of Nottingham, July 1986.

52 See note 3, p. 25.

53 'Submission from British Psychological Society', reported in *Report on Family Law, Scottish Law Commission*, (HMSO, Edinburgh, 1992) p. 21.

54 *Beating the devil out of them: corporal punishment in American families*, Murray A Straus, (Lexington Books, New York, 1994) p. 186.

55 *Report on Family Law, Scottish Law Commission*, HMSO Edinburgh, 1992, contains details of opinion poll of Scottish adults showing that over 90 per cent believed it should be unlawful to hit a child with a belt, stick or other object, p. 31; 'Spanking dad is cleared of assault on sons', *Wolverhampton Express and Star*, 20 March 1993; 'Victory for mother who spanked girl', *Daily Express*, 20 April 1993.

56 Education (No. 2) Act 1986, Section 47; House of Lords *Hansard* (10 May 1993).

57 See note 4, p. 249.

58 See note 5, p. 23.

59 See note 4, p. 97.

60 See note 5, p. 26.

61 See note 4, p. 96.

62 See note 33, p. 167.

63 *The roots of delinquency*, Michael Wadsworth, (Martin Robertson, 1979) see note 35, pp. 18 and 82.

64 See note 35, p. 19.

65 *Ibid.*

66 See note 5, p. 24.

67 *Household below average income (HBAI) statistics for 1992/93*, (Department of Social Security, June 1995).

68 *Juvenile Violence in a Winner-Loser Culture – Socio-economic and Familial Origins of the Rise of Violence Against the Person*, Oliver James, (Free Association Books, 1995).

69 See note 5, p. 25.

70 *National Child Development Study*, the National Children's Bureau. A follow-up study of children born in a particular week of 1958, held at the Social Statistics Research Unit, City University, London.

71 See note 4, p. 84.

72 *Programmatic intervention with aggressive children in the school setting,* J D Coie, M Underwood and J E Lochman, see note 41, pp. 389-410.

73 'Familial and temperamental determinants of aggressive behaviour in adolescent boys: a causal analysis', Dan Olweus, *Developmental Psychology* 16, (1980) pp. 644-60.

74 'Bullying in the Junior School', Pete Stephenson and Dave Smith, 1989, in *Bullying in schools,* Delwyn Tattum and David Lane (eds.), (Trentham Books, 1988) pp. 45-57.

75 See note 7, p. 370.

76 See note 40, p. 404.

77 See note 45.

78 See note 33, pp. 165 and 166.

79 *Fifteen thousand hours*, Michael Rutter *et al*, (Open Books, London, 1979).

80 *Discipline in schools: Report of the Committee of Enquiry,* chaired by Lord Elton, Department of Education and Science and Welsh Office, (HMSO, 1989).

81 See note 5, p. 29.

82 See note 4, p. 75.

83 Tenth version, (World Health Organisation, 1992).

84 *Alcohol policy and the public good*, G Edwards, P Anderson, T F Babor *et al*, (Oxford University Press, Oxford, 1994).

85 *Adolescent drinking*, OPCS, (HMSO, London, 1986).

86 *Alcohol drinking and family life in Europe: a pilot study;* Report to Alcohol Education and Research Council, London, 1995; *Views and behaviour of 11, 13, and 15 year-olds from 11 countries*, A J C King and B Coles, (Ministry of National Health and Welfare, Ottawa, Canada, 1992).

87 See note 5, p. 28.

88 See note 4, p. 86.

89 See note 9, p. 14.

90 *Alcohol in human violence*, Pernanen, Kai, (Guildhall Press, New York, 1991).

91 *The 'video violence' debate: media researchers respond*, Dr Martin Barker *et al*, (unpublished, 1994).

92 See note 4, pp. 80-2.

93 See note 5, p. 33.

94 *Ibid*, p. 33 et seq.

95 'The effect of easy availability of pornography on the incidence of sex crimes: the Danish experience', *Journal of Social Issues*, vol. 29 (1973) pp.163–181.

96 See note 7, p. 371.

97 'TV Violence - don't cloud the issue with common sense', Dr Guy Cumberbatch, *Health at school,* vol. 1, no. 6, (March 1986) p. 190.

98 See for example *Children talking television*, David Buckingham, (Falmer Press, 1993).

99 *Video violence and the protection of children*, Elizabeth Newson, Professor of Developmental Psychology, Child Development Research Unit, University of Nottingham, (March 1994).

Section 2

Reducing violence involving children
discussion and recommendations

The Commission's priority recommendations are set out on pages 18-27. In the following major section of the report, the Commission provides detailed discussion and expands these and other recommendations for reducing violence involving children. The Commission emphasised in section 1 that many factors are involved in the development of violence, and that their interaction is complex. This is reflected in the range of issues covered in the following section, which is divided into three inter-related parts:

1 Working towards a non-violent society:
  national and local commitment and co-ordination

2 Policies for children and families which support violence prevention

3 Other issues.

PART 1

Working towards a non-violent society:
national and local commitment and co-ordination

Making a commitment to non-violence

Nobody wants a violent society. This is an issue about which it is reasonable to seek and expect national consensus. We need to turn that consensus into an overt and stated commitment which leads to consistent action. If we wish to become a less violent society, we need to encourage and promote non-violent values in a comprehensive and consistent way.

Quotes boxed in the text are from children and young people who took part in discussions based on a questionnaire circulated by the Commission – see Appendix 5, page 286.

The Commission emphasises working **towards** a non-violent society. Banishing violence completely is not a realistic expectation in the face of the strong social and personal pressures which impel some individuals to violent actions. Nevertheless, we believe that the volume and seriousness of violence in society could be greatly reduced by commitment and action at all levels, from central government to individual parents.

'I think violence is stupid and dangerous. The people who use violence need to get their lives sorted out.'

'Parents shouldn't be violent themselves, should show kids that it is wrong to fight. Schools should be harder on bullies, councils should have more things for kids to do, the government ought to give people more jobs and money and the media shouldn't make violence in films look unreal, like in a fight someone falls out of a window and then walks away.'

'Adults should learn to cool down.'

The Commission proposes that the adoption and development of a UK-wide **commitment to non-violence** should be given similar priority to adopting equal opportunities statements and developing equal opportunities policies, and given the links between discrimination and violence, and the pronounced gender factor in violence, there will be corresponding links between the two processes. The Commission emphasises that this is not a pacifist statement or commitment. We recognise that violence may sometimes be necessary to restrain violence, whether on an individual or international scale, when all reasonable attempts to resolve the conflict have failed. Those who use violence as a restraint should use it only as a last resort, should use only the necessary minimum force and should take all possible steps to avoid injuring innocent bystanders.

We distinguish between positive forms of aggression and the negative aspects which lead to violence. Human beings need drive, self-assertion and competitiveness in order to prosper — or even survive — in modern societies. They are qualities which, if properly channelled and used, can benefit society as well as the individual.

The commitment to work towards a non-violent society needs to be adopted and appropriately applied within all services which affect children and families. The aims of services and the ways in which they are provided, the content of services and all training for those involved should be reviewed in the light of the commitment.

Recommendation
Individuals, communities and government at all levels should adopt a 'commitment to non-violence', of similar standing to existing commitments to equal opportunities.

The aims of the commitment are to work towards a society in which individuals, communities and government share non-violent values and resolve conflict by non-violent means. Building such a society involves in particular reducing and preventing violence involving children, by developing:
- *understanding of the factors which interact to increase the potential for violence involving children, as well as those which prevent children from becoming violent*
- *action to prevent violence in all services and work with families and children*
- *consistent disavowal of all forms of inter-personal violence – in particular by opinion-leaders.*

[Aimed at central and local government; opposition parties; voluntary and private agencies and groups]

Translating the commitment into action
Checklists for working towards a non-violent society

The Commission wants its proposals to be seen as practical and immediately relevant to the everyday lives of children, families and those who seek to support them. To turn the commitment to non-violence into a practical programme, families, children and all those working with and for them need to consider their relationships and work with children in the light of it. The Commission therefore proposes a series of *Checklists for working towards a non-violent society*. Their purpose is to demonstrate how to develop practically and in detail the commitment to non-violence.

The Commission believes that available research on the antecedents of violence, coupled with the value-base of the UN Convention on the Rights of the Child (see Appendix 2, page 251) make it possible to devise in some detail strategies for prevention targeted in particular at children, parents, other carers and those working with and for them.

'I think that you should show people the consequences of being violent and should learn that violence solves nothing.'

'People should learn to get on with each other. Parents teach children to 'stand up for themselves': if anyone hits you – hit them back. Adults should learn not to fight. Sometimes fighting is related to drinking.'

While the overall aim is the creation of a safe, non-violent society for all and the prevention of all forms of inter-personal violence, our focus is on children not simply because this is also the focus of the Commission, but because there is ample evidence to show that early intervention is vital to prevent the development of violent attitudes and actions; that what happens in the early years, and in particular within the family and in schools, is most influential in determining attitudes to violence. Violence to children is inextricably linked to violence by children. The current level of apparent public concern about violence involving children makes it a good moment to launch such an initiative.

Interventions to reduce and prevent violence involving children will be of benefit to the whole community. And since many of the factors implicated in the development of violent attitudes and actions are also linked with other forms of anti-social and criminal behaviour, effective action to prevent or minimise violence can be expected to increase general levels of socialised behaviour.

Since violence is widely recognised as 'a failure of socialisation', programmes to prevent it – whether directed at children themselves or at their parents – are often directed at correcting negative behaviours, and focused on what is wrong. But much of the work against violence must be positive: 'good' childcare protects children from developing violent attitudes, even when they face many other risk factors. Children and young people can be taught pro-social attitudes and behaviour.

At the moment our society professes abhorrence of individual violence – and other forms of anti-social behaviour – but tolerates, even rewards many societal manifestations of violence, not only in entertainment and in sport, but generally in admiration for 'macho' male attitudes. The confusions to which these contradictions give rise lessen the impact and sustainability of existing strategies against violence. Anti-bullying programmes in schools, for example, often have to struggle against the open approval of influential members of staff for children 'standing up for themselves' and their disapproval of 'telling tales'. Many parents, even those who profess themselves against violence, encourage children to 'hit back' and hit and humiliate children themselves in the name of discipline.

Positive parenting is the foundation of a non-violent society. It minimises the chances of children experiencing violence and, consequently, minimises the likelihood that they will behave violently. Furthermore the effect should be self-perpetuating as such children are likely to grow not only into non-violent adults but also into positive parents in their turn.

Any programme that contributes to timely and realistic preparation for parenthood, to practical and emotional support for parents and carers and to opportunities for optimal health and development for all children, is relevant to prevention of violence (and the Commission makes more general recommendations for the development of such programmes in Part 2 below, page 129). Taken together, such programmes may produce a social context which is generally unsympathetic to violence. But to review programmes, and the services that produce them, from a specifically anti-violence perspective is to go much further. Such reviews take the programmes' overall purpose and content for granted but focus narrowly on what is being done, or could be done, within them to prevent and combat violence and to replace it with positively non-violent attitudes, aspirations and behaviour. It is that process of review at every level of practice that the *Checklists for working towards a non-violent society* are intended to facilitate.

Parents and parent-figures are the first, and arguably the most compelling, influence on children. However parents are not the only influence and do not act in isolation. A commitment to non-violence and a violence-prevention perspective is important in all services that can influence and impact on children and families: most obviously for those in health services, daycare, education and youth services.

Thus the first generic *Checklist for working towards a non-violent society*, set out in Appendix 1, page 241, addresses itself to parenting, but is aimed not only at parents and future parents, but also at those working with them, supporting, educating and informing them in many different settings. The Checklist addresses the following issues in sections:

1 Expectations of, and demands made on, children should realistically reflect their maturity and development
2 All discipline should be positive, and children should be taught pro-social values and behaviour, including in particular non-violent conflict resolution
3 Non-violence should be clearly and consistently preferred and promoted
4 Adults should take responsibility not only for protecting children from violence done to them but also for preventing violence done by them.

These principles should be taught to, and observed by, anyone who is involved in any capacity with children of any age. The principles are equally relevant to parents, childcare workers and teachers, and to infants, pre-school children and older children. They become doubly relevant in adolescence when young people have parallel roles as 'children' in relation to the adults on whom they depend, and as 'adults' in relation to those younger than themselves.

Help and advice on reducing and preventing violence should be available to all involved in care and education of children, and should be sought if violence threatens to escalate.

Checklists with similar aims and using the same structure should

---

A Merseyside youth leader comments following discussion of the Commission's questionnaire with four groups of young men aged between 14 and 18:

'Listening to these young people writing their quotes and re-reading them, it is obvious they know where the education should start – the parents. Their schools also do not come high on their list of doing anything positive. They do give indications that at least their school helps to reinforce the macho image. The girls have the brains, the boys do the fighting.

'The police and the social services hardly came into the discussions as they were seen as the enforcing agencies.

'It appears from the young people's comments that some families hold to a culture of violence. They believe that corporal punishment is a necessary discipline and that winning a fight confirms your masculinity, giving you "respect" in a society that is finding very little use for young juvenile males.'

now be drawn up adding items of particular relevance to particular services or settings. The following areas might be covered initially:

- pre-school, early years and family support
- health, mental health and social services for children and families
- schools
- police, probation service, system of juvenile justice
- environmental planning, housing.

Making a commitment to non-violence: working towards a non-violent society

Adoption of the commitment to non-violence and use of *Checklists for working towards a non-violent society* will be particularly important for the following services and individuals working in them:

Health

- Members, administrators and officials in health authorities and trusts; Northern Ireland Boards
- Health education and promotion; preparation for parenthood; pre-conceptual care; ante-natal and post-natal services, midwives and obstetric staff; family health service authorities, GPs and health visitors; community and school nurses; community paediatricians
- Purchasers and providers of public health, primary and community health, child health services, mental health services; psychological and psychiatric services
- Private health care.

Education

- The Schools Curriculum and Assessment Authority, Scottish Consultative Council on the Curriculum, NI Council for the Curriculum, Examinations and Assessment, for inclusion in appropriate parts of the National Curriculum
- Local education authorities, NI Education and Library Boards, members and officials
- School governors
- Pre-schooling; primary and secondary schools and special schools and units, including private, grant-maintained and voluntary sectors
- Care staff in residential education
- Education social workers, educational psychologists and other support staff
- Office for Standards in Education, school inspectors.

Social services

- Child protection; child care, residential and other; daycare; services for disabled children; family support; family violence
- Social Services Inspectorate
- Probation service.

Police
- Child protection/ domestic violence units; neighbourhood and community policing.

Juvenile justice system
- Crown prosecution service, the judiciary, lawyers and other advocates working with or for children.

Housing and planning authorities and agencies

Voluntary sector
- Voluntary organisations working with or for children and families, and involved in community safety, crime prevention, victim support.

Private sector
- As above.

Training institutions and services
- Covering all above and any others working with or for families and children.

Recommendation

A series of Checklists for working towards a non-violent society, following the framework developed in the Commission's report, should be prepared and disseminated for parents and all those working with or for families and children, in conjunction with appropriate working groups of practitioners.

[Aimed at parents, carers, and all practitioners working with families and children]

The Commission has started this process by drafting the first generic checklist on parenting – see Appendix 1, page 241. The Gulbenkian Foundation has agreed that it will consider co-ordinating the process of developing further checklists with small working groups of practitioners, involving Commission members, and a partnership of major organisations is being formed to help promotion and dissemination.

A UK-wide media campaign to promote non-violent values and attitudes

All major commissions on violence have identified the need to challenge the strong social attitudes which condone violence. The Commission emphasises too the need for opinion leaders of all kinds to denounce all forms of violence involving children.

The Australian National Committee on Violence identified as the first major objective for its recommendations the adoption of a national strategy for the promotion of non-violent attitudes:

'The degree to which many Australians condone violence is one of the fundamental impediments to achieving a non-violent society. The Committee considers that a strategy should be launched to promote non-violent attitudes, beginning with a national media campaign ... The Committee believes that Governments and all opinion leaders must denounce violence forcefully and unequivocally, taking special care not to tolerate some forms of violence while condemning others.'[1]

In the UK, parliamentary and other political debates about law and order and youth crime are still peppered with sentiments that condone or propose violent 'solutions' like corporal punishment for violent offences, which if implemented would undoubtedly exacerbate the problem. The same is true about debates concerning discipline within the family. The media, and in particular the tabloid press, frequently still reflect and encourage these attitudes. In particular, they promote macho male images, often with an implied approval of violence. Many individual columnists, of course, take a more enlightened view. On page 53 we identified other ways in which UK society currently condones inter-personal violence.

Linked to the arrangements for ensuring national and local action for violence prevention as part of community safety strategies (outlined below, page 96), the Commission believes that a sustained public education campaign is required consistently to promote non-violent attitudes and values. Our recommendations for a commitment to non-violence and checklists for working towards a non-violent society relate to building these values permanently into services and work with and for children and families. There is also a strong case for a government-led and -funded media campaign to provide a high profile position statement and to seek to lead public opinion. The campaign should take full account of the gender factor and the need to challenge macho male images, and should highlight those groups particularly at risk of violence: infants, young people, people with a disability and minority ethnic groups.

Planning of the campaign should be influenced by evaluations of other similar public health campaigns (e.g. on smoking, drink driving etc.), and evaluations of the NSPCC's public information campaigns on child abuse prevention, and, for example, the 'Zero Tolerance' campaign against violence in the family.[2] The campaign should be planned to be ongoing, with a high profile launch using television, radio, posters and other channels of communication. Materials should be prepared which can be used or adapted within local community safety strategies. The Commission also proposes (page 208) that the media should be encouraged to maximise its huge potential for promoting pro-social and non-violent attitudes, through direct educational contributions and through programme planning generally.

Recommendation
The Department of Health and other appropriate government departments should plan and implement a media campaign aimed at developing individual and community responsibility for achieving a non-violent society, and in particular for reducing and preventing violence involving children.

[Department of Health and other government departments; opposition parties]

Co-ordinating a UK-wide strategy against violence

A UK-wide strategy to promote non-violent values and attitudes, and in particular to reduce and prevent violence involving children, demands leadership from government and co-ordination at local level. Research on risk factors for violence and other anti-social behaviour and on effective interventions underlines the importance of a multi-agency approach.

While the emphasis of the Commission's recommendations is on empowering communities, families and children themselves to reduce and prevent violence, there is a need for national and local leadership and co-ordination. The increasing fragmentation of children's services following local government reorganisation adds importance to this.

Before drafting recommendations for national and local co-ordination to prevent violence involving children, the Commission considered relevant existing structures. The following sections briefly summarise these before making recommendations for change or development.

Central government

At central government level, responsibility for responding to violence involving children, and for services relevant to interventions to reduce violence is split among many departments, including the Home Office, Department of Health, Education and Employment, Environment, Transport, Scottish, Northern Ireland and Welsh Offices etc. In many areas of policy affecting children, lack of communication and co-ordination between departments appears to cause problems which have been well-documented in other reports. There is currently no co-ordinating committee or mechanism for all inter-departmental work on violence prevention The most relevant structures at ministerial level appear to be:

Inter-Departmental Group on Child Abuse, on which the Department of Health takes the lead. The Group was set up in 1987 in recognition of the need for a permanent mechanism to facilitate inter-departmental co-operation in child protection: inter-personal violence involving children is among the matters considered by the Group

Ministerial Group on Crime Prevention, which is chaired by a Home Office Minister of State, and supported by an inter-departmental group of officials. The Ministerial Group seeks to ensure that the policies of various departments which have a crime prevention perspective are co-ordinated and that departments pursue crime prevention objectives in the implementation of their policies and programmes

Ministerial Group on Domestic Violence, chaired by the Home Office and bringing together the Lord Chancellor's Department, the Law Officer's Department, Crown Prosecution Services, Departments of Environment, Health, Social Security, Department for Education and Employment, Welsh, Scottish and Northern Ireland Offices and the Treasury, and supported by an interdepartmental group of officials

Inter-Departmental Consultative Group on Provision for Young Children, chaired by a Parliamentary Under-Secretary of State at the Department of Health, and bringing together representatives of the Department of Health, Department for Education and Employment, other departmental observers and the voluntary and private sector. This group has no specific violence prevention function, but its consultative role in relation to early years care and education is relevant.

It is clear that the major responsibility is centred in:
- the **Department of Health,** which oversees child protection, child care aspects of youth justice and development of family support services and
- the **Home Office,** responsible for crime prevention, the law on violent and sexual offences against children and the sentencing powers of the courts dealing with young offenders.

Both the Department of Health and the Home Office plan and support relevant research programmes. **The Scottish Office, Welsh Office** and **DHSS Northern Ireland** have similar responsibilities and are represented on the various inter-departmental groups.

In May 1993 the **National Board for Crime Prevention** was set up by the then Minister of State at the Home Office, Michael Jack. The aim of the 12-member multi-disciplinary Board is

'To find new ways of involving all sections of the community, including business and the voluntary sector, in the development and delivery of crime prevention, both locally and nationally'.

Its remit is to advise on the development of measures to reduce crime and the fear of crime, to suggest local practical strategies, and to recommend ways in which all sections of the community can be involved in crime prevention. At early meetings the Board decided to direct its initial efforts at retail crime, car crime and young people and crime. In relation to the latter, it has established a Working Group on Young People and Crime, chaired by the Director of the National Youth Agency and focusing on the contribution of youth service agencies in diverting young people from crime.

In England and Wales, the **Children Act Advisory Committee** is also relevant, including as it does the concept of children in need and child protection. It is currently (1995) chaired by Mrs Justice Bracewell and reports to the Lord Chancellor, Home Secretary, Secretary of State for Health and the President of the Family Division.

While responding to crime and crime prevention has become a high profile area of government (and opposition) policy, there is no sign of this leading to a co-ordinated, knowledge-based approach to reducing and preventing violence involving children. The Commission does not seek to minimise the anti-social nature of property crime, but it does believe that within the overall field of crime prevention, aiming to reduce and prevent inter-personal violence must be seen as the priority. There is ample evidence that to achieve this aim, the major focus for interventions must be on families, carers and children. It is clear that many of the factors associated with a growth of violent attitudes and actions are also associated with other anti-social behaviour. This means that planned interventions focused on the factors are likely to have other beneficial effects.

Various government-supported bodies are already actively involved in co-ordinating and supporting relevant work with local bodies. **Crime Concern** is the crime prevention body for England and Wales, formed in 1989 to work with local agencies on reducing crime and creating safer communities. Crime Concern has placed an important emphasis on child-centred violence prevention in various aspects of its work, including:

- promoting non-violent child-rearing techniques
- preventing violence against children in the home through family support and parenting education initiatives, actively promoted with various organisations
- preventing violence against children in schools through support for Youth Action Groups, its newspaper for school-age children YX, and an emphasis on anti-bullying strategies
- teaching children how to recognise and deal with dangerous situations through the *Crucial Crew* scheme.

Crime Concern has made a point of consulting children and young people directly about their concerns in its fieldwork.[3]

Crime Concern Scotland has a similar role. **Victim Support** provides a service to victims of crime (see page 216).

The Commission bases its recommendations not only on available knowledge of the origins of inter-personal violence involving children, but on the value-base of the UN Convention on the Rights of the Child. It notes with concern the lack of a co-ordinated approach to full implementation of the Convention, which the Government ratified in 1991. Other countries have developed formal co-ordinating structures within government to respond fully to the Convention, and many have set up statutory offices – ombudspeople or commissioners – to promote the rights and interests of children (who, after all, have no vote and no say in the political process) at government level. A previous Gulbenkian Foundation report, *Taking children seriously*, provided a detailed blueprint for a statutory children's rights commissioner.[4] In relation to violence involving children, the office would, as in other areas of policy, provide a powerful independent voice for children, working to the principles in the UN Convention, and in close co-operation with children and organisations of children. The Commission welcomes the decision of an increasing number of local authorities, health authorities and trusts, and voluntary and professional organisations formally to 'adopt' the Convention and commit themselves to using its principles and standards as a basis for all policy development affecting children.

Our recommendations for action at central government level aim to provide a supportive framework for co-ordinated action to develop a non-violent society, and to ensure proper respect for the principles and standards of the Convention in the development of government policy which affects children. We propose a Ministerial Group for Community Safety which should be chaired by a Cabinet minister and serviced by appropriate inter-departmental groups of senior officials covering England, Wales, Scotland and Northern Ireland. Sub-groups of Ministers and officials should consider particular aspects of community safety. Departments involved should include the Department of Health, Home Office, Department for Education and Employment, Departments of Environment, Social Security, Lord Chancellor's Department, Law Officers' Department, Crown Prosecution Service, the Treasury and Welsh, Scottish and Northern Ireland Offices and Departments.

The Inter-Departmental Consultative Group on Provision for Young Children should also adopt the commitment to non-violence, and take on a key role in promoting preventive work with families and young children, within the context of the overall community safety strategy set by the Ministerial Group. We recommend elsewhere improvements in the collection of statistics and other information related to violence involving children (page 227), and more consistent evaluation of interventions (page 231). Such information should be reported at least annually in appropriate form to the Ministerial Group on

Community Safety, and appropriate sub-groups, which should consider it and make recommendations.

Recommendations

An inter-departmental Ministerial Group, covering the whole of the UK and reporting to a Cabinet Committee, should agree and oversee implementation of an ongoing community safety strategy, whose first commitment should be working towards a non-violent society. A key segment of its work should be to reduce and prevent violence involving children.

[Government; opposition parties]

The National Board for Crime Prevention should be re-constituted as the National Board for Community Safety, and its aim, remit and membership reviewed to ensure that reduction and prevention of violence involving children is a priority concern within the wide range of crime prevention strategies. Children and young people should be appropriately represented, and consulted.

[Home Office; National Board for Crime Prevention]

The Commission strongly supports the proposal for an independent statutory office of Children's Rights Commissioner, to promote children's rights and interests at government level. It commends the detailed blueprint for such an office set out in another Gulbenkian Foundation publication, Taking children seriously.

[Government; opposition parties]

Principles for implementation

The Commission emphasises that all initiatives aiming to reduce and prevent violence should:
- *encourage children's active participation: children's views should be sought and given careful consideration, and their active participation should be promoted. This and other principles in the UN Convention on the Rights of the Child should be used as a framework for policy development (see Appendix 2, page 251).*
- *challenge discrimination: the violent victimisation of particular groups in society should be recognised, and protection from violence and prevention of violence should be sought without discrimination. Information and materials for violence prevention should be available in appropriate forms and languages for all communities.*

[All agencies]

Regional co-ordination

In April 1994, the Government brought together regional offices of the Departments of Trade and Industry, Employment, Environment and Transport in England, setting up 10 new regional offices, which are to prepare annual regeneration statements setting out key priorities for regeneration and economic development, and bidding for resources from the Single Regeneration Budget. The intention is that these offices should develop close links with Departments without a regional structure, including the Home Office, Department of Health and Department for Education and Employment.

A Ministerial Committee for Regeneration will consider regeneration policies and their co-ordination, and give guidance to the Secretary of State for the Environment who has lead responsibility for implementing regeneration policy. The Single Regeneration Budget brings together 20 separate funding programmes from the Departments of the Environment, Trade and Industry, Education and Employment and the Home Office and amounted to £1.4 billion in 1994/95. The Commission believes that the Department of Health, as the Department with lead responsibility for children, should be represented in these structures. Current objectives include:

- enhancing the job prospects, education and skills of local people, particularly the young and those at a disadvantage
- tackling crime and improving community safety
- improving the local environment and infrastructure
- promoting initiatives of benefit to ethnic minorities
- encouraging tenant and community participation.

Action to reduce and prevent violence involving children falls clearly within the scope of the regeneration initiative. One of the expressed aims of the new regional structure has been to ensure co-ordination between crime prevention and other relevant initiatives. It is essential that regions share information, skills and experience on a UK-wide basis. There should be close co-ordination with the Ministerial Group for Community Safety proposed above, and the related inter-departmental groups of officers. Each regional office should have designated senior staff responsible for initiatives aimed at children and young people. These senior staff should develop regional strategies for community safety giving scope for action to reduce and prevent violence involving children, drawing on local community safety strategies and children's services plans (see page 104). A network of representatives from the regions should share information, experience and ideas.

Recommendation

The Ministerial Committee for Regeneration should ensure that action to reduce violence involving children Is a specific priority within its responsibility for community safety, and within the objectives of the Single Regeneration Budget.

[Government; opposition parties]

Local co-ordination

Local community safety strategies

A recent report of an independent working group on *Safer communities – the local delivery of crime prevention through the partnership approach* (the Morgan Report) proposed that

'in the longer term local authorities, working in conjunction with the police, should have clear statutory responsibilities for the development and stimulation of community safety and crime prevention programmes, and for progressing at a local level a multi-agency approach to community safety.'

In the shorter term, the Working Group proposed a Code of Practice to encourage full involvement of local authorities in local partnerships.[5]

The Working Group, chaired by Mr James Morgan, proposed that the term 'community safety' rather than the narrower 'crime prevention' (often interpreted as a police responsibility) could encourage greater participation from all sections of the community in the fight against crime:

'Community safety should be seen as the legitimate concern of all in the local community.'[6]

The Commission echoes the Working Group in believing that 'community safety' is a valuable concept which should encompass the prevention of violence involving children. In justifying its central proposal that local authorities should have a statutory responsibility for community safety together with the police, the Working Group lists several advantages:

• 'The first is that responsibility for the development of a programme for community safety is a proper role for the local authority which controls important services and resources which need to be committed in accordance with a multi-agency strategy for community safety. The local authority also rightly has concerns about its total environment.

• 'Second, the active participation of the local authority will encourage a wider acceptance of responsibility amongst the potential partners in the multi-agency arrangements and will discourage the community from assuming that the police can and will do all that is required.

96

- 'Thirdly, it provides for permanency, continuity and a clear focus for involvement of the business and voluntary sectors.

- 'Fourthly and crucially it provides for the legitimate and productive involvement of elected members.'[7]

The development of a local Community Safety Strategy should take place at a level equivalent to the highest tier of local government. The role of a multi-agency Community Safety Strategy Group would be to formalise a joint commitment to community safety and crime prevention, formulate objectives based on an analysis of local problems, identify the responsibilities of different departments and organisations, monitor progress and report regularly.

More locally, the report proposes that a wide group of organisations would be brought together to form local Action Groups responsible for policy implementation (see also proposals for co-ordinating neighbourhood responsibility for child protection, page 107). It does not propose any particular priority for action on violence involving children, nor does it suggest any co-ordination with existing child protection structures, already organised on a local multi-agency basis (see page 101).

The proposed role for local Action Groups is relevant to prevention of violence, though the Morgan Report lays emphasis on its 'crime prevention' aspect and the need:
- to assess the nature of the problem locally
- to formulate objectives and a strategic plan for community safety within the area
- to consult local communities and organisations about the strategy
- to appoint either topic-based groups or neighbourhood-based groups to plan and implement the detail of the strategic plan
- to monitor, review and report publicly on progress.

The report gives examples of 'a portfolio of community safety initiatives', many of which are relevant to the prevention of violence involving children.[8]

The increasing fragmentation of local children's services following local government reorganisation makes it all the more vital to ensure co-ordination at local level. There are concerns, as there are with Area Child Protection Committees, that current reorganisation, purchaser/provider splits and so on may inhibit the development of effective co-ordinated community safety programmes.

The Commission undertook a survey of chief executives of local authorities, seeking information on the development of community safety strategies and the extent to which they included particular strategies for reducing/preventing violence involving children. We received a very substantial and valuable response, summarised in Appendix 4 (page 267). About half the 152 authorities which responded had adopted a community safety strategy, and of these, 46 included particular strategies for reducing/preventing violence involving children. But only about a quarter had views on how such action should be co-ordinated locally, and only a very small minority reported any co-ordination between community safety activities and the Area Child Protection Committee. Many expressed active interest in the outcome of the Commission's proposals, and all will of course receive summaries of the Commission's report.

The Commission's survey of local community safety strategies (see Appendix 4 for full report, page 267) found that while reducing and preventing violence involving children was an explicit priority in a small minority of schemes, many strategies included relevant initiatives. For example:

- School involvement police groups providing personal safety talks and training

- holiday play schemes with a priority of promoting personal safety

- parental seminars on issues of violence, drugs and solvent abuse

- school youth action and crime prevention panels

- diversion projects for young offenders, including vehicle offenders

- early years provision and after-school clubs

- parenting skills training

- development of local 'no physical punishment' policy

- psychological service providing behaviour management training

- anti-bullying and mediation schemes in schools

- home safety checks

- designated teacher for child protection in all area schools

- a booklet listing all local sources of support and advice for parents

- family centres to act as focuses for social change

- pilot project to reduce neighbour disputes

- counselling in anger management, men's groups

- support project for 16-18 year-olds who have been in care or are homeless

- secondary school Student Council to represent the interests of young people and respond to consultations about local services

- development of leisure facilities for children

- media campaign to 'improve relationships by managing family conflict'

- environmental improvements – such as street lighting, video surveillance.

It appears to the Commission that the prevention of inter-personal violence must be seen as the highest priority for community safety strategies. Within that priority, prevention of violence involving children needs to be highlighted because of its potential for reducing all forms of inter-personal violence. Our recommendations in relation to community safety strategies are intended to achieve this by providing a local framework for inter-agency work. Such frameworks will need to be sensitive to the varying structures of local government in different jurisdictions. They should in our view be set out in legislation. Until such legislation is enacted, an inter-departmental circular should encourage the development of community safety strategies which are explicitly committed to working towards a non-violent society and have as major components the reduction and prevention of violence involving children, and work with child victims and perpetrators of violence to children. Strategies should be developed with the participation of and in consultation with appropriate groups of children. The circular should set out ways of ensuring appropriate co-ordination and integration with the work of Child Protection Committees (see page 101).

Recommendations

The government should introduce legislation to make the formation and implementation of a community safety strategy a statutory duty of local authorities, setting out the duty in such a way as to encourage an inter-agency community-based approach. The legislation should be sensitive to the structure of local government in all jurisdictions, and should ensure participation of all authorities and the voluntary and private sectors.

Working towards a non-violent society should be a key aim for local community safety strategies, involving a particular focus on reducing and preventing violence involving children. Local strategies should set out ways of ensuring co-ordination of relevant preventive work including:
- *local planning (see page 100)*
- *child protection (see page 101)*
- *prevention of family violence (see page 106)*
- *suicide prevention (see page 189)*
- *accident prevention (see page 155)*
- *prevention of sport violence (see page 218)*
- *victim support and rehabilitation (see page 215).*

National and local media and regulatory bodies for the media should be appropriately represented in the development of community safety strategies to reduce and prevent violence involving children.

[Government; opposition parties]

Training and Enterprise Councils should be alerted to the perspective of violence prevention, involved in Community Safety Strategies and encouraged to ensure appropriate opportunities for vulnerable and difficult-to-place groups of young people, including those identified in schools as having emotional and behavioural difficulties.

[Training and Enterprise Councils]

Local planning initiatives

Within the planning sector, there have been attempts to co-ordinate action on crime prevention, but with no particular priority for violence prevention. A joint circular from the Department of the Environment and the Welsh Office issued in 1994, *Planning out crime*, emphasised the contribution that good planning, when co-ordinated with other measures, can make to crime prevention:

> 'Desolate, sterile and featureless surroundings can engender feelings of hostility, anonymity and alienation. Used sensitively the planning system can be instrumental in producing attractive and well-managed environments that help to discourage anti-social behaviour. It can also be used to make it harder for criminals to find targets. It can do this by encouraging developers to adopt designs for new developments that take the security of people and property fully into account ...'[9]

In particular the circular emphasises that development plans can be used to encourage the provision of leisure and social facilities for the young.

A Junior Minister for the Environment, Sir Paul Beresford, emphasised in a recent speech that the 'fortress mentality' is largely self-defeating:

> 'Generally speaking, the more people there are about, the safer any environment is likely to be.'[10]

A recent project studied the problems of revitalising public and social life in town centres. It proposed that councils should consider establishing a Town Centre Policy Sub-committee, and appointing a Town Centre Manager. In co-operation with police and the local business sector, councils should develop policies on safety and security in town centres during the day and night:

> 'Such policies should be also informed by the principle that it is a right of

people to walk the streets as and when they wish, in safety, rather than a provocation or undesirable character trait.'[11]

There is a need to ensure that planning initiatives for crime prevention take priority action on violence involving children, and are properly integrated into community safety strategies at all levels.

Recommendation

The Department of the Environment should issue guidance requiring planning authorities:

- *to adopt the commitment to work towards a non-violent society*
- *to take action to reduce and prevent violence involving children and*
- *to play a full and co-ordinated part in community safety strategies.*

[Department of the Environment; opposition parties]

Local co-ordination of child protection

In England and Wales, Area Review Committees were created following publication of a DHSS Circular on *Non-accidental injury to children*, to provide an inter-agency management framework to respond to child abuse.[12] In 1988, following publication of new guidance *Working together: a guide to arrangements for inter-agency co-operation for the protection of children from abuse*, the committees became Area Child Protection Committees (ACPCs).[13] Further guidance, *Working together under the Children Act 1989*, was issued in 1991. This states:

'There needs to be a recognised joint forum for developing, monitoring and reviewing child protection policies. This forum is the Area Child Protection Committee.'

The guidance emphasises that members of the ACPC

'will be senior officers or senior professionals from all the main authorities and agencies in the area which are involved in the prevention and management of child abuse.'

It lists main tasks, including 'to scrutinise progress on work to prevent child abuse and make recommendations to the responsible agencies.'[14]

In Scotland, Area Review Committees, generally covering a region or islands area and the corresponding Health Board, were set up to:

- ensure the establishment, maintenance and review of local inter-agency guidelines on procedures to be followed in individual cases
- receive and review regular statistical information concerning the child protection register and also to review its use
- review significant issues arising from the handling of cases and reports from inquiries

- review arrangements to provide expert advice and inter-agency liaison
- promote and review progress on work to prevent child abuse
- review and identify inter-agency training needs and take a leading role in the development and promotion of an inter-disciplinary training strategy.

As in England and Wales, the name was changed a few years ago to Child Protection Committees. In Scotland the relevant guidance is *Effective interventions on child abuse: guidance on co-operation in Scotland.*[15] The 1993 White Paper *Scotland's children* promised a revised and updated version of guidance on inter-agency working, now presumably delayed until implementation of new children's legislation: the Children (Scotland) Act 1995 received Royal Assent in July 1995.[16]

At local level child protection committees have a co-ordinating role in responding to and seeking to prevent child abuse. Represented on committees are many if not all of the professions and services relevant to violence prevention. Surprisingly, these committees have no statutory basis, although their functions are linked to the investigative duties and statutory powers given to local authorities under the Children Act (for England and Wales), the Children (Northern Ireland) Order and in Scotland, where the relevant law is under review, in the Social Work (Scotland) Act 1968.

While the role of child protection committees is clearly focused on protection of children from those forms of violence that are commonly defined as child abuse (which includes by no means all violence to children) it is relevant to the whole scope of the Commission's concerns, because child abuse is clearly implicated as a significant factor in the development of violent attitudes and actions. Violence to children is inextricably linked to violence by children. There are widespread concerns within child protection committees about their role, structure and finance, and in particular about the development of preventive work.

Particular concerns include:
- the threat posed to collaborative working by reorganisation in the health and education services, the pressures of a growing internal market and the purchaser/provider split
- lack of any statutory authority to enforce decisions
- lack of sufficient funding and no statutory basis for funding (recent research in England found half ACPCs had no significant budget, despite their substantial responsibilities[17])
- difficulties in developing preventive services.

The English ACPCs generally believe that it is in reviewing child deaths and in developing child protection procedures that they have been most consistently 'successful'. Identification and investigation of individual cases is universally given priority, and attracts the highest proportion of stretched child protection budgets.

A report for the Welsh Office on the role and effectiveness of Welsh ACPCs suggested there was general agreement that inter-agency relationships had improved as a result of committees' work:

'However, ACPCs continue to focus largely on investigative work. Child protection operates separately from the rest of children's services and family support. There is as yet little attempt to engage the energies or motivation of extended families and communities in the interests of prevention.'[18]

The report suggests that at a strategic level there needs to be closer co-ordination between child protection services and those services designed to provide support for children in need and their families.[19] Amongst proposals for change which ACPC members have identified as beneficial are:

- the need to prioritise prevention and actively redirect resources to preventive services; creation of prevention sub-committees
- the need for ACPCs to evaluate the effectiveness of their work as part of an inter-agency monitoring programme integrated with existing agency monitoring programmes.

In the Commission's view, local child protection committees should become a fully-integrated but distinct part of local community safety strategies, whose development and implementation should become a statutory responsibility of local authorities, linked to statutory child protection duties. We see them working as a crucial and high priority segment of a co-ordinated community safety strategy in each area. The preventive role of the committees, which would be enhanced by integration into the overall strategy, must be adequately resourced and not developed at the expense of necessary interventions to protect children. The Commission believes a detailed review of the role, structure, powers, funding and accountability of ACPCs is overdue. The Commission draws attention to the National Commission of Inquiry into the Prevention of Child Abuse, convened by the National Society for the Prevention of Cruelty to Children, which is looking at these and connected issues in more depth and is due to report in 1996.

Such a review should consider in particular how inter-agency work, in order to protect children from violence, work with child victims of violence and with perpetrators of violence to children can best be integrated into national and local community safety strategies.

Children's own assessment of investigations and interventions following abuse and allegations of abuse should play an important part in evaluation of child protection services. Consultation with children should be built into monitoring and planning services.

Recommendation

The Department of Health together with appropriate departments in each jurisdiction should review the role, structure, powers, funding and accountability of Area Child Protection Committees. In the Commission's view, local child protection committees should become a fully-integrated but distinct part of local community safety strategies, whose development should become a statutory responsibility of local authorities, linked to statutory child protection duties.

[Government; opposiiton parties; local authorities; Area Child Protection Committees]

Children's services plans

The Commission welcomes the development of comprehensive local children's services plans, and believes that their preparation, publication and monitoring should become statutory duties of local authorities. In a circular issued in November 1992 the Department of Health first asked local authorities' social services departments to produce such plans.[20] The 1991 report *Children in the Public Care* had proposed that the Secretary of State should ask local authorities to prepare plans.[21] The 1992 circular sets out some general guidance on content of plans, which should be

'the product of collaboration between local authorities, health authorities, local education authorities, voluntary organizations, the private sector and other appropriate interests.'[22]

Information from which plans should be derived includes the child population, children on the child protection register and the range of family support services.

A draft circular sent out by the Department of Health in June 1995 indicated that the Government proposes to issue an order to make the preparation and publication of plans a social services function. An accompanying letter stated that a review of the first published plans by the Social Services Inspectorate had found that few contained strategic statements or action plans for the future:

'We want to encourage local authorities to consider widening the scope to take account of – for example – Citizens' Charter principles, the views of users and the UN Convention on the Rights of the Child so that children's services plans become a comprehensive planning tool as well as a position statement.'[23]

The Commission's proposals for children's services plans are intended to ensure joint planning and action across all relevant authorities and bodies, and to link the production and implementation of such plans to broader community safety strategies, and to the functions of the ACPC. (There will need to be some integration with existing reviewing and reporting duties of local authorities, for instance in relation to daycare and special educational needs). It is disappointing that the plans outlined in the draft circular relate only to children in need, rather than to all children. This focus is likely to intensify the risk of stigmatising services.

The 1994 Audit Commission Report *Seen but not heard – Co-ordinating community child health and social services for children in need* – proposed that all relevant local authority departments as well as voluntary bodies should be responsible for developing a joint strategy for children, set down in a children's services plan 'which should be jointly published by health, social services and education in much the same way as community care plans are now.'[24] Work on preventing or reducing violence involving children, and helping child victims of violence, clearly fits within such a strategy.

In Scotland, the 1993 White Paper stated:

> 'At a strategic level the Government will introduce a new requirement on local authorities to publish plans in relation to child care services. The plans will be:
> - a clear appraisal of the strengths and weaknesses of current services
> - an assessment of future needs
> - an estimate of likely available resources
> - a statement of strategic objectives for service development and
> - a review of innovative developments.

> 'The plans will cover a three year period and will be rolled forward annually. They will reflect consultation with education, housing, health, police, the children's panel, and the voluntary sector. Consultation with local and national organisations representing children or families using the services will also be required. The plans should be succinct, and authoritative, with targets and timetables. Summaries of the plans should be widely published. Children and families should be informed of what services are available.'[25]

Further guidance from the Department of Health (and other appropriate departments) should ensure that local children's services plans are committed to working towards a non-violent society, outlining the local dimensions of violence involving children and inter-agency plans to reduce and prevent it. The relevant sections of children's services plans would also form part of the local community safety strategy (as, presumably, would other parts of children's services plans related to prevention of non-violent crime). The plans should also cover the narrower functions of child protection committees. The development of plans should involve consultation with children (it is welcome that the 1995 draft circular does stress the need to have a system for users to be consulted and have their views taken into account).

Recommendation

The Commission welcomes the decision of the Department of Health to require local authorities to prepare and publish plans for their children's services and to monitor their implementation. These plans should be comprehensive, rather than limited to children in need, and should include proposals for assessing, reducing and preventing violence involving children.

[Government; opposition parties]

Domestic violence forums

In Autumn 1994 the Home Office and Department of Health circulated for comment a draft circular on *Inter-agency co-ordination to tackle domestic violence.*[26] This arose from recommendations in the February 1992 report of the House of Commons Home Affairs Select Committee. The circular emphasises the importance of inter-agency co-ordination to enhance the local response to domestic violence, seeing the establishment of a local domestic violence forum as one model (these already exist in an increasing number of local areas). Domestic violence was defined in the Home Affairs Select Committee report as

> 'any form of physical, sexual or emotional abuse which takes place within the context of a close relationship. In most cases the relationship will be between partners (married, cohabiting or otherwise) or ex-partners.'[27]

While the circular does refer to the potential ill-effects on children of witnessing domestic violence, it does not appear to include actual violence to children within the home as domestic violence. Such a compartmentalised approach to violence within the family seems to the Commission unhelpful, as does the lack of any proposal for co-ordination between multi-agency domestic violence initiatives and child protection structures. Of course the Commission does not seek in any way to undermine attempts to reduce violence to women. But they are inextricably linked to and should be properly co-ordinated within community safety strategies, and in particular with action on violence involving children.

The term family violence seems preferable to the Commission, defined to include all violence between family members and its effects (for further discussion and recommendations on family violence, see page 162).

Recommendation

Arrangements for co-ordinating responses to domestic violence should become part of community safety strategies, include all violence within families, and be appropriately linked to child protection.

[Government; opposition parties; local authorities; all concerned with prevention of domestic violence]

Neighbourhood responsibility for child safety

Several submissions to the Commission have referred to the significance of the accounts of witnesses in the Bulger murder trial, who did not intervene when they saw an evidently distressed James being led through the streets by his two eventual murderers. Was this is a vivid reflection of the lack of community and individual responsibility for child protection?

The Commission believes that creating a non-violent society is everybody's responsibility. Encouraging neighbourhoods to organise themselves to help reduce and prevent violence involving children is essential. But it is vital that such schemes are seen to aim at mutual support rather than invasion of privacy.

Of course much exists already, including informal child care and supervision arrangements between families and friends and school-, estate-, street- and neighbourhood-based schemes. They may not have an identified violence-prevention role, but they can contribute significantly. Below, we also discuss family and community support proposals which interlink with neighbourhood schemes (page 108).

In other countries, recent major reviews of child protection services have emphasised the danger of systems which are reactive and investigatory rather than proactive and preventive. In the USA, the Advisory Board on Child Abuse and Neglect, having identified a 'national crisis' of child maltreatment has advocated a policy which is comprehensive, child-friendly, family-focused and neighbourhood-based, and adequately resourced to allow for prevention and treatment as well as investigation and adjudication:

> 'In neighbourhoods that have low maltreatment rates one is likely to find friendship among neighbours, watchfulness for each other's families, physical safety, common knowledge of community resources, visible leadership, and a sense of belonging, ownership and collective responsibility. Offering people respect, involvement and support can help overcome the isolation and depression that can result in abuse and neglect.'[28]

In New Zealand, a Neighbourhood Support Group was established in an area because neighbours had ignored cries from a house in their midst where a murder was being committed. In Australia, the National Association for the Prevention of Child Abuse and Neglect (NAPCAN) picked up the idea and in 1988 launched *Neighbour Network*, a flexible scheme aimed at encouraging neighbours to come together to assist each other. NAPCAN has provided booklets, leaflets and videos to encourage local developments, suggesting such networks could grow out of existing neighbourhood or community centres, neighbourhood watch groups or other crime prevention initiatives. The Federal Government is now supporting a pilot scheme in a rural area of New South Wales, which will be fully evaluated.[29]

Volunteers in violence prevention

A specific proposal was submitted to the Commission by the Volunteer Centre to *Enhance voluntary effort in the prevention of abuse of children*. This would identify ways in which formal and informal volunteers could be enabled to promote and adopt sensible practices which will prevent opportunities for the abuse of children in the community by for example:

- action on the physical environment to secure lighting for an unlit alley regularly used by children on dark evenings
- improving supervision, e.g. by establishing a rota of informal volunteers to keep an eye on children using an unsupervised play area
- changing public attitudes and behaviour, e.g. promoting debate on what is safe and acceptable behaviour for an adult who sees a child in distress in a public place.

It is also important that individuals and groups should receive advice on appropriate immediate interventions to prevent violence involving children.

The Volunteer Centre's submission to the Commission outlined another scheme to increase the involvement of volunteers in children's lives – 'a deliberate move to provide children with access to other adults who have a genuine and spontaneous interest in them, and who have no statutory locus in their lives': an experiment to introduce carefully selected, well-trained and supported volunteers into families and into nurseries and schools, to explore the extent to which volunteers might intervene helpfully in children's lives.

The Centre points to a number of volunteer-based projects which introduce parents into families in need of contact and support:

> 'In proposing an extension of the involvement of volunteers in children's lives, the assumption is made that providing a child with access to an interested "outsider" will provide them not only with an alternative model, but also with a person in whom to confide, a control element, a visitor who comes in and out of their lives, and who, merely by being there, may serve to prevent or reduce opportunities for violence. Of course they may also be

helpful in assisting children in devising coping avoidance strategies, as well as acting as a contact or a "whistle-blower" in emergencies.'

The Centre goes on to propose the creation of some experimental local projects where volunteers could be invited to take part in 'programmes for child safety', based on education, training and confidence-building, all designed 'to make our town/village/neighbourhood a safer place for children'. The projects could involve professionals in supporting local adults through a carefully planned programme.

The Commission cautiously welcomes such a scheme. Schemes are operating in some other countries and should be reviewed before proceeding here. We also note the need for some vulnerable children, in particular in residential care, to have independent visitors or representatives. These are volunteers specifically recruited and supported, and may have a crucial violence-prevention role in relation to institutional care (see also *One scandal too many* ... [30]).

Kidscape aims to provide practical help to children, parents, teachers and others to keep children safe from dangers and particularly from sexual assault. It provides books, videos, posters and other materials and training programmes on child safety and bullying prevention. The Suzy Lamplugh Trust, 'the national charity for personal safety', seeks to reduce fear and enable people to live safer lives. It provides personal safety leaflets, books, videos and training manuals which stress a welcome non-violent approach to conflict resolution as well as self-protection. It is now working with disabled children and young people and focusing on assertiveness training as well as on personal safety advice. Mothers Against Murder and Aggression (MAMAA) was formed following the murder of James Bulger, as a campaign to increase awareness of child safety. The organisation has lobbied for a 'national safety procedure' to provide a code of practice for anyone whose child goes missing, or who finds a missing child.

The Commission has proposed that community safety strategies should be developed to facilitate inter-agency work; they should encourage neighbourhood support initiatives, including initiatives which directly involve children, to adopt the commitment to work towards a non-violent society, to help reduce and prevent violence involving children, and to ensure that their work is properly evaluated.

Recommendation
Appropriate voluntary organisations (the Volunteer Centre, CSV (Community Service Volunteers), NSPCC, Community Development Foundation, Kidscape, Suzy Lamplugh Trust, Mothers Against Murder and Aggression and others) should come together to review any existing initiatives in the UK or other countries which aim to

reduce and prevent violence involving children, and to consider how best to encourage the development of voluntary and volunteer neighbourhood initiatives, including initiatives involving children, within the overall framework of community safety strategies.

[Voluntary organisations concerned with volunteering and neighbourhood initiatives to reduce violence]

PART 2

Policies for children and families
which support violence prevention

Challenging inequality and poverty

As reported in section 1, page 56, international studies have found violence to be more common in societies characterised by widespread inequalities. An American study in 1988 stated:

> 'Harsh inequalities in living standards in both "developing" and developed countries are closely associated with high levels of violence.'[31]

From many perspectives, including that of prevention of violence involving children, the very substantial increase in numbers of children living in poverty in the UK, and the steeper gradient of inequality, must cause concern, as does related information about homelessness and youth unemployment. According to recent official statistics 4.3 million children, almost one in three, live in poverty (using the definition accepted across Europe: families living on less than 50 per cent of average income after housing costs have been discounted). The poorest 10 per cent of the population suffered a real drop of 14 per cent in their living standards at a time when average incomes went up by 38 per cent, and incomes of the top 10 per cent by 62 per cent, after housing costs. Thus inequalities have become sharper, and a regional picture shows that poverty is not evenly distributed, with Northern Ireland consistently emerging as one of the poorest areas, closely followed by areas of Scotland and Wales. Within Northern Ireland, there are regions suffering the most severe deprivation. Thirty-nine per cent of children in Northern Ireland live in families receiving less than half average income, compared with 19 per cent of children in the whole of the UK. In 1992 the average gross weekly household income was £281.25 in Northern Ireland, compared with £342.95 in the UK as a whole (and Northern Ireland has on average a larger household size).[32]

The Joseph Rowntree Foundation study into Income and Wealth reported in 1995 that the pace at which inequality had increased in the UK was greater than in any other industrialised country with the exception of New Zealand. After taxes and benefits, the incomes of the richest 20 per cent of the population at the start of the 1980s were four times larger than those of the poorest 20 per cent, but by 1991 these differences were six-fold. These findings were quoted in a report of the independent Crime and Social Policy Committee published in 1995 which concluded:

'Exclusion and poverty are not evenly spread. In recent years hardships have fallen particularly heavily on families with children, on particular neighbourhoods and on young people setting out in the world. A society which excludes a growing number of its members from the expanding opportunities available to the majority of citizens will pay a price …'[33]

Recent economic trends that have increased the relative poverty of the lowest-income quarter of the whole UK population have particularly affected parents and young children, and have affected lone parents most of all.

A UNICEF report monitoring the social well-being of children in 10 industrialized countries over a 20-year period through a set of international indicators found that only in the US and the UK did children end the period with lower levels of social health, on every count, than when they started.[34]

Family poverty has been clearly identified as the principal risk factor in children's lives:

'… inexorably correlated with premature delivery, postnatal, infant and childhood mortality, malnutrition and ill-health; childhood neglect; educational failure; truancy; delinquency; school-age pregnancy and the birth of babies who are victims of premature delivery, postnatal, infant and childhood mortality …'[35]

> **Residential social worker comments following discussion on the Commission's questionnaire with five young people aged 16–19 living in a semi-independent unit in Sunderland.**
>
> 'The group had difficulty identifying ways in which they could help children or siblings not to get involved with violence. Again they saw adults as the ones who should take the lead in this. Parents were seen as the ones who should take control and be supportive. They felt that schools do not do enough to protect children from bullying etc. It was felt that local councils do not do enough to help channel their energies into more positive and structured activities to alleviate boredom and aggression as youth clubs catered mainly for children up to 16 and after that there was nothing for older teenagers. This inaction leads to destructive, deviant and aggressive behaviour. The group felt that the media were guilty of causing fear in the minds of the general public by sensationalising crime and violence on TV and in the newspapers. The female member of the group felt that too much violence via films etc was shown on TV and this has a detrimental effect on young people as it portrays violence as exciting and fascinating and this kind of exposure to young people has an anaesthetic effect …'

The health implications of poverty and homelessness are well documented. Additional stress is placed on parents by financial worries, and a majority of very poor families live in areas characterised by overcrowding, impoverished public services and lack of positive opportunities. These factors all increase the pressure and potential for inappropriate parenting, which itself increases the potential for violence involving children.

There is no doubt that in UK society today, having a child places parents at a substantial financial disadvantage. If the parents are poor, and substantially or completely dependent on state benefit, the disadvantages become acute. Research published by the Child Poverty Action Group in 1993 demonstrated that a low cost budget representing a very minimal standard of living for a couple with two children was 30 per cent higher than the rate of income support.[36] Recent inquiries, including that of the Social Justice Commission established by the Institute of Public Policy Research, have analysed in detail the extent of poverty and inequality affecting children and the adequacy of the benefit system.[37]

Measures are needed that publicly acknowledge the economic burden of caring for children; redistribute some of this burden from parents to non-parents and from women to men; and support the unpaid work of caring.

In 1988 the Government introduced legislation which withdrew entitlement to income support from most 16 and 17 year olds; young people were promised that if they had left school and were unable to find employment, they would be offered a training place and training allowance. A Labour Force survey in the summer of 1992 found that an average of 195,000 16 and 17 year olds were without work, an unemployment rate of about 24 per cent.[38] Youthaid estimated in April 1993 that 76,700 young people of this age group were without any income at all (severe hardship payments are difficult to claim, and there is no appeal against a rejected claim).[39] There is evidence that young people identified at school as having emotional or behavioural difficulties are particularly unlikely to be offered appropriate training places. It appears that this age group is a high-risk one for victimisation through violence, and involvement in some violent offences. This strengthens the arguments for benefit entitlement from the Commission's violence prevention perspective.

Recommendation

The Commission adds the perspective of violence prevention to the many other powerful reasons for recommending urgent and concerted government action to challenge the extent and growth of child poverty in the UK. Economic and taxation policies should seek to reduce inequality and ensure that basic benefit levels for those dependent on benefit match the actual costs of children. 16 and 17 year olds should be entitled to income support if they are unemployed and are not offered an appropriate training place. Benefit levels for those under 25 living independently should be the same as those for over 25 year olds.

[Government; opposition parties]

Discrimination

As indicated in section 1 (page 56) discrimination and prejudice are linked to violence involving children in various ways. Relevant to the pressures discussed above, there is a clear relationship between race and deprivation.[40] Certain groups of children are particularly at risk of violence, including disabled children and children from some minority ethnic groups. Victimisation statistics in crime surveys and other interview research provide *prima facie* evidence of discrimination. Racial harassment, always a form of violence and often involving physical violence, threatens many children in the community and in schools. The Commission for Racial Equality has proposed detailed strategies for combating racial harassment in schools and colleges. A report *Learning in terror* concluded:

> 'Abuse, graffiti and violence as both threat and actuality serve as a constant reminder of the intolerance in white society and the vulnerability of ethnic minority people ... If our society is to restore its reputation for justice, and if the potential of the whole community is to be realised, and if schools, homes, streets and public transport are to be made safe for everybody, then urgent action is called for by all agencies concerned with the well-being of all our people, on a national as well as a local basis.'[41]

'Children should have a secure family life without violence and teach them that is one of the worst things you can do – to be violent to someone.'

A recent Court of Appeal judgment found that a proven racial element in an offence of violence 'was a gravely aggravating feature justifying an increase in sentence.'[42]

There have been suggestions that there should be a specific offence of racial violence. The Court of Appeal took the view

> 'that it was perfectly possible for the court to deal with any offence of violence which had a proven racial element in it, in a way which made clear that the aspect invested the offence with added gravity and, therefore, had to be regarded as an aggravating feature.'

Discrimination takes a number of forms in Northern Ireland, including

115

discrimination against minority ethnic groups and also sectarianism. It is currently legal to discriminate on the grounds of race in Northern Ireland. There are various minority ethnic groups in Northern Ireland including the Chinese community, numbering approximately 8,000. The Traveller community numbers approximately 1,200 and there are about 500 people of Indian origin. Over two years ago the government consulted on anti-racism legislation, and recently (1995) indicated that legislation would be introduced, along the general lines of the Race Relations Act 1976, and would refer to the Traveller community.[43]

The Commission has aimed to cover issues of discrimination within all relevant sections of the report, underlining the UN Convention's requirement that all rights within it, including protection from all forms of physical or mental violence, must be available to all children without discrimination on any grounds.

Recommendations

All those involved in planning, co-ordinating and implementing violence prevention programmes at all levels should have regard to the particular violent victimisation of certain groups, and protection from violence and prevention of violence should be sought without discrimination.

Information and materials for violence prevention should be available in appropriate forms and languages for all communities.

[All]

The Commission welcomes the intention of the Government to introduce anti-racism legislation in Northern Ireland; there should be a monitoring body to ensure it is effectively implemented.

[Northern Ireland Office]

Parental responsibility for children

The slogan for the International Year of the Family (1994) was 'Building the smallest democracy at the heart of society', and the UN body responsible for the year stated:

'The family must become the medium for promoting new values and behaviour consistent with the rights of individual family members, as established by various UN instruments.'

The articles of the UN Convention on the Rights of the Child provide a framework for assessing children's status and relationships within the family as well as beyond it, and also for assessing the state's supportive relationship with families. The Convention underlines the concept of parental responsibility for children, whose best interests should be parents' 'basic concern' (article 18). The Children Act introduces the concept into family law, but defines it in a circular and unhelpful fashion.[44] Proposals from the Scottish Law Commission for reform of Scottish family law in 1992 suggested an expanded definition. Parents should be responsible

'so far as is practicable and in the interests of the child:

(a) to safeguard and promote the child's health, development and welfare

(b) to provide, in a manner appropriate to the stage of development of the child, direction and guidance to the child

(c) if the child is not living with the parent, to maintain personal relations and direct contact with the child on a regular basis

(d) to act as the child's legal representative.'[45]

Responsibilities defined in (a) and (b) would apply up to 18; those in (c) and (d) up to 16. The Scottish Law Commission proposed defined rights for parents to enable them to fulfil these responsibilities, and in addition proposed that

'before a person reaches a major decision which involves fulfilling parental responsibility or exercising a parental right, the person shall, so far as practicable, ascertain the views of the child concerned regarding the decision, and shall give due consideration to those views, taking account of the child's age and maturity.'

These proposals have been adopted with some amendment by the Government in the Children (Scotland) Act 1995 which received Royal Assent in July 1995: this is hopefully the beginning of comprehensive reform to define parental responsibilities adequately in laws applying throughout the UK, as part of the process of implementing the UN Convention.

Other countries, notably Finland, Norway and Sweden, have developed the definition of parental responsibilities considerably in their family law.[46]

The Commission supports proposals made by a previous Gulbenkian Foundation Working Group in its report *One scandal too many ...* that family law should include a statement of positive principles of care, addressed to parents, others with parental responsibility and all those having care and control of children.[47] It is important to ensure that the 'public' parents of children in care have a clear understanding of parental responsibility and the elements of good parenting. The Commission believes that the concept of parental responsibility should be properly developed in the law in all jurisdictions, as a basis for encouraging changes in attitudes and practice towards children which reflect principles in the UN Convention, and which would undoubtedly lead to a reduction in violence involving children. The purpose of such reforms is not to increase prosecutions of parents, or formal interventions in the lives of families, but to set society-wide standards. Given the complexity of factors which interact to 'cause' violence, we do not support crude attempts to make parents specifically responsible before the courts for children's violent or offending behaviour.

The Commission is also interested in seeking ways of encouraging a more thoughtful and informed commitment to parental responsibility. It welcomes the launch of the Family Covenant Association which aims to promote celebration of birth, naming ceremonies and formal commitment to community responsibility for all sorts of families, and also to encourage fathers in non-marital couples in England and Wales to use Children Act procedures to gain parental responsibility. The Association is

'a completely independent non-party body, whose aim is to help generate mutual support for families of any shape or size, by providing an informal way of meeting members of other families, young or old, and by broadening community support for children.'[48]

The Commission would like to see further attention given to the need to promote and develop the concept of parental responsibility. This is an educational process which needs to happen before conception as well as around the time of birth. One idea worth exploring would be to link formal acceptance of parental responsibility to registration of birth, at present a necessary but drab and bureaucratic process. A 'birthrights contract', used as an educational tool, could include a reflection of the rights of the new child as set out in the UN Convention, and of the corresponding responsibilities of parents and the wider community.

Recommendations

Laws concerning the upbringing of children in all jurisdictions should provide a definition of parental responsibility, and of parental rights necessary to exercise responsibility, based on the principles of the UN Convention on the Rights of the Child.

Arrangements for registration of birth should be reviewed to consider how best to use them to promote the concept of parental – and wider – responsibility for children.

[Government; opposition parties]

Family support

There is no unitary structure or set of relationships that is uniquely 'a family'. Parents, relations in- and out-of-law, step-, adoptive and foster-parents along with extended families of all those individuals in an almost infinite variety of configurations and combinations can, and often do, meet children's needs, and function as good families to them. Children are neither the private possessions of parents, nor are they the *raison d'être* of families.

The UN Convention defines 'family' widely, to include

'parents, or, where applicable, the members of the extended family or community as provided for by local custom, legal guardians or other persons legally responsible for the child'. (article 5)

Its preamble emphasises that the family

'as the fundamental group of society and the natural environment for the growth and well-being of all its members and particularly children, should be afforded the necessary protection and assistance so that it can fully assume its responsibilities within the community'.

Article 18 emphasises that parents together with other carers

'have the primary responsibility for the upbringing and development of the child. The best interests of the child will be their basic concern ...'

It goes on to underline the State's duty to support parents:

'States Parties shall render appropriate assistance to parents and legal guardians in the performance of their childrearing responsibilities and shall ensure the development of institutions, facilities and services for the care of children'.

States must also ensure that working parents 'have the right to benefit from child-care services and facilities for which they are eligible'.

The recent report of a Carnegie Corporation Task Force on *Meeting the needs of young children* concluded:

'We can now say with greater confidence than ever before, that the quality of young children's environment and social experience has a decisive, long-lasting impact on their well-being and ability to learn. The risks are clearer than ever before: an adverse environment can compromise a young child's brain function and overall development, placing him or her at greater risk of developing a range of cognitive, behavioural and physical difficulties'.

But it also underlined that the opportunities to reduce risk were equally dramatic:

'Adequate pre- and post-natal care, dependable caregivers, and strong community support can prevent damage and provide a child with a decent start in life'.

It referred to the crisis among young children and their families as 'the quiet crisis: after all, babies seldom make the news.'[49]

As in the section above on challenging inequality, the Commission seeks to add the violence prevention perspective to the many-sided case for doing much more to support parenting and in particular to enhance both parents' roles.[50] The Commission has already indicated that it sees positive parenting as the foundation of a non-violent society. We have also indicated that inadequate supervision of children can lead to a potential for violence being realised.

Societal support for individual parents

Going out to work or staying at home with children is no longer a meaningful long-term choice. Almost all parents, women as well as men, need to earn. Almost all parents, men as well as women, need time with their children. The ideal time-balance varies for different individuals, and changes as children grow. Unless government ensures that flexible choices are available to parents, acute time-conflict can mean poverty when, perhaps, a lone mother cannot seek work for lack of childcare provision; or child neglect, if children must spend the hours between the end of their school day and their parents' working day without adult supervision. Whenever children are unable to attend their usual daily care arrangements – because of illness or upset on their part or that of their caregiver – a parent needs time to care for them and/or make new arrangements. Parents of some disabled children will have multiple hospital and other appointments. Their lives may be constantly disrupted by meetings with professionals, and by the greater likelihood of the child having periods of illness or hospitalisation. Support entitlements must properly reflect such situations. They must also be responsive to changing working lives, including more self-employment.

The Government has reluctantly complied with the European Union (EU)

Directive giving women who have been employed for six months by the same employer the right to 18 weeks paid maternity leave and to return to their previous job within 29 weeks of the birth or adoption. Although new in the UK, these are minimal concessions in European terms. The Government has vetoed EU proposals for statutory paternity leave. The UK is alone in rejecting the European Directive on Working Time, in favour of a cumbersome partial opt-out.

Many variants of the 'standard working week' are proving beneficial to firms who need flexible staffing, as well as to families who need flexible parenting. During the current recession, new entrepreneurs and small-scale businesses have provided a larger number of new jobs than all other sectors put together. Many of these are especially suited to parents needing shorter-time and more flexible working. The Department for Education and Employment should review its incentives for such businesses, and review and publicise the use of voluntary short-time working and the costs of state maintenance of pension rights at full-time level; a range of schemes for job-shares and flexitime and home-working should be promoted.

Recommendation

The Government should review arrangements for supporting working parents in order to establish rights:

- *to paid parental leave following maternity leave, for either parent*
- *to paid paternity leave and job reinstatement following birth or adoption*
- *to paid family leave for illness and other emergencies.*

[Government; opposition parties; employers; trades unions]

Community-based support for parents and their children

A coherent, comprehensive approach to community services for families is urgently needed. It should emphasise but not be confined to daycare for children under school age while their parents are at work. Integrated support services for families should be brought together in centres, which might incorporate infant health and immunisation clinics, and early years educational and recreational services including libraries and children's theatres. Support services should be planned with the active participation of parents and children. A start towards developing such an approach has already been made, for example, by Manchester City Council whose children's centres provide part-time and full-time daycare, parent and toddler sessions, pre-school playgroups and out of school care for older children.

A survey in 1989 found 352 'family centres' in the UK, offering a variety of services including playgroup activities for children and opportunities for parents to develop parenting skills. Many also provide counselling and opportunities for community meetings. Some are open to all families in an area; others are restricted; some are run by local authorities, some by voluntary bodies. A 1994 Audit Commission report proposed more family centres as a crime prevention measure, and called for them to be open to all.[51]

A recent review of policy and practice in parent education and support published by the National Children's Bureau, *Confident parents, confident children*, found a wide range of support services for children:

'However, there is little evidence of a co-ordinated approach to such provision in a locality; concern about cuts in funding for statutory services; emphasis on targeted rather than universal services; and extensive reliance on a sometimes insecurely funded voluntary sector. In order for parent support to be available to all who want it, at the time they want it, and in the way they want it, it will be necessary to move beyond this somewhat *ad hoc* approach.'[52]

One rare example of an evaluated comprehensive parent support project is the Henley Safe Children Project, started in 1991 with funding from the Home Office Safer Cities Project, in the Henley Ward of Coventry, chosen because it was a deprived area with the highest number of children on the Child Protection Register in Coventry when the project was planned in 1989. Two thirds of families in the area are on low income, with high levels of unemployment, and accidents, crime and danger on the streets. Health statistics underline the deprivation of the area. The project is jointly managed by the NSPCC and the University of Warwick.

Its aims are to:

- 'identify and promote preventive initiatives aimed to reduce levels of concern about child protection in the Henley area
- to work with parents to identify their own needs and problems in bringing up children, identify resources needed and preferred solutions
- help parents provide written accounts of their experiences which can be used in training health and welfare professionals
- through collaborative work with local people and professionals, to increase awareness of the range of difficulties faced by parents in deprived neighbourhoods and so improve the sensitivity and effectiveness of local health, education and social services policy and practice
- demonstrate the need for and usefulness of self-help and family support programmes as a major priority in child protection
- work with other professionals and local groups to develop self-help groups and other initiatives which aim to improve support for parents.'[53]

An interim evaluation up to the end of 1992 reported that parents had identified the need for a wide range of readily accessible preventive and support services for families and children, and also for urgent work within the community to challenge and change negative, destructive and discriminatory attitudes and behaviour shown by some families and groups – in particular groups of young males:

'Ways are needed to change the negative, hostile and destructive energy and initiative which many young people show, into positive work to change the Henley area from being one of the most dangerous places for children (and adults) into the safest place to bring up children ... In the same way as parent support requires commitment to partnership, work with young people will involve principles of partnership and ownership. It will involve listening to and working with young people themselves as experts on their own situation.'

The evaluation identified the need for community wide strategies, agreed between voluntary and statutory agencies and local people, to give close attention to the following:

1 Family support

a) practical, such as child care: daily, evening, respite, emergency 'sitting' services; user friendly hospitals, surgeries, clinics; safe play areas; help with transport
b) social and emotional support: local social networks; counselling for parents and children, available when they say they need it; behaviour management courses; preparation for parenthood classes

2 Social environment

Attention to: safe constructive play and activities; safety on streets; crime, violence, bullying; 'macho' destructive street culture, racism, sexism, prejudice; negative attitudes of some young people; intimidation of children with disabilities; aggressive assertion of power by white people; male attitudes to power and sexuality

3 Partnership, participation, ownership

Commitment to needs-led flexible services; recognition of the power of local people to identify needs and control resources, using local skills and building networks, in partnership with local residents, families and young people
Provision of training and job opportunities, linked to a common sense of purpose for the neighbourhood; long-term view of community development, responsibility and support.[54]

There are well-developed voluntary home visiting schemes offering support to families, of which Home-Start is probably the best known, working with families with at least one child under five, who are experiencing difficulties or suffering stress. They are offered support and friendship in their own homes for as long as needed. Families are self-referred, or referred generally by health visitors or social services. An evaluation of a Home-Start scheme in Charnwood, Leicestershire found that 84 per cent of the families studied in the scheme received emotional support, 65 per cent practical support, and 13 per cent were given a respite from their children. 19 per cent of the families had mental health problems; 44 per cent reported depression. Over two-thirds of the families suffered from loneliness and isolation.[55]

The latest 1993-94 statistics show that Home-Start supported 9,507 families, of which 3,489 were one-parent families with 22,533 children of whom three-quarters were under five. Of these, 1,041 were on the Child Protection Register. Such schemes cost relatively little, and promote the concept of neighbourhood and community mutual support. The average cost to Home-Start of supporting a family and child in 1993/94 was £484 and £204 respectively. The expansion of these and similar schemes is hampered by lack of resources.[56]

In the US, a 1990 review of research into major parent support programmes aimed at disadvantaged families concluded:

'Parent support can produce meaningful short-term effects on discrete parenting behaviours, and on parents' efforts at coping, adaptation and personal development. But the modest long-term evidence that exists suggests that parent support may not set in motion causal processes leading to improved long-term child development outcomes for environmentally at risk children ... programmes that combine parent support and direct developmental services to young children appear to hold out the most promise of promoting improved long-term child development outcomes, while not neglecting parents' own developmental and support needs.'[57]

Daycare

Providing good quality daycare is relevant to the prevention of violence both as a key form of parental support and as an experience which can reinforce non-violent attitudes for children. Although 47 per cent of UK mothers with children under five go out to work there are publicly funded daycare places for less than one per cent of them. Such places are confined to 'children in need' and thus stigmatised. Eighty-six per cent of daycare places in the UK receive no public funding. High fees put good non-subsidised daycare out of the reach of many families.

According to Kids' Clubs Network one in five UK children between the ages of five and 11 are 'latchkey children', spending after school hours and holidays without adult supervision or companionship.[58] No comparable figures are available for secondary school students but it seems likely that the proportion for whom such provision is made is even lower and that the need is just as great. An adolescent may not require adult attention to ensure physical safety, but without it may be lonely, and consequently particularly vulnerable to the influences of street culture and gangs.

Until all daycare can be publicly funded, rates and a sliding scale for payment should be centrally or regionally set by government in consultation with local authorities and daycare providers. Parents should be charged on a sliding scale according to their ability to pay. Children in private daycare – with childminders or nannies – should be freely entitled to use publicly-funded educational, play or library resources. Local authorities should be encouraged not only to register childminders and inspect them effectively but to offer the kind of back-up and support (including guidance and training on working towards a non-violent society) that is currently available only from the best.

In England, Wales and Scotland, the Children Act obliges local authorities' education and social services departments jointly to review their daycare provision for under eight year olds every three years. The second report to Parliament on progress in implementing the Act suggests that such reviews are less than adequate. A study of 25 review reports by the Social Services Inspectorate found 'a general lack of specific targets and, not surprisingly, less than a third described the arrangements for monitoring progress'; only a tiny minority had a costed action plan. Less than half the reports indicated targets for quality assurance in services. The study also concluded that:

> 'Discussion around the development of services for children in need, including disabled children, and for meeting the distinctive needs of ethnic minority groups was not found in the majority of reports.'[59]

Reviews should specifically address the needs of all children, including disabled children and ethnic minority children. Reviews should adopt a commitment to non-violence, and use the *Checklists for working towards a non-violent society* to develop appropriate detailed policies (see Appendix 1, page 241). Reviews should be incorporated into the proposed legislation and arrangements for local children's services plans (see page 104).

In each area, there should be co-ordination between those involved in planning and reviewing daycare and the community safety strategy: living in a supportive and safe community is a key protective factor for positive child development, which in turn is a key factor in the prevention of violence involving children and building safe communities.

In Northern Ireland, the 1994 report of the Chief Inspector of the NI Social Services Inspectorate stated:

'Provision of daycare in Northern Ireland is piecemeal and is lower than in other European countries. While there has been a significant increase in the number of day nursery places, total provision is negligible relative to demand.'[60]

The Standing Advisory Commission on Human Rights has emphasised that all Northern Ireland children should as a matter of right have access to early childhood services.[61]

Recently a review group chaired by a senior official of the NI Department of Health and Social Services produced a policy statement to provide a framework for the development of services for young children in Northern Ireland, endorsed by Ministers of the NI DHSS and the Department for Education (the statement reaffirms the principles of the UN Convention on the Rights of the Child, and also the European Community Recommendation on Childcare (31 March 1993)).[62] The new Children (Northern Ireland) Order, due to be implemented in 1996 places a duty on Health and Social Services Boards to provide appropriate daycare and out of school care for children in need, and the authority to provide it for other children. The statement emphasises the need for quality standards and proper training, accreditation, registration and inspection for all aspects of provision; for available resources to be targeted at those most in need, including those at risk of abuse or neglect, and those within communities who are experiencing stress, social, economic or educational disadvantage, or childcare-related problems. The daycare and educational needs of children with behaviour problems should be taken fully into account.

It promotes consultation with and participation by parents in all aspects of care and education programmes, securing a range of 'reliable, affordable services', and 'supporting parents in balancing their family, work or other commitments, thereby helping to ensure equality of opportunity for parents of young children'. The statement emphasises that employers should consider providing various forms of flexible working arrangements, career breaks, childcare facilities and other means to help all their employees combine domestic and career responsibilities. In addition, the new policy statement emphasises as policy objectives:

'ensuring equality of opportunity and equity of treatment for all sections of the community; and encouraging and facilitating cross-community contact among parents, providers and children, while recognising the diversity of cultural traditions in Northern Ireland.'[63]

'Curriculum' for daycare
In relation to the content of daycare, the Early Childhood Education Forum has embarked on a project, due to be completed in 1995/96, to develop

curriculum guidelines for children from a few months to eight years, entitled *Quality in diversity* and aiming to be appropriate to all settings. The forum has identified the following framework for a curriculum for young children, which should:

- support and extend their learning through a system of observation, assessment and planning
- use children's existing knowledge and interests to develop their understanding, attitudes, skills and knowledge across all areas of experience
- be based on first hand experience and on playing and talking
- provide opportunities for children to develop social relationships and extend their creativity and imagination
- foster aspiration, motivation and self-esteem
- respect cultural and physical diversity and promote anti-discriminatory practice
- build on the relationships between children and their parents, recognising that parents are their children's first educators.[64]

Such curriculum guidelines must develop a violence prevention perspective, reinforcing positive non-violent experiences and attitudes for children.

Recommendations

Local authorities should be encouraged to develop integrated support services for families and bring them together in centres so that the full range is flexibly available to all children and carers

[Government; opposition parties; local authorities; appropriate voluntary and private organisations]

Every local authority should offer a comprehensive information and advice service on community resources (including daycare) covering statutory, voluntary and private resources.

The daycare review duty placed on local authorities should ensure that all authorities develop costed action plans for the provision of good quality daycare for all who seek it.

The perspective of violence prevention needs to be integrated into all curricula for daycare. The Checklists for working towards a non-violent society *need to be applied consistently.*

[Local authorities; providers of daycare]

Parent education, preparation for parenthood and family life education

It is commonly accepted now that few parents are adequately prepared for the reality of parenting. In addition, many become parents in situations of the utmost stress. Education for parenting is much-discussed, and few would challenge its importance, but there is still very little of it. It needs to be a lifelong process. The purpose of recommendations in this area must be to aim for universal preparation for parenthood/parent education which encourages, informs, and empowers parents in ways which reduce children's involvement in violence and anti-social behaviour. This is the major aim of the development and application of the *Checklists for working towards a non-violent society* (see Appendix 1, page 241). A co-ordinated lead for the comprehensive development of parent education should come from the Department for Health, as the department with lead responsibility for children, from the Health Education Authority, from the Department for Education and Employment and the Schools Curriculum and Assessment Authority and from the equivalent ministries and government agencies in all parts of the UK. Programmes and materials, while sharing the same value-base and aims, should be adapted in culturally and linguistically appropriate ways for use with all families. Such programmes must not shrink from challenging childrearing practices and habits which do not respect the child's physical or personal integrity, and which are known to be conducive to developing anti-social behaviour, whether or not attempts are made to justify them by reference to culture, religion or tradition. In relation to reducing violence and other anti-social behaviour there are very clear key messages to get across to parents and prospective parents: the importance of positive interactions with children – listening to them and taking their views seriously – and of discipline which is rooted in the encouragement and modelling of good behaviour rather than the punishing of bad; and which, while setting clear limits and in particular not tolerating violent behaviour, completely avoids using violence and humiliation.

A welcome sign of increasing co-ordination in the voluntary sector was the formation in 1995 of the Parenting Education and Support Forum

'to bring together organisations working in parenting education and support to share expertise and information, and take forward issues of policy, practice, training, research and evaluation collaboratively.'[65]

The potential benefits of parent education extend of course far beyond the reduction and prevention of violence to and by children. Evaluations of parent training programmes have found them to be effective in reducing aggression and conduct disorders of all kinds in children, as well as increasing the self-esteem and confidence of parents.

A recent study of policy and practice in parent education and support, *Confident parents, confident children*, includes an *Agenda for action*, intended to ensure that parent education and support is available to all who wish to take advantage of it, within a coherent 'national family policy':

'Parent education and support comprises a range of educational and supportive measures which help parents and prospective parents to understand their own social, emotional, psychological and physical needs and those of their children and enhance the relationship between them; and which create a supportive network of services within local communities and help families to take advantage of them.
• It should be available to all parents and prospective parents, boys as well as girls, young men as well as young women, fathers as well as mothers.
• It is a lifelong process and as such will have a different emphasis at different stages of the life cycle.
• Its emphasis must be on individuals' roles and relationships in the here and now, as well as on their future roles and relationships.
• The overall aim of parent education is to help parents develop self-awareness and self-confidence and improve their capacity to support and nurture their children.'[66]

Confident parents, confident children suggests that beyond the family and community networks, there are three main ways of reaching parents; through the mass media, through group work and through individual approaches:

• mass media
books; pamphlets and leaflets; , magazines and journals; newspapers and general articles; TV and radio; videos, audio cassettes, film; talks and lectures
• group work
drop-in centres; informal self-help and parent and toddler groups; playgroups, nurseries family centres; parents' groups in churches and schools; semi-structured parent education groups; structured therapeutic groups
• individual approaches
informal network of family and friends; information and advice services;

telephone help lines; professional advice from health visitors, GPs, social workers, teachers and others; home visiting schemes; voluntary one-to-one schemes; counselling; family therapy.

A survey of current programmes designed to improve parenting skills is being funded by the Joseph Rowntree Foundation, and was due to be completed in June 1995.[67]

> 'Parents should set a good example, and also treat children fairly. Schools should have stricter rules about bullying or fighting. Shops and parents should enforce classification on video films and TV films as I don't think it is good for children to watch video nasties or too much violence.'

It appears that in the UK there has been no cost benefit analysis of parent support and education programmes. In the US, evaluations have shown as most notable outcomes: an increase in positive parent/child interactions, more extensive use of social supports, less use of corporal punishment, and higher self-esteem and personal functioning. For teenage mothers, outcomes also include fewer subsequent pregnancies, less welfare dependency and higher employment rates.[68]

There has been some evaluation of training parents in the management of 'difficult' pre-school children in the UK. A study of small samples of parents who received training through group methods, home visits and telephone support found that it was possible to train parents in more effective management by means of eight weekly sessions of no more than two hours a week; that the children became more manageable by comparison with a control group of children whose parents did not receive training; and that the effects of training persisted when evaluated 12-18 months later. There was little to choose between the three methods.

The study concluded:

> 'Parent training is a matter of urgent priority. This study has confirmed that it is a fairly simple and inexpensive matter to train parents in effective child management skills ... we should begin to train health visitors, social workers and other professionals in the skills of offering straight-forward and cost-effective help to parents in managing their children.'[69]

There is little evidence of any co-ordinated approach to parent education, whether open access or targeted training in behaviour management, at any level. In schools, family life education has been a victim of a series of legislative changes leading to the expansion of a prescribed core curriculum allowing less time for broader subjects related to education of the whole person.

The Open University has produced a series of parent education courses over the last 10 years, with study packs including audio-cassettes and posters linked to BBC radio and TV programmes. Extensive evaluations of courses and materials have concluded:

- 'an impressive number of parents have been reached and helped to develop their parenting skills

- a model of "learning for everyday life" and developing important lifeskills has been developed and refined

- an approach to facilitating learning groups in the community has been developed and disseminated.'[70]

The Health Education Authority has recently produced guidance for purchasers and providers of parent education in the health service. The publication covers the roles of purchasers, providers, health promotion departments and the training needs of professionals, and includes a model specification for parent education.[71]

The Agenda for Action in *Confident parents, confident children* creatively outlines a framework for developing parent education and support: family life education, through work with children and young people in schools, further education and the youth service; preparation for parenthood through pre-conceptual care, pregnancy and the transition to parenthood; and education and support for parents. But it appears unsatisfactorily non-prescriptive in relation to content: there is a clear need for a framework or curriculum for parent education based in particular on respect for children's rights, on the principles and standards in the UN Convention. In relation to violence prevention, there should be an explicit commitment to non-violence. The *Checklists for working towards a non-violent society* (see Appendix 1, page 241) should be integrated into all preparation for parenthood/parent education.

Recommendation

The Department of Health with other appropriate bodies should agree and promote a core curriculum for parent education. This should be based on principles in the UN Convention on the Rights of the Child, and include knowledge of child development and the development of violent and anti-social behaviour, and be informed by the Checklists for working towards a non-violent society *(see Appendix 1, page 241).*

[Department of Health; other key government departments; relevant agencies]

Physical punishment and deliberate humiliation of children

Within the UK, more than 60 major child welfare, child protection and professional bodies now support education and legal reform to end all physical punishment.[72] But physical punishment, and other forms of deliberate humiliation of children, remain very common. This was most recently confirmed by a very detailed 'Community study of physical violence to children in the home, and associated variables', funded by the Department of Health and involving interviews with all mothers and some fathers and children in over 400 families. It found that almost one in six of the children, and almost a quarter of seven year olds, had been 'severely' physically punished by their mothers. 'Severe' punishment was defined as involving 'intention or potential to cause injury or psychological damage, use of implements, repeated actions or over a long period of time'. The large majority (91 per cent) of children had been hit, and 77 per cent of them in the last year. Thirty eight per cent of children aged four, and 27 per cent of children aged seven were hit more often than once a week. Three quarters of the one year old children had been smacked in the year preceding the interviews. Most (88 per cent) of all severe punishment involved hitting. Children more frequently hit were more likely to have experienced other forms of physical punishment (see also page 51).[73]

> 'There is no excuse or circumstance where it is OK to hit any living thing or person.'
>
> 'They should bring out a law that dads are only allowed to shout and not raise their hands.'

The Commission has stressed the importance of not condoning any form of inter-personal violence. At present, the law on assault clearly condemns inter-personal violence – apart from physical punishment of children. The defence of 'reasonable chastisement' allows physical punishment and other humiliating forms of punishment by parents and other carers. Our courts still frequently interpret 'reasonable chastisement' as allowing parents and others to beat children with sticks and belts, causing injury. The law condones or even promotes concepts of 'discipline' which are known to be associated with violence. At present in the UK there remains a predominant belief that punitive discipline including physical punishments and humiliation is useful in reducing anti-social behaviour including violence. Some politicians and many commentators bear a heavy responsibility for promoting this belief. The evidence (see section 1, page 50) emphatically confirms that harsh and humiliating discipline are implicated in the development of anti-social and violent behaviour.

If we are to achieve a wholesale change in attitudes and practice, we have to remove the support the law currently gives to what in any other context would be a criminal assault. It is important to emphasise that if the criminal law applied equally to assaults currently approved as 'reasonable chastisement', this would not lead to prosecution of parents for 'little slaps or smacks'. Trivial assaults between adults, although they may technically amount to criminal offences, are not prosecuted, and trivial assaults on children would not get to court either. The purpose of such legal reforms is to change attitudes and practice, to make it clear that it is no more acceptable to assault a child than anyone else, and to provide a logical basis for education programmes and for child protection. There is evidence of rapid changes of attitudes and practice from countries which have achieved this reform. In the view of the Commission, the concept of 'reasonable chastisement' is inappropriate and anachronistic in the context of the developing emphasis on parental responsibility and respect for children's rights.

Outside the home, there has been substantial and accelerating progress to prohibit physical punishment, in schools (but see page 145), children's homes, foster-care and day-care. But, as set out in detail in the Gulbenkian Foundation Working Party report *One scandal too many* ..., the legislation is neither effective nor consistent.[74] As was demonstrated recently by the High Court decision in the case of the Sutton childminder, guidance alone is not adequate to implement the Government's stated policy that there is no place for physical punishment in the child care environment outside the family home.[75] The Commission deplores the Department of Health's decision to issue revised guidance on the registration of childminders which to some degree condones smacking.[76] In institutional and quasi-institutional settings (foster-care etc), there should be consistent legislation to prohibit not only physical punishment but other inappropriate sanctions, as now applies to children's homes in England and Wales.[77]

Several of the European countries which have attempted a detailed legal definition of parental responsibility have included in it a prohibition of physical punishment and other humiliating treatment of children. This has generally been in the context of family, ie civil, law. But its effect has been to emphasise that the criminal law protecting adults from assault applies equally to assaults of children which occur in the course of discipline.

Six European countries have prohibited all physical punishment of children: Sweden (1979), Finland (1983), Denmark (1984), Norway (1987), Austria

(1989) and Cyprus (1994)). In Germany, Switzerland, Poland, Canada, New Zealand and Ireland governmental bodies have proposed similar legal reforms. The Committee of Ministers of the Council of Europe has urged all member states to consider full legal reform in recommendations on strategies to reduce family violence.[78] Major commissions on violence which have reported in the last few years, in Australia, Germany and the US, have all proposed ending physical punishment of children as a key preventive strategy.

As indicated in Appendix 2, page251, the UN Convention on the Rights of the Child obliges states to protect children from 'all forms of physical or mental violence' while in the care of parents and others. The UN Committee on the Rights of the Child, in examining the initial reports which must be submitted within two years of ratification by states that ratify the Convention, has indicated that persisting legal and social acceptance of any level of physical punishment is not compatible with the Convention. When the Committee examined the UK's initial report in January 1995 it expressed concern about the legal provisions dealing with reasonable chastisement within the family:

'The imprecise nature of the expression of reasonable chastisement as contained in these legal provisions may pave the way for it to be interpreted in a subjective and arbitrary manner. Thus, the Committee is concerned that legislative and other measures relating to the physical integrity of children do not appear to be compatible with the provisions and principles of the Convention, including those of its articles 3, 19 and 37. The Committee is equally concerned that privately funded and managed schools are still permitted to administer corporal punishment to children in attendance there which does not appear to be compatible with the provisions of the Convention, including those of its article 28, paragraph 2.'

In its recommendations, the Committee stated:

'The Committee is also of the opinion that additional efforts are required to overcome the problem of violence in society. The Committee recommends that physical punishment of children in families be prohibited in the light of the provisions set out in articles 3 and 19 of the Convention. In connection with the child's right to physical integrity, as recognised by the Convention, namely in its articles 19, 28, 29 and 37, and in the light of the best interests of the child, the Committee suggests that the State party consider the possibility of undertaking additional education campaigns. Such measures would help to change societal attitudes towards the use of physical punishment in the family and foster the acceptance of the legal prohibition of the physical punishment of children.'[79]

The Commission emphasises the importance of education and information campaigns to discourage violent or humiliating punishments and promote positive discipline. Its proposals for a media campaign (page 87), for the development and application of *Checklists for working towards a non-violent society* (page 82), expansion of parent support (page 120) and parent education (page 129) and many other recommendations are relevant to fulfilling this need.

Recommendation

The current common law defence of 'reasonable chastisement' in so far as it justifies physical punishment or other humiliating treatment or punishment should be removed for the purposes of both criminal and civil proceedings. The Commission favours removing the concept of 'reasonable chastisement' altogether and replacing it with parental duties to guide and safeguard their children according to their evolving capacities, in conformity with the UN Convention.

[Government; opposition parties]

Pre-schooling

Currently in the UK only 28 per cent of three and four year olds are in nursery schools and classes. A further 19 per cent of four year olds are in infant school reception classes which are inappropriate for them, being designed for rising-fives and often staffed at a ratio of 1:20.

Advocated most recently by a succession of reports from the House of Commons Select Committee on Education, Science and Arts, the National Commission on Education and others, support for universal pre-school education is overwhelming. Pre-school education need not be full-time but must be delivered by fully qualified early-years teachers. Child development should be made a core component of all teacher training, as it already is in some courses. There is clear evidence that pre-school education makes a vital difference not just to children's performance in primary school, but to their lifelong personal competence and their own sense of it. The Commission adds the violence prevention perspective to the much broader case for universal pre-schooling; we also emphasise the use that can be made of pre-schooling to reinforce positive non-violent attitudes. We need an integrated system of childcare and education which is flexible enough to be user-friendly for every kind of family, and to all ages of children.

> **'If young kids are violent then they should get help then and not leave it until they are older. They should be told that it is wrong and bad.'**

Studies from several countries show that the most positive effects of early years education are not the comparatively shortlived benefits to children's academic performance in primary schools, but benefits to self-esteem that may last a lifetime. In the High Scope study, the most detailed of its kind, researchers monitored and costed the effects of pre-school education on the fortunes of children from poor African-American families, tracking them to the age of 27. Children who had pre-school education not only did better educationally and in employment but were five times less likely to be in repeated trouble with the law. It is estimated that every $1 invested in the programme saved $7, largely on police, probation and prison services.[80] Woodhead, analysing the relevance of these findings to the UK, describes the High Scope model as a 'virtuous circle' whereby higher teacher expectation, increased pupil motivation and increased parental aspirations became mutually reinforcing.

Pre-school programmes are powerful because of their potential for 'engineering, reinforcing and sustaining parental aspirations and interest in their children's education.'[81]

Four pilot schemes of High/Scope UK were founded in 1991, offering enhanced pre-school education at sites in Liverpool, Manchester Moss Side, North Tyneside and Lewisham. Training of teachers is backed by parent work at the sites; each site will then become a training centre. The four schemes are being carefully evaluated.[82]

In 1994, the Government set a target to provide over time a pre-school place for all four year olds whose parents wish to take it up; new places would have to be phased in over a number of years. A Task Force of officials, led by the Head of School Organisation Branch in the Department for Education, is working with other departments and providers, professionals and other groups.

> 'Schools should teach more about the effects of violence.'
>
> 'The adults should be more understanding about school, sometimes adults' action reflects on the child's attitude in school.'

In Northern Ireland, an official statement on 'Policy on Early Years Provision' takes as its ultimate aim the provision of one year of nursery education for all those children whose parents wish them to receive it. Compulsory education in Northern Ireland for most children starts at four (the Education Reform (Northern Ireland) Order 1989). The statement proposes that in the short and medium term available resources will need to be targeted on areas of greatest social and economic disadvantage.[83] In a 1994 report the Standing Advisory Commission on Human Rights questions the early start of compulsory education, and proposes that the age should be raised to five, and that three- and four year olds should have automatic access to state-funded nursery education on demand. It expresses concern that the restriction of the duty to provide daycare to children in need 'may have the effect of stigmatising the children and families concerned.'[84]

Recommendations

The Commission adds the violence prevention perspective to the case for rapidly expanding pre-school education, welcomes the Government's current (1995) commitment to some expansion, and endorses the target of the National Commission on Education that by the year 2005 pre-school education places should be provided for 85 per cent of three year olds and 95 per cent of four year olds.

All those involved in the provision of pre-schooling should adopt the commitment to building a non-violent society, and develop and use the Checklists for working towards a non-violent society *(see Appendix 1, page 241).*

Schools can either be a force for violence prevention, or can provide an experience which reinforces violent attitudes and adds to the child's experience of violence (see page 59). Evaluations of interventions to reduce anti-social behaviour including violence in the USA have found that programmes which involve schools as well as families are more likely to be effective. Comparisons of individual schools operating in urban areas with large numbers of high-risk children demonstrate that it is possible for schools to exert an independent effect on individuals' behaviour.

The American Psychological Association (APA) Commission in their report on Violence and Youth suggested that:

'Schools can become a leading force in providing the safety and the effective educational programmes by which children can learn to reduce and prevent violence. On the one hand, schools can often provide multiple opportunities for bullying, harassment, intimidation, fights and other forms of violence to occur. Students who feel that their personal safety is threatened may bring weapons to school with them. Students who show poor school achievement and poor peer relations show an increased risk of becoming involved in violence. On the other hand, schools also can provide children with repeated and developmentally appropriate opportunities to follow sound principles of personal safety, strengthen academic and social skills, develop sound peer relations, and learn effective non-violent solutions to social conduct.'[85]

Similarly, the Australian National Committee on Violence recommended that:

'Education authorities should include conflict resolution strategies as an integral part of school and other education curricula, and should evaluate their effectiveness... Teacher training institutions should incorporate materials relating to non-violent conflict resolution, including an analysis of the gender basis of patterns of violence and violent behaviour, in their curricula.'[86]

There has been considerable research into the links between school organisation and experience and delinquency. Schools which segregate children according to academic ability, categorise pupils as deviant and failures, refer such students to outside institutions to deal with, ignore repeated truancy and suspend or expel the most difficult students are the ones which are likely to contribute the most to delinquency.[87] The overall direction of current education policies is not promising, promoting a school system which operates on the principles of the market and is judged by league tables of success measured in narrow terms, and curriculum development which appears to marginalise personal and social education. There is evidence of increased exclusion from schools, with too much discretion to exclude remaining in the hands of the headteacher, and of increased segregation outside the mainstream system, in particular for children categorised as having 'emotional and behavioural difficulties'.

Education policy needs to be informed by what we know about child development and the development of anti-social behaviour including violence. It needs to reflect the basic principles of the UN Convention. Whole-school policies should be adopted that encourage self-esteem, a feeling of safety, ownership and active participation, behaviour policies which stress responsibility and the rewarding of good behaviour; and positive, non-violent discipline which reinforces pro-social, anti-violent attitudes. As the Department for Education has emphasised in relation to bullying, the various particular school policies need to dovetail together. A clear commitment to non-violence should be asserted in the school development plan, behaviour policy, and special educational needs policy. Whole school policies will need in particular to ensure that behaviour policies, rules and any sanctions are reviewed in the light of the *Checklists for working towards a non-violent society* (see page 82), and that the physical environment is reviewed and adapted as far as possible to inhibit violence. Training for all those involved in education needs to be reviewed from the same perspective.

Schools, providing a lengthy compulsory experience for almost all children, have a particular obligation to ensure that pupils have access to confidential advice, counselling and support on things that are worrying them, including violence.

Proper application of equal opportunities policies in education to challenge discrimination is clearly relevant to violence prevention. There is widespread evidence of discrimination in admissions and exclusions policy and access to the curriculum, in relation to disabled children, black children and other groups. In Northern Ireland there remains clear discrimination of various kinds in relation to provision of education. A large proportion of Traveller children receive inadequate or no education, in particular secondary education. The Department of Environment Travellers Census in 1993 found that children aged under 16 make up 53 per cent of the total Traveller population, compared with 28 per cent of the general population.[88] A recent Save the Children report, *Travelling people in West Belfast* contains detailed recommendations for improving educational opportunities for Traveller children.[89] There is little official encouragement for the Irish language and very few state-supported schools using Irish as their teaching medium at any level (and little if any provision for children whose first language is not English or Irish). There are continuing concerns over inequalities in funding between Catholic and Protestant schools.

In addition, while there is a lack of clear empirical data to show that the divided school system is a major cause of community conflict in Northern Ireland, a number of commentators have strongly maintained that it is. It is hard to disentangle the effects of family, peer group and schooling on socialisation. A 1983 review concluded:

'it is probable but by no means proved that the segregated school system exacerbates intergroup frictions ... it is highly probable that the segregated schools do nothing to neutralise hostile and prejudicial attitudes between religious groups.'[90]

Official statistics show that of the 1,200 schools in Northern Ireland, attended by 331,000 pupils, 21 are integrated, attended by approximately 3,500 pupils, which represents an increase since implementation of the Education Reform (NI) Order 1989. The Order places a duty on the Department of Education to provide and encourage integrated education.

Schools have been increasingly encouraged to conduct detailed self-evaluations, and it is important that the violence-prevention perspective should be built into such exercises. In Scotland, the Education Department and HM Inspectors of Schools have encouraged school self-evaluations, taking into account the views of pupils, parents and teachers, and showing how questionnaires and other approaches can be integrated into school development planning. Detailed materials for schools were developed on the basis of a pilot project in 23 Scottish schools. A series of 'ethos indicators' have been devised, several of which are concerned with pupil safety and harmonious relations between pupils and teachers.[91]

The curriculum

While violence prevention and encouragement of non-violent conflict resolution may form part of cross-curricular themes, there is no encouragement of it within the National Curriculum for England and Wales. Various bodies have produced relevant materials. For example, the Citizenship Foundation's 'Law in Education' Project, in association with the National Curriculum Council, has produced courses aiming at 'Education for citizenship', one of the cross-curricular themes, for pupils aged 11-14. It includes materials relevant to non-violent conflict resolution.[92]

In Northern Ireland there is a positive and developed example – unique in the UK – of use of the school curriculum to improve community relations and promote non-violent conflict resolution. This was first encouraged by the Department of Education in a circular in June 1982.

The Northern Ireland Curriculum, introduced through the 1989 Order, outlines six cross-curricular themes to be included in the curriculum for all pupils, which include 'education for mutual understanding' (EMU) and 'cultural heritage'. In guidance on EMU, the NI Curriculum Council states:

'In a divided community, EMU merits a place in the curriculum of schools because it is recognised that education has a significant contribution to make in dispelling prejudice and improving relationships.'

It indicates that the Department of Education in Northern Ireland and all major education bodies endorse its inclusion in the curriculum. The guidance suggests that EMU must involve all aspects of school life. It should be delivered mainly through the contributory subjects to the curriculum:

'Teaching and learning styles in support of EMU should be experiential and should be concerned with developing an appropriate ethos and quality of relationships which permeates the whole life of the school.'

It particularly mentions situations in which teachers are dealing with conflict in a variety of contexts, and can encourage constructive and non-violent ways of resolving it. A key aim is that children should 'learn the importance of resolving differences and conflict by peaceful and creative means.'[93]

> 'I think that men and boys should be encouraged to talk about their feelings and not be afraid to show if they are upset.'
>
> 'Boys should learn to cope with people teasing them about being wimps.'

The Northern Ireland Curriculum Council has issued planning guides for teachers, and an information booklet for parents. The FOCUS Group (Forum on Community Understanding and Schools) has produced a guide to statutory and voluntary bodies which can help teachers to plan and carry out work.[94]

The Standing Advisory Commission on Human Rights has welcomed the particular emphasis placed in the curriculum on education to improve understanding and tolerance between the communities in Northern Ireland. Some commentators suggest that there is a particular need in Northern Ireland to encourage in pupils an independence of viewpoint, an ability to question and if necessary challenge what they are told, to avoid the transmission of community conflict from one generation to the next. This has implications not just for the curriculum but for whole school policies designed to encourage active participation – policies which are of course supported by the principles of the UN Convention.

Otherwise in the UK there has been no consistent encouragement for violence prevention work within the curriculum, or in whole-school policies, although of course there are many positive initiatives with related aims in many individual schools, whether their particular perspective is crime prevention, anti-bullying, or anti-truancy. The curriculum needs to promote awareness of gender issues and issues of power and control, as well as personal safety, violence prevention and non-violent conflict resolution.

Bullying prevention

There has been a welcome focus on protecting children from bullying in schools. The Government has promoted research into school bullying and nationwide anti-bullying initiatives. These were encouraged partly by the success of a national intervention campaign against bullying in Norway in the 1980s. This emphasised positive involvement by teachers and parents, setting firm limits on unacceptable behaviour, and the use of 'non hostile, non-corporal' sanctions on rule violations (all physical punishment of children was prohibited in Norway in 1987). Not only did bullying decrease by 50 per cent over two years, but thefts, vandalism and truancy rates were also reduced, while student satisfaction with school life increased.[95]

There is still a need for detailed longer-term evaluation of the best methods of intervention to reduce and prevent bullying. The focus on bullying over the last few years has highlighted the right of students to feel safe in school, and of course this applies in all other institutional settings: bullying is particularly rife in young offender institutions (see page 173), and reported widely in residential care too. But these initiatives should not be seen in isolation from other society-wide moves to assert non-violent values. In particular action to prevent bullying at school must involve parents, who need to be encouraged to understand and support school policies. More important, they need to understand how inappropriate responses to their children and in particular violent and/or humiliating discipline may encourage bullying. A narrow focus within the school can only be limited in its effect.

> 'In school, older children could talk to young children and tell them of their experiences when they were bullied and some of the outcomes.'
>
> 'Schools should not only talk to the victims but also the attackers, more discussions should take place.'

The Department for Education circulated an anti-bullying pack to schools in 1994: *Bullying: don't suffer in silence*, and also made available an in-service training video. The pack identifies as key strategies: making prevention of bullying, and action against it, a high priority; promoting school values which reject bullying behaviour and promote co-operative behaviour; and involving the whole school community. A written whole-school policy against bullying should set out aims in relation to bullying behaviour, and a set of strategies to be followed:

'The policy needs to dovetail with other pastoral policies, play policies and the school development plan. Of particular significance are the relationships between the anti-bullying policy, and schools behaviour and equal opportunities policies. These three should underpin a coherent system for facilitating a healthy social and learning environment in and around the school.'

The pack also emphasises that families

'can be powerful allies for schools trying to resolve bullying situations. They can promote anti-bullying values within the home ...'[96]

The Commission proposes that all institutions including children should be required to have anti-bullying policies. Bullying should be defined broadly to include physical assault and intimidation, theft and extortion, verbal abuse including teasing, racial and sexual harassment or harassment on grounds of religion, gender, sexuality or similar.

These policies must cover:
• arrangements to ensure that everyone in the institutions is aware of the importance of reporting bullying and the importance of ensuring that those bullied are not blamed in any way
• specific strategies for preventing bullying
• provision of appropriate protection and support for those who are bullied
• appropriate responses for those who bully, with a strong emphasis on non-stigmatising and non-punitive approaches
• arrangements for responding to those forms of bullying that appear to involve criminal offences.

Children themselves should be actively consulted and involved in the drafting, implementation and monitoring of the policies. The policy should be made available to all those in the institution including children, in a form they can understand. Every school should be obliged to report on its anti-bullying policies and on a whole-school evaluation of its success within the obligatory report to parents.

Those responsible for inspecting the institution should be obliged to review the operation of the anti-bullying policy. Schools will already have behaviour policies and policies on special educational needs which will be reviewed as part of the four-yearly OFSTED (Office for Standards in Education) inspections. Schools' behaviour and special educational needs policies should be cross-referenced to anti-bullying policies to ensure the safety of children, and also to ensure that preventive strategies against bullying are seriously addressed.

Corporal punishment in private schools

The continuing legality of physical punishment for some pupils in private schools breaches their rights under the UN Convention on the Rights of the Child. In addition, by continuing to allow institutional physical punishment in these settings, the Government is seen to be at least condoning, if not actively supporting, a form of violence to children which increases the risk of their becoming violent. The Government's Initial Report to the UN Committee on the Rights of the Child states: 'The Government has decided that, on grounds of parental choice, corporal punishment should remain available for privately funded pupils in independent schools.'[97] This misguided justification entirely ignores the children's rights imperative for protecting children from an archaic practice. As indicated above (page 135) the UN Committee on the Rights of the Child expressed concern about the situation in private schools, indicating that the continuance of corporal punishment breached the UN Convention.

Although all well-known independent schools and their major professional associations no longer support the use of corporal punishment, as long as the law tolerates the practice for any pupils in any schools, there will remain an unhealthy association in the public mind of corporal punishment with education.

Abolition of corporal punishment in all state-supported education came into effect in 1987. The legislation removes any defence of reasonable chastisement which a teacher might have in civil proceedings, but leaves the defence intact in criminal proceedings. This means that in the eyes of the law, an assault by a teacher of a child that comes within the definition of 'reasonable chastisement' is not criminalised, whereas a similar assault of an adult by an adult is. This is another example of inconsistent attitudes to violence involving children which the Commission deplores. The Commission's recommendations for removing the defence of 'reasonable chastisement' in so far as it allows punishment involving physical or mental violence (see page 136), would give children the same rights to protection from assault as adults, in all schools and elsewhere. Until that reform is implemented, the Department for Education should issue regulations to extend abolition of physical punishment to cover all pupils in private schools.

Recommendations

Education services and individual schools should adopt the commitment to non-violence, and adapt and apply the Checklists for working towards a non-violent society *(see Appendix 1, page 241).*

[Government; opposition parties; education services and institutions]

The Schools Curriculum and Assessment Authority, Scottish Consultative Council on the Curriculum and the Northern Ireland Council for the Curriculum, Examinations and Assessment should adopt the commitment to non-violence and ensure that violence prevention is recognised as a priority within appropriate parts of the core curriculum (including it within education for citizenship, health education, family life education etc).

[Curriculum bodies]

Criteria to strictly limit exclusions from school should be defined in legislation.

[Department for Education and Employment; opposition parties]

Responsible government departments should require all institutional settings for children and young people, both day and boarding in the state, voluntary and private sectors to implement policies for preventing bullying and protecting children from bullying.

[Department for Education and Employment; Department of Health; Home Office; opposition parties]

Abolition of physical punishment in schools should be extended immediately to cover all pupils in independent schools.

[Department for Education and Employment]

Children's opportunities for play and leisure

Many recent reports from voluntary organisations have deplored the reduction in play and leisure opportunities for children and young people. The Commission adds the perspective of violence prevention to the powerful case for ensuring that adequate resources are devoted to play and leisure opportunities for all children and young people, essential to their health and positive mental and physical development. All such provision should be committed to non-violence, and should make a substantial contribution to working towards a non-violent society. The Commission notes that the UN Convention emphasises children's rights to appropriate play and recreation (article 31 recognises the right of the child 'to rest and leisure, to engage in play and recreational activities appropriate to the age of the child and to participate freely in cultural life and the arts').

It is clear that provision at present is unco-ordinated at both central and local level, ad hoc and under-funded, lacking any legislative basis. Recent changes in education legislation for England and Wales including Local Management of Schools and the National Curriculum have adversely affected the provision of play, recreation, sport, arts and culture for children. For example, while the National Curriculum is being used to ensure that all children take part in physical education, there is evidence that schools' resources for sport have been diminished. A Register of Recreational Land was launched in 1993, and should enable any future loss of land for play and sport to be accurately monitored. But sports bodies including the National Playing Fields Association and the Central Council for Physical Recreation have expressed concerns at the amount of playing fields and other recreational land which has been sold for development in recent years.[98] A survey by the National Youth Agency of local authority youth service budgets for 1991/92 and 1992/93 found that of the 69 authorities which responded, 29 reported a standstill budget, 27 a decrease and only 13 an increase.[99]

Overall, children and young people benefit from only a tiny proportion of the government expenditure on arts and leisure activities – far smaller than the 23 per cent of the population which under 18 year olds represent.

The Commission was particularly concerned at recent research suggesting that children's freedom of movement has been drastically limited over the last few decades. The major reasons given by parents for restricting their children's freedom of movement (for example, being allowed to cycle or walk to and from school) relate to fear of various kinds of violence, such as fear of a traffic accident, or, after dark, fear of 'molestation.'[100] Community safety strategies must aim to restore to children appropriate freedom of movement, through combating both violence and unrealistic fear of violence.

Lack of positive play and leisure opportunities tends to be most acute in inner city areas. A 1988 report from the National Association for the Care and Resettlement of Offenders (NACRO) stated:

> 'The level of social and recreational provision for children and young people on public sector housing estates in most areas is minimal. Many estates have no provision at all … These shortcomings have far-reaching consequences for everyone. Children are less safe. Their physical and social development can be seriously affected if they have no opportunity to play with each other.'[101]

> 'There ought to be more youth clubs and things for young people to do so that they are not under their parents' feet all the time.'

> 'They should make a club for violent males to meet and discuss about not being violent, or make them stay at home and out of trouble.'

It appears there has been little or no evaluation of youth and leisure projects in relation to their contribution to violence prevention (perhaps by comparing levels of service for comparable populations with their levels of violence). A recent report commissioned by ITV Telethon and the Prince's Trust concluded that there is little objective evidence to demonstrate a causal relationship between youth work and crime diversion generally, but

'there is a large body of subjective evidence which convinces us that there is a linkage. It has not been possible to estimate the strength of this linkage but it appears to be strongest for youth work which is carefully targeted at young people "at risk", has clearly defined objectives, offers an intense and long term process and provides a challenging and educational experience.'[102]

The report recommended that there should be an attempt to identify and establish a valid framework for monitoring and evaluating the effect of youth work, particularly its impact on crime diversion.

The report calculated that the benefit to society of preventing a single youth crime would be the equivalent of at least £2,300, just under half of which would be directly recoverable to the public purse. This calculation took no account of such benefits as the absence of psychological distress to victims or lower levels of fear of crime.

The National Board for Crime Prevention has set up a Working Group on Young People and Crime, chaired by Janet Paraskeva, Director of the National Youth Agency, which is focusing on the contribution of youth services to diversion from crime, and aiming to identify 'what works' in juvenile crime prevention.

In Northern Ireland, a major review of policies and practice on children's play, *Agenda for play: the way forward*, and *A charter for children's play in Northern Ireland* were jointly published by PlayBoard and Save the Children in 1994, arising out of a 'Playright' project, which emphasises the UK Government's obligations under the UN Convention. The Agenda suggests that sectarianism, which is 'inherent in the very fabric of society in Northern Ireland':

- artificially restricts children's outdoor play by creating no-go areas for play and leisure
- limits children's access to existing resources because those resources are located in areas identified with one community
- limits contacts between Catholic and Protestant children
- fosters negative and harmful stereotypes of the other group which can be translated into hostile behaviour.[103]

The report suggests that levels of play provision are among the lowest in Europe; only one in 12 under 16 year olds have access to holiday play provision, and only one per cent to an after-school scheme. It identifies certain existing local schemes in which partnerships have produced good delivery of play and recreation opportunities, for example the Belfast Healthy Cities Project and Brownlow Community Trust. On the other hand it found only one local council which had a policy covering all aspects of play.

The *Charter for children's play* emphasises children's active participation, and principles of non-violence and equal opportunities:

'Children of all ages should be able to play freely, confidently, on their own or with other children or with adults. Children should take care not to hurt themselves or others in their play ... All children should feel respected and valued and able to play free from racial or other types of harassment, or any abuse from either children or adults ... Play service providers ... should provide play opportunities which promote positive images of diversity ... Play practice should enable children to develop positive attitudes to difference of religion, culture, language, gender and ability and to perceived differences of race.'[104]

Play without frontiers, a policy document on community relations in children's play, produced by PlayBoard NI in 1990 reports that sectarianism is a widespread problem in playschemes and that workers would welcome guidance on how to deal positively with sectarian incidents. The report emphasises:

> 'Sectarianism is a problem affecting every one of us in Northern Ireland. Far from being unaware of the violence and hatred in our society, many children as young as five years old display sectarian attitudes and behaviour ... Promoting community relations is a long term process but by early intervention we have a chance to promote acceptance, understanding and respect for others before bigoted ideas become entrenched and form the basis for later inter-group conflict.'[105]

Recommendations

All those involved in planning and provision of youth and leisure services for children and young people should adopt the commitment to non-violence, and use the Checklists for working towards a non-violent society *to ensure that their policies and practice help in working towards a non-violent society. All play policies and the youth service curriculum should be reviewed in the light of the commitment to non-violence.*

[Play and youth services]

There should be central and local co-ordination of policy on play and leisure opportunities for children, and adequate funding to take account of the special needs of children and the proportion of the overall population which they form.

[Government; opposition parties]

Local authorities' corporate strategies must include planning of adequate play and leisure opportunities for children, and must be linked with community safety strategies; both must see reasserting children's appropriate freedom of movement, through reduction of violence and unrealistic fear of violence, as an essential aim.

[Local authorities]

The health service

What we know of the risk factors for violence involving children implies that prevention is a multi-disciplinary task, and one in which the health service clearly has a major role. The relationship with violence should be used to promote relevant programmes and to augment the arguments for adequate resources. There is a growing movement towards a focus on violence as a public health problem. The focus has been most developed in the USA, where the problem is acute. The World Health Organisation recently formed a Task Force on Violence and Health.

A recent paper in the *Journal of the Royal Society of Medicine* emphasised:

> 'It is surely better to reduce crime and violence through the positive aim of promoting health rather than through the negative aims of retribution, deterrence and incapacitation.'[106]

Adoption of the commitment to non-violence which the Commission proposes, and application of the *Checklists for working towards a non-violent society* could maximise the contribution of health services to violence prevention. Violence is certainly a significant threat to life and health, and a major cause of disparities in health between richer and poorer segments of the community. Public health aims to establish prevalence and incidence of disease, and to identify causes, risk groups and risk factors. If violence becomes recognised as a public health problem, detailed and consistent recording of incidents of violence by those involved in the health service could provide valuable information on which to base strategies for prevention.

Police and court statistics provide a very inaccurate picture of levels of violence. For example, a study in Bristol found that only 23 per cent of victims of assault treated in hospital had been recorded by the police as 'woundings'.[107]

In a joint paper, David Farrington from the Institute of Criminology at the University of Cambridge and Dr Frederick P Rivara from the University of Washington highlight:

> 'The health promotion approach of decreasing risk factors for diseases and strengthening protective factors is applicable to the problem of childhood aggression and youth violence ...'

151

In particular, health professionals can promote the 'resiliency' of children

> 'to "immunize" all children against lives of violence. By virtue of our early contact with all mothers and their children, we are perhaps in the best position of any group to intervene in meaningful and effective ways. In addition, because our contact is with all families across the entire socio-economic spectrum, we can avoid stigmatising and labelling families who might otherwise be singled out by various social service agencies and interventions.'[108]

The paper highlights ways in which the work of health professionals, in particular family doctors, paediatricians and health visitors, can contribute to primary prevention of violence involving children:

> 'Most of these interventions are familiar to paediatricians, albeit with an eye to different outcomes such as prevention of low birth weight, child abuse, school failure, teenage pregnancy or substance abuse. What is different is the link to violence prevention, which few paediatricians have considered as one of the important goals of these programmes.'[109]

Poverty and poor health go together. Increased income inequality in the UK in the 1980s has been accompanied by a widening in social class differences in infant mortality; the ratio between social classes V and I increased from 1.8 in 1978 to 2.0 in 1990.[110] A child born into a poor family in the UK is still almost twice as likely to die before he or she is one year old than the child from a better-off family. Although these inequalities were not addressed in the White Paper *The Health of the Nation* they are increasingly recognised in local health initiatives and infant mortality is regarded as a sensitive index to broader health inequalities.[111] Infants' physical and mental health and development also interact: 'failure to thrive' may be caused by relationship difficulties, while a sensory impairment, such as hearing loss, may cause problems between child and parents as well as delaying the development of speech.

Health visiting

Health surveillance by people trained and experienced in infant development is therefore crucial and it is health visitors, in the course of their 'well baby' work who are most likely to become aware of any increased risk of violence to a child, whether it is the risk to a young baby whose colicky crying causes stress which a parent finds intolerable, or the risk to a toddler of a parent's unrealistic disciplinary demands.

Health visitors aim to visit at home every baby born in the UK. Since the weeks after childbirth are usually a time when parents welcome support and advice, they are uniquely placed to participate in parent-education and to interpret and promote the *Checklists for working towards a non-violent society*. Early recognition and appropriate management of behaviour problems in children need to be built into all points of contact between the child and parents and the health service (see also mental health services, page ...).

A recent paper by David Farrington presents evidence that intensive health visiting programmes could ultimately cut the incidence of juvenile crime including violent crime.[112]

In the USA also, careful evaluations have supported home, or health, visiting:

> 'Strong support has emerged, on both theoretical as well as empirical grounds, for the expansion of home visiting services to new parents. Though not always conclusive, repeated randomized trials of this intervention, as well as quasi-experimental evaluations of various community-based home visiting programmes, suggest that intervention holds particular promise for altering parental behaviour. Positive outcomes include a reduction in reported cases of child abuse and neglect; children experiencing fewer accidents and being less likely to require emergency room care; less reported use of corporal punishment; and more stimulating and positive home environments.'[113]

At least three US longitudinal studies have found that comprehensive parenting services provided over two years not only produce initial gains but that these gains were strengthened over time. Areas showing improvement included parenting skills, parent-child relationships, educational achievement, employment rates and economic well-being. Intensity of service may be a far better predictor of positive client outcomes than duration or even service structure.[114]

School nursing

A modern school nursing service could play – and in some areas is already playing – a large part in child protection, in education for parenthood, in providing young people with confidential advice including contraceptive advice, and other work more directly related to building a non-violent society, including anti-bullying strategies and conflict resolution programmes. The service should be increased.

Parent education

Health services obviously have a crucial part to play in parent education (see also page 129). The *Checklists for working towards a non-violent society* should help to ensure that the violence prevention perspective is fully covered.

Discipline has been identified as a key area for positive advice, because physical punishment and humiliation, erratic responses and lack of monitoring and supervision are identified as key factors in the development of anti-social and violent behaviour. Within the health professions themselves there is a need for education in positive discipline; recent surveys of opinion amongst GPs found over 70 per cent supporting physical punishment.[115] But the British Paediatric Association, British Association for Community Child Health and the Health Visitors' Association support education and legal reform to end all physical punishment in the UK (see also page 133).

Teenage pregnancy

Low income teenage mothers are the group most at risk of low birthweight babies and poor perinatal outcomes. There is also some evidence that their babies are more at risk of serious abuse. Thus there is a violence prevention perspective to the problem of teenage pregnancy. The Government White Paper, *The Health of the Nation* has set a target of reducing the rate of conception amongst under-16s by at least 50 per cent by the year 2000 (from 9.5 per 1,000 girls aged 13-15 in 1989, to no more than 4.8 per 1,000).[116] There were 7,922 conceptions amongst under-16s in 1989, and indeed there has been a steady increase in numbers of under-16 conceptions since 1980.

There appear to be clear conflicts between the health target (and related targets which aim to reduce the incidence of HIV infection and other sexually transmitted diseases) set by the Department of Health for England, and the Department for Education's new policy and legislation limiting children's rights to sex education in schools (in the Education Act 1993). Primary school age pupils' right to sex education is dependent both on governors' discretion (they must devise a policy and can decide not to provide sex education at all) and parents' discretion. Parents can withdraw their children from any sex education provided in primary or secondary schools which goes beyond basic biological facts, which must be included in the National Curriculum. The compulsory elements of the National Curriculum must not include education about HIV/Aids or other sexually transmitted diseases, nor non-biological study of sexual behaviour. A recent major survey of the sexual experiences of 19,000 people, carried out in 1990/91 found that those reporting formal teaching as their main source of information had the lowest rate of sexual activity under the age of 16.[117]

Research in industrialized countries has found that countries with the lowest teenage pregnancy rates are those which have more liberal attitudes to sex, easily accessible contraceptive services for young people, and effective programmes of sex education.[118]

Accidents

Accidents cause a very high proportion of the deaths and serious injury suffered by UK children. The causes of accidents are often complex. By definition, accidents do not involve deliberate violence to children. But irresponsibility or neglect – by individuals, by institutions and by the state – may cause injury and death which is still defined as accidental. The borderline between such irresponsibility or neglect and deliberate harm is neither simple nor clear. The Child Accident Prevention Trust told the Commission:

'Accidents can be viewed as a form of violence against children perpetuated within an institutional framework when many can be prevented or avoided.'

The Commission felt it must highlight the threat posed to children by accidents, in particular in the home and on roads, partly to put the extent of deliberate violence to children in perspective, and partly to emphasise the importance of accident prevention, which should clearly be seen as part of community safety strategies.

In addition, brain injuries in children, as noted in the paper by Farrington and Rivara referred to above

'are one of the most preventable categories of risk factors which operate cumulatively and interactively to increase the risk of later psychopathology.'[119]

Head injury prevention programmes need to focus on the most common causes of brain injury: cycle accidents and falls (suggested strategies: wearing of cycle helmets; elimination of baby walkers, stair gates and other barriers; safe surfaces in playgrounds) and road accidents (suggested strategies: attention to pedestrian safety and occupant safety, wearing of seat belts).

Accidents to children in their home are the largest single cause of death and injury for children aged one to four. Numbers of children injured by burns and scalds, falls, 'foreign objects' and swallowing or inhaling poisonous substances have increased over the last five years, as have the numbers of children dying or being injured in uncontrolled fires, the most common cause of accidental death of children within the home. Children in low income families are at particular risk of accidents. Accident prevention may be limited by poor design of the environment in which they live (there are particular concerns over safety in temporary – bed and breakfast – accommodation) and by lack of money to buy safety equipment. Until 1988, families could claim one-off payments to buy safety equipment such as fireguards and stair gates. Since the introduction of the Social Fund, the only way to seek money for safety equipment is to apply for a discretionary loan, with repayment deducted from regular benefit.

Road accidents are the main cause of accidental death to school-age children; in 1991 they accounted for 61 per cent of the accidental deaths of 5-16 year-olds. Death rates in the UK among child pedestrians are among the highest in Europe (among under 10 year olds the UK death rate is three times that in Sweden). There are large social class differences: the chance of a child with unskilled parents being killed as a pedestrian is four times greater than that of a child of professional parents.

There has been a steady reduction in the under-15 year old death rate for accidents from about 18 per 100,000 in 1970 to 6.7 per 100,000 in 1990. The Government has set welcome targets for further reductions in accidents involving children and young people: to reduce the death rate for accidents among under-15 year olds by at least 33 per cent by 2005 (from 6.7 per 100,000 in 1990 to no more than 4.5 per 100,000) and to reduce the death rate for accidents among 15–24 year-olds by at least 25 per cent by 2005 (from 23.2 per 100,000 to no more than 17.4 per 100,000).[120]

Medical interventions which may constitute violence

Medical interventions without appropriate consent, or without full consideration of children's rights and interests and ethical principles, may come within the Commission's definition of violence. Treatment sometimes involves physical restraint, enforced medication and deprivation of liberty: such practices must be subject to detailed regulation and guidance: see also *One scandal too many ...*[121]

When available forms of treatment are invasive, but may result in considerable short-term gains in the quality of life, there are clear ethical dilemmas, intensified where the child concerned is judged incapable of giving or withholding consent.

Other examples which have caused public concern are cases of sterilisation of young women with learning difficulties, and the use of ECT on under 18 year olds. There have also been suggestions that children and young people are often not adequately prepared for painful forms of treatment, or given appropriate levels of pain relief. The Commission welcomes the advice booklets recently published by Action for Sick Children.[122]

Recommendations

The Department of Health should recognise that violence is a serious public health problem, and mount a new programme of prevention, based on research. Health services for families and children should adopt the commitment to non-violence, and develop and apply Checklists for working towards a non-violent society (see Appendix 1, page 241). A violence prevention strategy, devised on the basis of current knowledge of risk factors and effective interventions, should be built into training for, planning, commissioning and delivery of health services to families and children, and also used to justify targeting more resources at primary prevention. The strategy will of course contain many elements already adopted for improving public health in general and the health of children in particular.

The crucial surveillance and education role of health visitors should be protected and made available throughout the UK. Similarly, the school nursing service should be expanded appropriately to cover all schools.

[Department of Health; opposition parties; health authorities and trusts; relevant professional bodies]

Accident prevention should become an integral part of central and local community safety strategies. The Commission welcomes the Government's targets for reduction of accidents. From a violence prevention perspective, particular priority should be given to reducing accidents which may result in brain injury.

[Local authority community safety committees]

There should be provision for new parents of appropriate equipment to prevent home accidents, such as fire guards and stair gates, through specific grants and/or loan systems.

[Department of Social Security; opposition parties]

The Department for Education's policies on sex education should be reviewed immediately in the light of the Government's health targets and knowledge of effective strategies for reducing teenage pregnancy.

[Department for Education and Employment]

The right of children and young people with sufficient understanding to seek confidential advice on sex and contraception, confirmed by the House of Lords judgment in the Gillick case, should be upheld and confirmed consistently in statute.

[Department of Health]

Appropriate medical regulatory bodies should review ethical issues raised by those forms of treatment of children which may come within the Commission's definition of violence. Those involved in health services for children should ensure that advice on pain relief for children is appropriately disseminated.

[General Medical Council; professional bodies]

Mental health services

Violence involving children can sometimes be seen as a mental health problem. Some children behave violently as a result of a wide range of emotional problems and tensions within their families and communities. Many of these problems are persistent and cause significant distress to children and those responsible for them.

> 'Mental health problems in children and young people may be defined as abnormalities of the emotions, behaviour or social relationships which are sufficiently marked and sufficiently prolonged to impair the development of the child or young person and/or to cause distress or disturbance to the child, the child's family or community.'[123]

While child and adolescent mental health services are commonly understood to be specialist services, primarily concerned with the assessment and treatment of seriously disturbed children and adolescents, the contribution of the services in general is more comprehensive and includes work that is designed to promote mental health and to assist others in facilitating mental health as well as assessment and treatment.

Child and adolescent mental health services consist of a wide range of professionals from different disciplines, in psychiatry, psychology, social work, education and psychotherapy. The multi-disciplinary composition of the services is appropriate to meet the multi-faceted nature of children's mental health problems, including violent behaviour. The services operate at different levels or tiers of provision:

- a tertiary, specialist tier based in in-patient units and specialist clinics for severe mental health disorders
- a secondary tier based in the community in child psychiatry outpatient departments, child and family consultation centres, educational psychology services
- a primary tier consisting of many individuals and practitioners whose primary designated role is not that of mental health practitioner but whose direct work with families has considerable influence on the mental health of children.

Violent behaviour can occur in a wide variety of children with different kinds of mental health problems. It is important to recognise however that most violence in childhood forms but one part of a pattern of aggressive and rule-transgressing behaviour. The concept of 'conduct disorder' to describe this pattern, while it may misleadingly suggest an inappropriate medical approach to the problem, has nevertheless various distinct advantages. In particular, it has allowed the collection of information, especially through longitudinal studies, on the background of children and young people with such patterns of behaviour in a way that has strongly indicated significant links. These have been described in section 1, page 63. In addition, it has allowed the evaluation of various approaches to prevention and treatment.

The efficiency and effectiveness of child and adolescent mental health services in dealing with children's violent behaviour, especially among children with conduct disorders, needs consideration. A proportion, possibly a rather small proportion of those referred to the secondary level service, respond well to treatment. In general, these are the children who come from families well motivated to receive treatment and in whom a cause for the problem is reasonably readily identified. Other children may also respond, especially if the intervention is focused on an analysis of the situations in which the maladaptive behaviour is shown, and a planned programme is instituted accordingly. However, in many cases, children with conduct disorders come from families which are, at best, ambivalent about treatment. It should be stressed that ambivalence should not be seen as blameworthy. It often arises from fear of the child protection element of the service, from a concern about labelling, and from previous unrewarding experiences with similar services. Where conduct disorder includes offending, the use of supervision orders and probation orders may provide access to and encouragement for treatment without incarceration.

It is widely, though not universally, accepted that in the current state of knowledge, treatment in child and adolescent mental health services of many children with conduct disorders and their families has limited effectiveness.[124] This often results in children with these problems being given low priority by staff in the services. It is not thought to be efficient to do otherwise, despite the fact that some children do respond and all need adequate appraisal so that these can be identified. It is possible that if there were more collaborative work with other agencies in the community, for example with the youth service, intermediate treatment etc., such services could be more effective. There is a need for further evaluation of group and individual treatment and training for parents of young children with conduct disorders. Centres of research excellence in the mental health field could undertake this in collaboration with secondary care centres receiving referrals because of children's violent behaviour.

It is the Commission's view that health service provision in this field needs great improvement: our recommendation provides a framework.

Recommendation

Child and adolescent mental health services should continue to be developed as a comprehensive, multi-service, multi-disciplinary provision that includes specialist and non-specialist generic services. This comprehensive service should be operated at primary, secondary and tertiary levels of service. Within this tiered model, primary care professionals should receive consultation, training and support in the identification and first line management of children with violent behavioural problems, using methods which are not blaming or guilt inducing.

If children have not responded to primary care management, facilities for assessment and treatment at the secondary level should be available within six weeks for all children showing significant violent behaviour, especially those with conduct disorders. Parents and teachers should have the opportunity to consult secondary care professional staff, even if the children themselves do not wish to be seen. Every effort should be made to develop collaborative work with other organisations in the community, for example the youth service, child care, family support, education and criminal justice systems, to provide a comprehensive community-based treatment service.

[Department of Health; health authorities and trusts; all involved in child and adolescent mental health services]

Children in care and leaving care

Over the last few years there has been considerable concern over levels of violence to children in care in institutions, by both staff and other children, and in foster-care. Many of those in care have already suffered physical or mental violence. Regulations and guidance issued under the Children Act 1989 for England and Wales include welcome safeguards for children in residential and other settings, and positive advice for carers. But, as *One scandal too many* ... set out in detail, the safeguards are not consistent.[125] All those working in the care system should adopt the commitment to non-violence and use the *Checklists for working towards a non-violent society*.

The National Prison Survey found that 38 per cent of 17-20 year olds in custody had some experience of care before the age of 16, and other research has shown even higher proportions.[126] This is not a surprising statistic, given that many children enter care primarily because of offending – both those remanded to care while awaiting a court appearance, and those under a supervision order with a residence requirement. It appears there has been no analysis to determine whether there is a disproportionate number of ex-care violent offenders. But there is considerable evidence that care leavers receive inadequate support and represent a vulnerable group.

Recommendation
The child care system should adopt the commitment to non-violence and use the Checklists for working towards a non-violent society *throughout its services, including preparing and supporting care leavers.*

[Department of Health; local authorities; those involved in voluntary and private child care sectors]

'Domestic' or family violence

It is clear that there are various links between violence to adults, mostly women, in domestic situations, and violence to children in those situations. A major NCH Action for Children report published in 1994, *The hidden victims: children and domestic violence*, documented the issue in detail.[127] Children in the household frequently suffer violence from the same adult; children are affected not only by experiencing violence themselves, but by living in a violent situation, witnessing or hearing violence or noticing physical results such as bruises on their mother, and becoming fearful for their own safety. And the experience of violence including violent discipline within the home is a significant factor in the development of violent attitudes and the potential for violence in childhood and adult relationships (see page 50).

Approximately two out of every three women who come into Women's Aid refuges or seek advice and support have young children, many of whom will have themselves experienced violence in the home, and almost all of whom will have witnessed violence. One research study of women experiencing domestic violence where there were children in the home found that in 70 per cent of cases the child was also physically abused.[128]

> 'If my mum had told someone about what my dad did to us all sooner, something could of happened to stop him, but we were all too scared.'

Another study of physically abused children found that in 45 per cent of cases the mother also was being physically abused. The NSPCC's Child Protection Register Research has shown correlations between child abuse and domestic violence. For example, of the 9,628 registered cases during 1988/90, 23 per cent recorded marital violence as the family characteristic and a stress factor which may have precipitated the abuse. Closer examination revealed that of 2,786 physical injury cases, 25 per cent recorded marital violence, and of the 240 emotional abuse cases, 29 per cent recorded marital violence. These figures are likely to be underestimates of the incidence of marital violence and related stresses in 'registered' children's families, as little would be known about families at the point of registration. Research clearly establishes a significant link between child abuse and what is currently known as domestic violence.[129]

The Women's Aid Federation of England (WAFE) made a detailed submission to the Commission:

> 'Violence can also mean among other things: threats, deprivation of food, limiting contact with family or friends, constant criticism, being locked in the house, intimidation, threatening children to exert power and control over women, stealing money from women or depriving them of money. All of these have a direct effect on the children and are experienced by them as an abuse of power, which can therefore be considered to be violent.'

WAFE's Statement of Aims and Principles defines domestic violence as '… physical, mental or sexual abuse of women and children from known others …'

In its submission, WAFE described effects on children noted by refuge workers, including stress-related illnesses, confused and torn loyalties, lack of trust, unnaturally good behaviour, taking on the mother role, an acceptance of abuse as 'normal', guilt, isolation, shame, anger, lack of confidence, fear of a repeat or return to violence and so on. The mother's and children's problems are often exacerbated even when they are no longer living with violence by the need to sort out benefits, housing and legal matters. Children coming into refuges and into temporary accommodation suffer great disruption, leaving behind many of their possessions, losing contact with friends, and usually having to start at a new school.

While refuges are seriously under-funded, most now employ at least one part-time specialist children's support worker, who carries out a range of work – providing activities for children of all ages, liaising with local schools, nurseries, health workers and so on, being an advocate for children within the refuge, providing information and support for children and young people.

In 1993 the Federation adopted a detailed children's rights policy, including the right to be welcomed into the refuge, offered somewhere safe to stay with their mother and any brothers and sisters, to live in an environment that is healthy, safe and adequate for their needs, to have 'space she/he feels comfortable with in which to express feelings about their experiences', and to safety from violence which includes the right to safety from physical punishment. Guidelines show that all refuges have a policy of promoting non-violent discipline, and suggest that work with children could include promoting non-violent ways of resolving conflict amongst them.

Experienced refuge workers particularly challenge crude concepts of an inevitable cycle of violence, suggestions that those who are abused go on to abuse:

> 'The experience and analysis of Women's Aid workers leads to a rejection of

the cycle of violence theory as providing neither a useful nor an adequate understanding of domestic violence and its effects on children. The theory ignores the gender divisions and inequality that exist in our society, and offers men who abuse an excuse for their behaviour. It denies the experience of the majority of children survivors of abuse who do not go on to be abusers themselves. It does not examine the process of leaving abuse and the healing effects this will usually have on children in the long term, especially when given proper support and help. There is a need for research in the UK into the effects of domestic violence on children so that agencies working with children can become better informed and equipped to meet children's needs.'

The Federation emphasises that

'Empowering the non-abusing parent is one of the most effective ways of promoting the welfare and safety of the child, and is also substantially cheaper in the long term when compared with the cost of taking a child into local authority care.'

Local government policies and priorities should be informed by awareness of children's experience of violence in the family and its effects on them. There should be a greater emphasis on empowering and supporting non-abusing parents to enable the family to make a life free from violence without the need to take children into care. This requires better co-ordination of housing policies. Preventive duties of local authorities under section 17 of the Children Act, towards children in need, should be developed in relation to children in refuges. A survey in 1992 found that less than 10 local authorities were providing funds for work with children in refuges under this provision.

A 1990 Home Office Circular (60/1990) to all police forces encouraged the development and publicising of force policy statements and strategies. It stated:

'Violent assaults, or brutal or threatening behaviour over a period of time by a person to whom the victim is married or with whom the victim lives, are no less serious than a violent assault by a stranger.'

Forces were encouraged to set up dedicated domestic violence units or appoint officers to deal specifically with domestic violence cases and to liaise with other agencies in the field. HM Inspectorate of Constabulary reports show that all forces do now have policies which emphasise:
• the over-riding duty to protect victims and children from further attack
• the need to treat domestic violence as seriously as other forms of violence.[130]

The recently promoted 'zero tolerance' campaigns provide an exciting model for violence prevention. The first Zero Tolerance Campaign was developed by

Edinburgh District Council's Women's Committee, in consultation with groups working with victims and survivors of domestic violence; its aim was to challenge social attitudes towards physical and sexual assaults against women and girls. This involved a poster and media campaign and public debate. Evaluations found that the campaign

> 'succeeded in attracting the attention and gaining the approval of most of the people who were questioned in the street survey. It has also provoked considerable public debate... Looking on the Zero Tolerance Campaign as a "first step" in attempting to challenge the social climate within which abuse occurs would suggest that it has been a success.'[131]

Following the inquiry by the Home Affairs Select Committee into domestic violence and its 1992 report, inter-departmental working groups of ministers and officials were set up to promote a co-ordinated approach to the issue at a national and local level. A draft circular issued for consultation in October 1994 proposed local inter-agency action 'to enhance the local response to domestic violence' (see page 107 for recommendations on local co-ordination).[132]

While the circular reflects the growing acceptance at government level of the scale of the problem of domestic violence, and the need for inter-agency action, it also illustrates problems over the definition in relation to children. It would seem common sense to assume that the term 'domestic' violence included any children affected by violence within the domestic situation (as it does in the WAFE definition). But in fact the term is generally used only to refer to 'adult' violence, mostly by male husbands or partners to women. The draft circular, for example, defines it as:

> 'any form of physical, sexual or emotional abuse which takes place within the context of a close relationship. In most cases the relationship will be between partners (married, co-habiting, or otherwise) or ex-partners.'

While this definition could be taken to cover 'domestic' abuse and violence to children, the text makes it clear that it does not. The Commission believes that much current usage of the term domestic violence tends to hide the extent of violence to children within domestic situations, and to ignore the various links between adult-to-adult violence in the home and violence to children. In the view of the Commission, it would be more valuable from the perspective of prevention and intervention to use the general term 'family violence' (given a wide definition of 'family' – see page 120) to include violence between adults, between adults and children, and between children. Where the focus is on violence within particular relationships, like violence to women, or violence to children, it should be explicitly defined.

Recommendations

All organisations concerned with violence within close relationships should consider fully the safety and welfare of children at all times, including episodes in which violence occurs only between adults.

Community safety strategies should include measures to prevent family violence and arrangements for a co-ordinated response (see also recommendations on local co-ordination, page 107)

[All involved in challenging family violence, including police, local authorities, voluntary organisations]

Training for the judiciary should include gender and violence awareness, as proposed by the Home Affairs Select Committee 1992 report on its inquiry into domestic violence.

[Lord Chancellor's Department; appropriate bodies in Scotland and Northern Ireland]

When courts are considering making orders on residence and contact under section 8 of the Children Act, there should be consideration of the safety of the non-abusing parent, given that this affects the welfare of the child, and also of the effects of domestic violence on children.

[Department of Health]

Funding for refuges, including their services for children, aftercare and outreach work should be adequate and centrally co-ordinated.

[Home Office; Department of Health]

Hospitals and Accident and Emergency Departments and GPs need to liaise with refuges, and provide information and advice about refuges to women and children affected by domestic violence. Health visitors should have awareness training on effects on children of violence between adults in the home, and maintain up-to-date information on services and options for children.

[Health authorities and trusts; GPs; health visitors]

Sexual abuse

For child protection purposes sexual abuse is defined as 'actual or likely sexual exploitation of a child or adolescent. The child may be dependent and/or developmentally immature.'[133]

The activities encompassed by such a definition include those such as rape and other sexual assaults which would be deemed violent if committed with an adult, let alone a dependent child or adolescent. Other activities, such as fondling, or consenting intercourse, that would be acceptable between adults, are deemed victimising in the case of children because of their immaturity and dependency. The former activities are distinguished from the latter in that the motivation for them seems to be primarily aggression rather than sexual gratification, though that may also have played a part.

This distinction is clearly illustrated in a recent American survey of children as victims of violence. In a national survey of two thousand children aged 10-16 in the USA, Finkelhor and Dziuba-Leatherman distinguished between physical assaults, sexual abuse/assaults and violence to genitals. Using the question: 'Has there ever been a time when anyone intentionally tried to hurt your private parts by hitting you, kicking you there, or trying to hit them with an object?' they found some 9 per cent of the sample had had such an experience and 5 per cent in the last year. Boys were much more likely to have experienced such violence than girls.[134]

Where the main motivation appears to be aggression there is no problem in defining such sexual acts as violence to children. Where the motivation appears to be the sexual gratification of the perpetrator, no force is used and the child is not physically hurt, the abuse still falls within the Commission's remit. The working definition of violence agreed by the Commission is 'behaviour by people against people liable to cause physical or psychological harm'.

The vast majority of evidence indicates the generally harmful effects of sexual abuse on children.[135] Different factors such as the closeness of the relationship with the perpetrator, a high frequency of sexual contact, a long duration and penetrative sexual acts were all associated with increased symptoms in child victims. Given this body of evidence, all sexual abuse of children, both aggressive and non-aggressive, has a strong probability of causing physical or psychological harm. All sexual abuse of children therefore fulfils the Commission's working definition of violence.

Some studies have reinforced grey moral and definitional areas of child sexual abuse. In 1979 Finkelhor argued against basing the prohibition against adult-child sex on the belief that it would cause harm to the children. He felt that such an empirical presumption had not been sufficiently firmly established. He felt that a stronger ethical position against adult-child sex lay in the fact that children were incapable of full and informed consent to such activities.[136] Since then a number of follow-up studies (eg Caffaro-Rouget et al, 1989; Conte and Schuerman, 1987[137]) have found a surprisingly large percentage of victims of child sexual abuse who showed no symptoms of disturbance on their assessments. More recently Sandfort (1992) has reported on a retrospective survey of young people between the ages of 18 and 23.[138] Over a third of the sexual experiences they had had with adults when children were reported by them as being consensual and satisfying. These studies would seem to bear out Finkelhor's caveats.

Society's response to the disclosure of child sexual abuse

There is a great deal of concern that the response to the disclosure of child sexual abuse may, in some circumstances, be more harmful to the child than the abuse itself. A Scottish research study on the impact of sexual abuse on children and their parents asked the children what had been the worst part of what had happened to them. Nearly half the children detailed the fear and uncertainty connected with the abuse itself and the continuing fear of the abuser but there were also comments on unpleasant medical examinations, negative peer reactions and difficult court appearances.[139]

The criminal justice system and sexual abuse

Within the past few years a number of reforms have been introduced by the Criminal Justice Acts 1988 and 1991 which aim to reduce the trauma of the system and bring more cases into the courts.[140] Such reforms have included the introduction of 'livelinks' which spare the child from the formal and forbidding atmosphere of the courtroom, and also pre-recorded videotaped evidence-in-chief, which preserves the child's allegations on tape, reducing the number of times she or he has to be questioned.

In spite of these reforms, much remains about the criminal justice system that causes concern. Children who have made an allegation of abuse are subjected to delays of months or even years before their cases come to court. Recent research has shown that although procedures have been implemented to reduce delays for child witnesses, delays are in fact increasing, with an average delay of about 10 months.[141] Related to this is the concern that children who have made an allegation are often denied therapeutic support until after their case is heard, as prosecutors fear that defence counsel may suggest that the therapist 'coached' the child.

A Home Office *Memorandum of Good Practice* details the way in which potential child witnesses should be questioned about their alleged abuse.[142] Critics argue that this document is itself insensitive to the needs of young, disabled and traumatised children yet it does at least offer guidance and may be used with a degree of flexibility. There is no such guidance for practice in the court, and one of the fiercest criticisms of the system may be levelled at the manner in which barristers are able to cross-examine children. Lawyers, defending those accused of abuse, in their attempt to win their case, rely heavily on confusing and accusatory language, which typically leaves children bewildered and distressed.[143] Many cases collapse because children are not able to give their evidence, and this experience in itself can be as damaging as the original abuse. The 1991 Act reforms have compounded this problem, since with the introduction of pre-recorded videotaped evidence-in-chief, the first person the child will usually face in court (or via livelink) will be the hostile defending barrister. There is strong support among professionals for the proposals in the Pigot Report, whereby child witnesses would not have to appear in court at all, unless they wanted to.[144] Under the proposals, the child's cross-examination would also be conducted ahead of trial, in judges' chambers and videotaped. The child would be free to then receive therapy and would not spend anxious months waiting for the case to come to court. In Scotland, the Prisoners and Criminal Proceedings (Scotland) Act 1993 makes provision for the evidence of children in criminal proceedings to be 'taken on commission' in some circumstances. The significance of this is that it takes the place of cross-examination as well, so the child might never need to be questioned in court. It appears that the provision has not been used much as yet.

A 1993 report gives useful guidelines on investigative interviews with severely disabled children, with particular reference to interviews when the child cannot use ordinary communication, and the need for careful preparation and recording to avoid any subsequent invalidation of the child's testimony.[145] There is a need for special training for interpreters and facilitators for disabled children in child protection investigations.

In view of the distinctly child-unfriendly nature of the criminal justice system, it is hardly surprising that professionals should be increasingly reluctant to expose children to it.

Recommendations

Process

Policies and procedures should be reviewed to seek to reduce disruption to a child's everyday life following disclosure of sexual abuse. For example, children should not be brought out of school for interviews or have attention drawn to them at school. Children should be encouraged to lead as normal a life as possible.

Peer support groups should be made available for sexually abused children and non-abusive parents.

Courts

The proposals in the Pigot Report should be implemented in full.

There should be better training for judges, greater use of judicial discretion in controlling cross-examination, and central funding and organisation of preparation programmes for child witnesses.

There should be a real reduction in delays in cases coming to court.

Offenders

There should be more treatment programmes for sexual offenders, in custody and in the community. Sexual offenders who have not received appropriate treatment should not be housed, on release from prison, on estates containing large numbers of children.

Child prostitution

Since 1991 there has been a 35 per cent increase in the annual number of cautions administered to young people for soliciting.[146] There is widespread agreement that sexual abuse and neglect, problems at school, unemployment, homelessness and other factors are associated with the incidence of youth prostitution. Few commentators regard the usual entry to child prostitution as the result of a free unconstrained choice. A recent American study of youth on the streets demonstrated persuasively that shelter and unemployment are the two most important situational factors promoting youth prostitution, and that coercive parental control, sexual abuse and violence at home are the main background and development factors that directly influence taking to the street and becoming a prostitute, either male or female.[147]

Young people's own accounts of their involvement in prostitution present a consistent picture of an impoverished and uncertain lifestyle, filled with risks to health and to personal safety. The issue needs to be addressed both nationally and locally through specialised services within the inter-agency context of community safety strategies. As well as addressing the reasons why young people are selling sex, policies and service responses that seek to minimise the risks of harm facing those involved in prostitution need to be considered.

Recommendation
Children's and young people's involvement in prostitution needs to be addressed through specialised services provided within inter-agency community safety strategies nationally and locally.

Criminal justice

The criminal justice system is relevant in a variety of ways to violence involving children: the prosecution and treatment of people for violent offences against children, and the prosecution and treatment of children for violent offences. There is the particular issue of violence within penal institutions for children.

The Commission's concerns are over the effect that the criminal justice system has on children and its implications for violence prevention. It regrets in particular the yawning gap that appears to exist between research knowledge of the outcomes of custody for children and young people, and current legislation and policy. It appears to the Commission that an emotional response to the trial of the young murderer Mary Bell in the late 1960s put back progress towards reform of the criminal justice system for young offenders, and that a further period of reform in the late 1980s and early 1990s has now been reversed following a media-generated panic about a perceived youth crime wave, focused by the response to the murder of James Bulger by two 10 year olds.

As NCH Action for Children emphasised in the introduction to a 1993 report *Setting the record straight: juvenile crime in perspective,*

> 'The British Crime Survey shows that for every 100 crimes committed only 41 are ever reported, and just three ever result in a conviction. If we are to have a real impact on the root causes of crime, we therefore need to recognise the limits of the criminal justice system. The central aim of policy-makers should be to foster and support the capacity of home, school and community to respond effectively and to "hold on" to young people in trouble.'[148]

In a graphic demonstration of the choices available, NCH Action for Children worked out that for the minimum estimated capital cost of establishing five 'secure training centres', taking a maximum of 200 young offenders, an alternative national programme could be established including 26 'alternative to custody' projects, 85 bail support schemes, 52 remand fostering schemes and 117 'open access' family centres.[149]

Aims of the criminal justice system

The Commission believes that social policy generally should seek to minimise the need for intervention under the law. Once the juvenile justice system is brought into play, rehabilitation and, where necessary, protection of the public must be its aims. Reparation may (in some circumstances) be an effective element in rehabilitation.

The relevant provisions of the UN Convention which the UK Government has ratified, and the three UN instruments on prevention of juvenile delinquency and treatment of juvenile offenders which the UK has accepted clearly support this policy. Thus the UN Convention emphasises:
- that children must be treated in a manner 'consistent with the child's sense of dignity and worth, which reinforces the child's respect for the human rights and fundamental freedoms of others and which takes into account the child's age and the desirability of promoting the child's re-integration and the child's assuming a constructive role in society'
- the importance of measures for dealing with young offenders without resorting to judicial proceedings, providing that human rights and legal safeguards are fully respected
- the need for a variety of positive dispositions
- that there must be no arbitrary or unlawful restriction of liberty, and arrest, detention or imprisonment must be used only as a last resort and for the shortest appropriate period of time.

In addition there are the United Nations Standard Minimum Rules for the Administration of Juvenile Justice (the Beijing Rules), the United Nations Guidelines for the Prevention of Juvenile Delinquency (the Riyadh Guidelines), and the United Nations Rules for the Protection of Juveniles Deprived of their Liberty.

Together, these provide a detailed framework on which to base law, policy and practice. Until a few years ago it looked as though social policy in relation to juvenile offenders in the UK was hesitantly developing within such a framework. But the Commission notes with concern the recent return to an apparent belief in custody for young children, and a lack of adequate legislative support and resources for diversion from the criminal justice system. These directions appear to be in conflict with our international obligations under the Convention and other instruments, and are certainly in conflict with available research on the outcomes of custody versus diversion. There is evidence that use of custody, for young offenders in particular, increases the risk of violent offending; most young offender institutions are violent institutions, with high levels of bullying and self-harm.

The recent report of the Howard League Commission of Inquiry into Violence in Penal Institutions for Teenagers under 18 found that

'The nature of prison life breeds bullying. In most prisons tobacco, cannabis and trainers are currency. Violence and aggression are entrenched as normal behaviour. Those not inclined to violence before entering prison are forced to use it in order to survive. Many victims of bullying turn into bullies themselves ... The Prison Service anti-bullying strategy is not widely implemented. Some prisons do little more than put up posters. Very few prisons are segregating bullies rather than victims. Those that do are not systematically addressing the causes of bullying behaviour.'

The Inquiry also found that physical control and restraint is used routinely whether or not there is a serious danger of personal injury:

'Restraint measures are potentially dangerous and a number of prisoners complained of injuries and excessive force.'[150]

In a preface to the Inquiry report, Helena Kennedy writes:

'Prison does have the temporary effect of removing an offender from our midst but used with too much zeal it leads to increased and more sophisticated criminality. Some young people need to be contained in secure accommodation, of that there is no doubt, but adult prisons or institutions managed along traditional prison lines which reinforce machismo are not the answer. What is needed is a little vision and a willingness to look at the alternatives seriously.

'Behind this report are many stories of pathetic young lives. As soon as faces and histories are given to the young people who are steadily filling our youth prisons, one is left with an overwhelming sense of hopelessness and wretchedness of their prospects. Creating bins for society's problems and locking up children invites the sort of bullying and violence we have encountered in the course of our inquiry. The whole approach is wrong. We have to be bold enough to say so.'[151]

Scotland as yet appears to have escaped the negative direction of policy for England and Wales. For some time there has been international interest in and admiration for the Scottish children's hearing system. The increasingly admired New Zealand model of family group conferences (FGCs) poses another non-judicial system for resolving juvenile offending, as well as child protection and child care issues, involving victims and preserving legal rights. In the UK, the Department of Health has commissioned a study of the development of FGCs in child care (there is as yet no statutory framework for them), and the Family Rights Group has been prominent in promoting the idea to social services and related professionals.

The Commission believes that if the dual aims of rehabilitation of young offenders and necessary protection of the public are accepted and enforced consistently in legislation, the criminal justice system can become an effective but small part of the national strategy to prevent violence. Currently, the involvement of many young people in the court and sentencing procedures, and in particular the use of custody which is not justified by consideration of protection of the public, contribute to the problem of violence rather than to its solution. The anonymity of children and their families in the criminal justice system must be protected, in line with international instruments, as an essential prerequisite for rehabilitation. Spurious justifications of public or media interest must not prevail over the interests of children. We do not perceive the changes we propose as a 'soft option' for children, but as a principled and research-based way of reducing violence to children and thus increasing community safety. It will also fulfil our international obligations under the UN Convention and other instruments.

A public information campaign is needed to seek to influence public opinion to recognise the counter-productive results of a punitive criminal justice system and the use of custody for young offenders who do not pose an immediate risk of danger to the public.

Recommendation
The criminal justice system for under 18 year-olds should be reviewed to ensure full compliance with the UN Convention and relevant UN instruments. Rehabilitation and necessary protection of the public from serious harm should be the sole aims of the system. Diversion should be promoted through legislation, guidance and financial incentives. The aims and content of rehabilitation programmes for any children who come within the criminal justice system should include a commitment to non-violence and adoption of the Checklists for working towards a non-violent society.

[Home Office; Chief Inspector of Prisons; boards of visitors; young offender institutions; attendance centres; local authorities]

Age of criminal responsibility

There has been growing debate over the age of criminal responsibility, and the fact that in the UK it is currently much lower than in many other countries: 10 in England, Wales and Northern Ireland, eight in Scotland. The trend elsewhere has been to raise the age – in Canada from seven to 12, in Israel from nine to 13, in Norway from 14 to 15, in Cuba from 12 to 16 and in Romania from 14 to 18. The Children and Young Persons Act 1969 set the minimum age for prosecution in England and Wales at 14, but this section of the Act was never implemented, and was finally repealed by the Criminal Justice Act 1991.

The Commission notes that in consideration of reports from States Parties to the UN Convention, the UN Committee on the Rights of the Child has suggested that 12 is certainly too low an age, and in considering the UK's initial report, the Committee proposed that serious consideration should be given to raising the age throughout the UK.

Some commentators have suggested that it is anomalous that a child should be regarded as fully responsible for criminal actions at the age of eight or 10, but in civil proceedings not considered competent to take responsibility for decisions that affect them. The official commentary to the UN Standard Minimum Rules for the Administration of Juvenile Justice notes the wide differences in age of criminal responsibility and states:

> 'The modern approach would be to consider whether a child can live up to the moral and psychological components of criminal responsibility; that is, whether a child, by virtue of her or his individual discernment and understanding, can be held responsible for essentially anti-social behaviour. If the age of criminal responsibility is fixed too low or if there is no lower age-limit at all, the notion of responsibility would become meaningless. In general, there is a close relationship between the notion of responsibility for delinquent or criminal behaviour and other social rights and responsibilities (such as marital status, civil majority, etc.).'

The Rules and the Riyadh Guidelines also emphasise the well-researched fact that most young offenders 'grow out' of offending.

We have emphasised that acts of criminal violence are by definition acts of individual choice. Children who act violently, like those who act violently to children, are immediately 'responsible' for their actions. If we wish to move as we do towards a society in which everyone takes responsibility for reducing violence, it is not helpful to cloud or confuse the issue of individual responsibility. But the general acceptance of the concept of individual responsibility for violence does not mean that juvenile offenders should be tried as adults. The process must be one that they can understand and respect. Nor does it mean that once regarded as responsible, young people should face retribution. It is for these reasons that the Commission proposes raising the age of criminal responsibility.

Recommendation
The age of criminal responsibility should be reviewed and raised to at least 14 throughout the UK in the light of UN instruments and European experience.

[Government; opposition parties]

Restriction of liberty

The Commission accepts that some young people must have their liberty restricted for periods to protect the safety of others. Children are currently locked up in both the penal and welfare systems; new legislation – the Criminal Justice and Public Order Act 1994 – is likely to significantly increase the numbers in both sectors. The Commission deplores this, because there is no evidence that the expansion is justified by a need to protect the public, and there is evidence that it is likely to increase the potential of individual children to be violent. As the Association of Chief Officers of Probation wrote to the Commission:

'Re-establishment of secure training centres which seem very much modelled on the old reformatories are likely to increase substantially rather than reduce violence to children and by children and young people.'

Only five years ago, a Government White Paper on *Crime, justice and protecting the public* stated:

'Imprisonment makes it more difficult for offenders to compensate their victims and allows them to evade their responsibilities ... The prospects of reforming offenders are usually much better if they stay in the community, provided the public is properly protected.'[152]

In most European countries, the proportion of the prison population that are young offenders is only a quarter that of the UK. Given that most countries make far less use of prison for all age groups, the difference in terms of numbers of young offenders locked up is even greater. Regional and racial variations put certain groups of young people particularly at risk of custody: of all male young offenders serving custodial sentences on 30 June 1990, 14 per cent were black, and black prisoners accounted for 18 per cent of those serving sentences in excess of 18 months. There are also great regional variations in sentencing policy; approximately two-thirds of the 600 juvenile courts in England and Wales passed no custodial sentences in 1990, whereas courts in Greater Manchester accounted for 10 per cent of the custodial sentences passed on boys aged 14-16, and 17 per cent of those passed on girls aged 15 and 16.

The Commission does not accept that the seriousness or violence of a crime is in itself a reason for restriction of liberty of a juvenile; to allow such considerations to determine sentencing and placement is incompatible with the aim of rehabilitation. Considerations of retribution, and retributive public opinion should play no part in sentencing or treatment. It is also vital that sentencing is removed entirely from the political arena (for example to end the role of the Home Secretary in determining the 'tariff' for those receiving indeterminate sentences under section 53 of the Children and Young Persons Act 1933).

The sole consideration, in relation to restriction of liberty of children, should be the degree of risk of actual danger to the public, and it should be constantly reviewed. Lack of adequate staff or other resources cannot be a justification for restriction of liberty. Nor is it necessary or legitimate to lock up children who pose a danger only to themselves: they are normally better protected by constant supervision than by locks and bars (and if detention appears the only option for adequate protection, then it should be under mental health legislation).The present criteria for restriction of liberty of children in secure accommodation in the child care system (Children Act 1989 section 25 etc.) provide a constructive model to build on, but need to be more narrowly defined. See more detailed discussion in *One scandal too many* ...[153]. The National Children's Bureau report *Safe to let out?*, published in 1995 indicated that many of those working directly with children in secure accommodation and managing secure units (lock-ups in the care system) believe that restriction of liberty is unnecessary for a substantial number of the children in their care (almost one in three of the children studied who were in secure units on 31 March 1994)[154].

There is a clear need for a comprehensive review of all restriction of liberty of children, in the penal system, child care, health including mental health, and education. Alongside this review the Government should review and encourage alternatives to lock-ups. Legislation and guidance should ensure that there are financial incentives for avoiding the use of, rather than providing and using, secure accommodation. Relevant government departments must collect and publish regularly information on all children whose liberty is restricted, in penal, childcare, health, education and any other settings, covering the statutory, voluntary and private sectors. Such information is vital for research and planning purposes and is currently not collected and published consistently.

The Commission commends local and voluntary initiatives which seek to meet young offenders' needs without further damaging them, and collaborative working by social services, health, education, police, probation and voluntary sectors.

The 1993 report of the House of Commons Home Affairs Committee into *Juvenile offenders* proposed the establishment of a new national agency to manage the custody and supervision of persistent juvenile offenders and others who receive custodial sentences:

> 'We recommend that the agency be funded centrally, and be given wide discretion to manage the young people in its care on an individual basis up to the age of 18, with the intention of stopping the juveniles concerned committing further crimes and helping them by education, vocational training and therapy to live law-abiding adult lives.'[155]

The agency would be responsible for a defined group of persistent offenders aged between 12 and 17, and would be responsible for managing secure units throughout the country. One added advantage of the new agency would be that it would help end

> 'the confusion which is inevitable when both the Home Office and the Department of Health have responsibility for policy relating to the custody of young offenders.'[156]

The regimes and all programmes provided within locked institutions should have a particular focus on non-violence. This has implications for the training of all staff. The structure, training of staff, rules and procedures, methods of care and control and education programmes – including training in family life and preparation for parenthood – in all secure settings should be carefully reviewed to ensure a commitment to non-violence, the promotion of non-violent values and non-violent conflict resolution, and the challenging of male macho images and attitudes. The *Checklists for working towards a non-violent society* will be relevant to the development of curricula. In 1994 a training package aimed at prison service staff on *The nature of adolescence: working with young people in custody* was commissioned by the Prison Service from the Trust for the Study of Adolescence. It aims to advance knowledge of the nature of adolescence and help staff to use their increased understanding to help prevent re-offending.[157]

Recommendation

The Government should review the criteria for detaining children in conditions of security in the penal and all other systems, and the provision and management of all secure places, in order to ensure that children are locked up only as a last resort for the shortest possible time compatible with defined considerations of public safety, in line with the UN Convention and other UN instruments. The review should consider the proposal for a national agency to take responsibility for all custody for under-18 year olds; it should also consider the introduction of Family Group Conferences and other alternatives to conventional forms of juvenile justice.

[Home Office; Department of Health; inspectorates; institutions]

Car crime

Crime involving the theft and reckless driving of motor vehicles represents a particular threat to the safety of children and young people, and the Commission decided that some (but not all) car crime falls within its definition of violence. The 1980s and 90s have witnessed a dramatic increase in crime involving motor vehicles. Thefts of vehicles rose by 50 per cent between 1989 and 1993. It is estimated by the Association of British Insurers that, on average, a car in Britain is broken into, stolen or vandalised every 25 seconds and that a stolen car is 200 times more likely to be involved in an accident than one driven by its owner.

The statistics indicate that a high proportion of thefts of cars are committed by young offenders. In 1990, 78 per cent of those found guilty or cautioned for theft of and from cars were aged between 10 and 20; 40 per cent were aged between 10 and 16.

Media attention has focused on the incidence of young people driving powerful cars at great speed and a number of fatal accidents involving very young drivers in stolen vehicles and sometimes children playing or walking nearby. The Government responded to this concern with tougher sentences. The Aggravated Vehicle-Taking Act of 1992 represented a move to increase the courts' powers to impose custodial sentences on car thieves; to 'toughen up' on the offenders, curbing car crime through the use of deterrent sentences. The legislation has been ineffective in stemming the rise in car crime amongst young people. Nationally, over 70 per cent of young offenders released from custody re-offend within two years. Local studies suggest that with regard to young offenders sentenced to custody for vehicle-related offences, the re-offending rate can be nearer 100 per cent.[158]

Some research studies have sought to examine the persistence of car theft as a delinquent activity. A study of 100 car crime offenders aged between 14 and 35 indicated that car theft provides a degree of excitement and status for young people otherwise disaffected. Light et al (1993) suggested that excessive levels of car theft are akin to adolescent infatuation or obsession.[159] A study undertaken by The Children's Society in South Wales interviewed young offenders, some of whom had been involved in serious car accidents. Self-injury following a car accident appeared to deter few from continuing to put their and other people's lives at risk. One young man, when asked whether an accident had ever deterred him from stealing cars, replied:

'No. You've got to die some day, so you may as well die young. It's better than living 'til you're older.'[160]

The Children's Society study also emphasised the disaffection expressed by young people involved in car theft and high speed driving. Unemployment, the lack of benefits and training opportunities and restricted leisure facilities were all seen as factors contributing to a lack of hope amongst young people who felt they had little or no investment in a future. The researcher commented:

'The young people who took part in the research were on the whole young people who felt they had no future, no hope and certainly nothing to aim for.'

Crime and particularly car crime was seen as providing young people with an opportunity to 'succeed':

> 'Stealing cars, driving at high speeds and initiating chases involves a fair degree of skill and daring which are likely to be fully appreciated by the offender's peer group.'[161]

The official statistics indicate that most young people 'grow out' of crime. Strategies to combat car crime will need to focus on improved crime prevention and community safety measures and effective responses to the young offender's behaviour. Motor projects which provide young people with a legitimate outlet for their interest in driving and cars have demonstrated some success in reducing re-offending amongst known offenders. The National Association of Motor Projects (NAMP) indicates that:

> 'Eight out of 10 sent to prison for auto crime re-offend within two years. Seven out of 10 who stay with a motor project for over three months do not re-offend within two years.'

NAMP suggests that the impact and long term viability of motor projects is substantially enhanced by collaboration and partnership between the various statutory agencies and community groups.

Basic crime prevention measures can also reduce the incidence of car crime. Figures published by the Home Office show that 30 per cent of people forget to lock their cars and 70 per cent of all cars parked on the street have no security device fitted. Practical security measures such as improved lighting in car parks and voucher parking schemes appear to have reduced car crime in some areas.[162]

In 1990 there were 7,042 reported incidents of joy-riding in Northern Ireland and in 1991 this increased to 8,455 incidents, an overall increase of 20 per cent. Young people involved in car theft in Northern Ireland have been in particular risk of death or injury, including the risk of being shot at by either the security forces or paramilitaries. Young people have also suffered punishment shootings and beatings by paramilitaries for involvement in car theft and other crime. Paramilitary groupings on both sides have taken on this 'policing' role. Approximately 1,680 teenagers have been the victims of punishment shootings by paramilitaries. Clearly, dealing with car theft through such responses represents a breach of human rights. It has also proved to be ineffective. Fear of death or injury has not acted as a deterrent to young people engaged in joy-riding.

The responsibility for managing youth crime falls on a number of different local authority and government departments. On a local level, a successful strategy to reduce car crime will require a multi-agency approach within a statutory framework.

A local car crime strategy will need to include:

i) an effective response to known offenders; deterring young people from the need to steal cars by providing an opportunity to pursue their interest in driving and cars in a safe and legitimate environment. Such opportunities should also be made available to young people generally

ii) programmes designed to educate young people about the dangers of car crime should be introduced into all secondary schools. Families, schools, youth clubs and other community institutions should be encouraged to assist boys and young men in challenging the powerful stereotype that associates driving fast cars with manhood

iii) encouragement of more balanced and responsible media reporting regarding car crime

iv) initiatives designed to raise the public's awareness of car security issues; nationally, car manufacturers need to be encouraged to improve car security, with purchasers making it clear that increased security is a specification in demand

v) other environmental measures to make stealing cars more difficult, such as better street lighting, and security in car parks.

Recommendation
Local authority community safety strategies should include measures to reduce the incidence of car crime, based on local analysis of the problem.

PART 3
Other issues

Child death inquiries

Babies under the age of one are the people most at risk of homicide in the UK (and many other countries where such statistical analysis is available). This to many people surprising and horrifying fact clearly demands special analysis and attention within overall concern for violence reduction and prevention. The majority of child homicides are committed by parents or other caretakers: Home Office analysis of the 285 under-18 homicide victims from 1989 to 1991 included 170 (60 per cent) killed by their parents; 43 (15 per cent) by friends or acquaintances; 29 (10 per cent) by other associates, and only 38 (13 per cent) by strangers.[163]

It is also important to underline that there is much dissatisfaction with the analysis and recording of causes of death of children and particularly young babies, and thus with published statistics. Many observers believe that the recorded statistics of homicide of young children seriously understate the real situation. A death is classified as a homicide only where criminal proceedings have found someone guilty of the offence. Violent deaths of children are classified by the external cause of injury (E-Codes). E- Codes particularly relevant to child abuse are:

E 904:   Hunger, thirst, exposure, neglect

E 960-969: homicide and injury purposely inflicted by other persons (of which E 967, introduced in 1979, is child battering and other maltreatment)

E 980-989: injury undetermined whether accidentally or purposely inflicted.

Suspicious child deaths, where parents deny injuring the child and there is insufficient evidence for a prosecution, are usually given 'open' verdicts by coroners, and would be classified under E 980-989; consideration of these deaths should be included in any attempt at estimating the total number of deaths from child abuse or neglect. In addition there are deaths where the child is recorded as dying from 'natural causes', but where violence or neglect is an underlying cause (for instance by weakening the child's natural resistance to disease). Detailed studies of samples of child deaths where the main cause of death was non-violent find a significant number of these cases. In addition there will be some cases of misdiagnosis.[164] Most recently there has been a particular focus on child deaths caused, or possibly caused by Munchausen's Syndrome by Proxy, leading to calls for more covert video surveillance of children in hospital, where it appears that a child's symptoms may have been deliberately caused by a parent or other carer (most often by suffocation). The current *Confidential Inquiry into Stillbirths and Deaths in Infancy* set up by the Department of Health may provide further insights into the extent to which child abuse and neglect is implicated in infant deaths.

The official guidance on inter-agency responses to child abuse for England and Wales, *Working together*, states that:

'Whenever a case involves an incident leading to the death of a child where child abuse is confirmed or suspected, or a child protection issue likely to be of major public concern arises, there should be an individual review by each agency and a composite review by the Area Child Protection Committee (ACPC).'[165]

Such reviews have become known as 'section 8 reviews', referring to the section of *Working together*. There is no statutory requirement to hold such inquiries.

A survey of a sample of ACPC reviews published in 1994 indicated that while reviews generally make recommendations, the question 'How could this death have been avoided?' is not asked. 90 per cent of the children covered in the sample of reviews had been identified as at risk by case conferences, but subsequent action had not prevented death or serious harm.[166] The survey confirmed that mental illness is a factor in serious abuse: eight children in the surveyed reviews had apparently been killed as a direct result of mental illness. There were 11 cases in which a known male schedule 1 offender (convicted of offences of violence etc.) or men with known violent records had joined the family before the death. In some, the full extent of the man's record had been identified only after the child's death. The survey found some evidence in the case review reports of excellent work in joint investigations:

'in other cases the outcomes were less pleasing. The dangers are that lack of sufficient evidence for prosecution is taken as meaning that no steps are necessary to protect the child(ren).'

The Commission heard that in several states of the USA, legislation sets out an obligation to hold a formal inquiry into all 'unnatural' deaths of children. In New Zealand, the statutory Commissioner for Children has recently been given the task of reviewing all such deaths. From the perspective of prevention, such arrangements could provide valuable information in a consistent form.

For example, the South Carolina Child Fatality Review and Prevention Act creates a Department of Child Fatalities within the State Law Enforcement Division, and a State Child Fatality Advisory Committee. The Act places a duty on coroners and medical examiners to notify the Department within 24 hours when a child dies as a result of violence, when unattended by a physician (unless a physician has before death provided diagnosis and treatment following a fatal injury), in any suspicious or unusual manner, or when the death is unexpected or unexplained.

The purpose of the Department is to:
- investigate child deaths throughout the state
- develop a protocol for child fatality reviews
- develop a protocol for the collection of data regarding child deaths
- provide related training to local professionals etc.
- undertake a study of all local investigations of child fatalities
- develop a Forensic Pathology Network available to coroners and medical examiners for prompt autopsy findings and
- report their activities and findings to the Child Fatality Advisory Committee.

The purpose of the Advisory Committee is to decrease the number of preventable deaths by developing an understanding of the causes and incidence of child deaths; to develop plans and implement changes to prevent child deaths; to advise the Governor and General Assembly, and to educate the public regarding the incidence and causes of child deaths. 'Preventable death' is defined as 'a death which reasonable medical, social, legal, psychological or educational intervention may have prevented'. An amendment to the aims of the Act adopted in 1993 reads:

'It is the policy of this State that:
(1) Every child is entitled to live in safety and in health and to survive into adulthood
(2) Responding to child death is a state and a community responsibility
(3) When a child dies, the response of the State and the community to the death must include an accurate and complete determination of the cause of death, the provision of services to surviving family members, and the development and implementation of measures to prevent future deaths from similar causes, and may include court action, including prosecution of persons who may be responsible for the death and family court proceedings to protect other children in the care of the responsible person ...'

Since implementation of the legislation, the number of child deaths under investigation has multiplied, with child abuse or neglect identified in far more cases than previously.[167]

The particular risks of homicide and serious assaults faced by young children, the need for more effective interventions and prevention, and concern over the recording and reviewing of such cases, and the accuracy of available statistics all point to the need for a more rigorous, consistent, and statute-based response.

Infanticide

The existence of the crime of infanticide denotes a distinct attitude to the murder of young children. In one sense, its existence stems from an historical attitude which undoubtedly placed less value on the life of a baby than that of older people. Its purpose is to signal a particular defence: that the mother's mind was

> 'disturbed by reason of her not having fully recovered from the effect of giving birth to the child or by reason of the effect of lactation consequent upon the birth of the child ...'[168]

But this defence is adequately covered within the defence of 'diminished responsibility' to a charge of murder or manslaughter. There has been a decline in the number of prosecutions for infanticide. It is time the law was reviewed in the light of the child's equal right to life.

Recommendations

As a matter of urgency, the government should set up a UK-wide review of law, policy and practice relating to child deaths (birth to 14), with appropriate inter-departmental observers. The review should cover:
* *the law on child homicide including the various relevant offences, and policy and practice over prosecution;*
* *law, policy and practice on recording and investigation of all child deaths, by coroners, medical personnel, social services etc.;*
* *collection and interpretation of statistics relating to child deaths.*

Its terms of reference should enable it to make recommendations for law, policy and practice designed to promote a better analysis and understanding of the causes of child deaths, and to prevent child deaths.

[Government; opposition parties]

Without prejudice to the results of a such a review, the Commission believes that the guidance in Part 8 of Working together *and equivalent guidance in Scotland and Northern Ireland should be revised to ensure that all deaths of children from birth to 14 are formally reviewed when the child appears to have died as a result of violence, when unattended by a doctor, in any suspicious or unusual manner, or when the death is unexpected or unexplained or appears preventable. The form of* such reviews, and who should be involved should be the subject of detailed guidance, and the review should be required to consider how the death could have been prevented.

[Department of Health and equivalents]

Additionally and in the short term, the Commission supports the view of the British Paediatric Association that in all cases of sudden or unexplained death in childhood there should be full assessment of the circumstances and the history by an experienced clinician, preferably a consultant paediatrician, and that the autopsy should be performed by a paediatric pathologist (there is a national shortage of this specialism). There should be liaison between these two experts in order to determine the probable cause of death.

[Department of Health; health authorities and trusts]

Suicide and self-harm

As indicated in Appendix 3 (page 264) while overall the suicide rate has dropped slightly over the last decade, there has been a clear increase in deaths from suicide and self-inflicted injury among young men in the UK aged between 15 and 24, from 320, or 7 per 100,000 in 1982 to 500, or 12 per 100,000 in 1992.[169] For this age group of males, suicide is second only to accidents as a major cause of death. A further analysis published in 1994 found that the particular and only age group to show an increase since the 1970s is males aged 15-19, with no increase in the 10-14 age band.[170] There are very few suicides by children aged under 15, but seven per cent of callers to the Samaritans are in this age group (amounting to one call every 15 minutes). As with other statistics of violence, there are concerns that official figures may understate the problem, with the causes of many deaths recorded as 'undetermined'. Young people in Northern Ireland are one and a half times more likely to kill themselves than their counterparts in the rest of the UK (but the actual figures are very small). The overall trend is common to almost all European countries and the US. The highest rates of suicide are in the 25-54 and over-85 age groups. While around 80 per cent of suicides in all age groups are male, 80-90 per cent of those who attempt suicide (parasuicides) are female: one in every 100 young women aged between 15 and 19 attempts suicide. A recent Department of Health *Key area handbook on mental illness* notes however that rates of suicide in immigrant populations are higher among women than men.

The Handbook notes that:

'Causes of suicide can be many and various, but are fundamentally the inter-action of life events, psychological state, lack of effective treatment and social support and access to the means to commit suicide.'

People who have attempted suicide are 100 times more likely than the general population to attempt it again within a year. The Handbook suggests that people at increased risk of suicide could be signified by 'alert status' on comprehensive mental health information systems.[171]

Considering explanations of the very marked gender differences in suicide rates, the recent Health Advisory Service (HAS) report on suicide prevention notes that aggressive and anti-social behaviour, alcohol abuse and depression in young people are risk factors for eventual suicide. There are substantial differences in the susceptibility of boys and girls to these factors, with girls more likely to suffer depression, and boys at greater risk of alcohol and substance abuse (which have increased in young people in close parallel to the increase in suicide rates).

The HAS report also notes that boys show a predilection for more lethal methods of self-harm, in parallel with the higher rate of risk-taking behaviour:

> 'This risk-taking behaviour has been linked with increasing male concerns about keeping up with contemporary "tough guy" masculine stereotypes.'[172]

The report lists specific risk factors which should be considered: economic and social pressures; alcohol and substance abuse (approximately one in three adolescents who commit suicide is intoxicated, and a further number are under the influence of drugs); custody (within the prison population, young people represent the largest group of individuals at risk, see below); bullying in schools, armed services and similar situations; rural isolation; and physical and sexual abuse.

An analysis of suicide in children and adolescents published in 1994 re-emphasised that it is the consequence of 'a highly complex interaction of predisposing and precipitating factors'.

Among factors known or thought to be associated with suicidal behaviour which have worsened, the author cites increase in family break-up, often with loss of father, pressures on the family such as poverty, unemployment and homelessness, and abuse related to family dysfunction. The paper also suggests that the changing role of men and women in society may affect the propensity to commit suicide:

> 'The change in the role of young women may have enhanced their self-perception and thus protected them from suicide. Conversely, new roles and expectations of young men in society may lead to loss of self-esteem if they are unable to live up to expectations.'

In relation to method, the report finds increases in poisoning using vehicle exhaust gases, and hanging and strangulation. The analysis of statistics referred to above underlines the importance of examining not only the records of those given a verdict of 'suicide', but also 'undetermined' or 'accidental' deaths by causes similar to suicide.[173]

Young women are three to four times more likely to be involved in deliberate self-harm (defined to include parasuicide, deliberate self-poisoning and attempted suicide). The vast majority involves intentional overdoses, and the report emphasises that up to 11 per cent of teenagers who take overdoses will commit suicide within a few years.

Certain groups are at particular risk of suicide: between 10 and 15 per cent of those diagnosed as schizophrenic commit suicide. There has been particular concern over suicides in young offender institutions, with an overall increase in both suicide and self-inflicted injury by prisoners in the last decade. In 1991, according to Home Office figures, there were 2,963 recorded incidents of self-injury, of which 1,208 were by prisoners aged 21 or under. A recent survey found 17 per cent of young offenders had considered suicide. Here again, recording is inconsistent and not detailed enough to be useful in informing preventive strategies.

Reports by the Chief Inspector of Prisons, and by the Howard League for Penal Reform (into the suicides of four young men aged between 15 and 20 at Feltham Young Offender Institution and Remand Centre between August 1991 and March 1992) have made a series of detailed recommendations for suicide prevention.[174] The Home Office has responded with a range of initiatives which aim at achieving a multi-disciplinary approach to suicide prevention involving the full range of prison staff and external agencies. All prisons now have a Suicide Prevention Management Group. The Howard League inquiry into violence in penal institutions referred to above reported that there were record levels of suicide and self-harm in prisons in 1994:

> 'This cannot only be attributed to better record-keeping. It is a product of overcrowding, the failure of key elements of the Prison Service self-harm and suicide prevention policy and the increasing levels of violence and alienation affecting young prisoners.'[175]

Inquiries into individual cases make it clear that factors such as barren regimes, degrading conditions, widespread bullying, and detention a long distance from home exacerbate the risk of suicide and self-harm. They are also incompatible with the Government's obligations under the UN Convention and other international instruments specifically relating to juvenile offenders (see page 173). Proposals to increase the use of custody, and allow longer terms of custody for very young offenders, enacted in the Criminal Justice and Public Order Act 1994, will involve locking up some children as young as 12 long distances from their homes.

One of the targets set in the Government White Paper *The Health of the Nation* is to reduce suicide by 15 per cent by the year 2000.[176] The report from the Health Advisory Service, referred to above, called for concerted action, with all staff in touch with young people who have threatened or attempted suicide taking an active preventive stance. A focus on alcohol and drug abuse would have a greater impact than any other primary prevention programme: one in three adolescents who commit suicide is drunk at the time of death, and a larger number use drugs (90 per cent of suicide attempts are through overdosing).[177] One practical proposal in the report is to lower the toxicity of paracetamol and combine it with an emetic.

It is clear that those who attempt suicide are most at risk of trying again within a year, and a long-term follow-up study of young attempted suicides in Manchester showed that those teenagers least likely to try to kill themselves again were those whose parents had clearly accepted the attempt as serious and demonstrated that they wanted to understand and help.[178]

It is important that those involved in the media and regulation of the media should be aware of the potential effects of reporting or depicting suicidal behaviour.

Various voluntary bodies, including the Trust for the Study of Adolescence and Young Minds have recently sought to focus debate on prevention of adolescent suicide, and provide information and training.

Recommendations

The Government's Health Target should be amended to include a particular focus on reducing suicide and attempted suicide among young people.

[Government; opposition parties]

Community safety strategies both centrally and locally should include suicide prevention as a segment of their work.

[Local authority community safety committees]

On the basis of available research, the Department of Health should prepare information materials and ensure wide circulation to appropriate professionals, voluntary agencies, parents and young people on identification of risk of suicide and self-harm including eating disorders, and prevention. This should include clear information on when and how to seek specialist help and counselling, lists of relevant statutory and voluntary agencies etc.; all those involved in developing programmes in schools and communities should be particular targets for information and training.

[Department of Health]

Arrangements to prevent people who threaten children's welfare gaining inappropriate access to them

There has been some progress towards putting in place consistent arrangements for recruiting and checking the backgrounds of people who apply to work in situations which will give them substantial unsupervised access to children – in schools, residential settings, youth clubs etc. None of the arrangements for checking on the possible criminal background of those applying to work with children is mandatory, but there has been increasing pressure on employers through government circulars. There is no consistency of policy relating to police checks: it is clear that resource considerations rather than safety have limited their extension to cover many voluntary and private schemes involving work with children. Recently an independent company, 'Faircheck', has been launched to provide information on prospective employees who will be working with children. This raises further concerns.

Evaluations of vetting procedures have indicated that the use of police checks of possible criminal background must not be regarded as a panacea, and that other recruitment and employment procedures (such as adequate supervision) may be much more significant for child protection. Current arrangements, details of evaluations and proposals for improving safeguards are considered in detail in *One scandal too many* ...[179]

The recent Mental Health Foundation *Inquiry into community care for people with severe mental illness – Creating community care* recommends that the Department of Health should issue further guidance about child protection in relation to parents or other responsible adults with severe mental illness, and review the guidance in *Working together*. It also noted that 'speedy communication is needed if a crisis develops.'[180] The inquiry report also recommends that the Department of Health should give further consideration to the transmission of relevant information about severely mentally ill people at risk of self-harm or violence to others when they move from one area to another: it emphasises 'a need for greater professional honesty on the issue of dangerousness.'[181]

> **'Keep a close eye on adults which are thought to be able to be violent to children.'**

In September 1994 a revised circular and guidance notes were issued by the

Prison Service to prison governors, setting out revised arrangements for notification about prisoners convicted of offences against children. They require that the prison service should notify local authority social services departments and the probation service at the start of a period of custody, during custody when consideration is being given to releasing the prisoner or transferring him to less secure conditions; and towards the end of a period in custody. This is to ensure that services concerned can consider the implications for protection of children and, where needed, take necessary steps to safeguard children who may be at risk from the prisoner's release.

Recommendation

The Commission supports the recommendations in One scandal too many ... *for improving safeguards for children in the recruitment, induction and supervision of people working or volunteering in situations which may give them substantial unsupervised access to children.*

Alcohol and drug abuse

As indicated in section 1 (page 67) the link between alcohol and violence involving children is not simple; alcohol abuse by parents and other adults may be implicated in violence to children, and alcohol abuse by children themselves may be implicated in violence by children. A recent research review in the USA has suggested that associations between alcoholism, drug use and child maltreatment are not well understood; in particular 'the severity and chronicity of intoxication and substance abuse remains poorly documented in studies of child maltreatment'. The review concluded:

'For example, although alcohol often is cited as a principal risk factor in the etiology of child maltreatment, its relationship to child abuse and neglect remains uncertain. More needs to be known about the unique and immediate effects of alcohol, its co-occurrence with other problem behaviours such as anti-social personality disorder and substance abuse, the circumstances under which different types of drinking situations lead to or sustain violence against children, and cultural factors that mitigate or exacerbate connections between substance use or abuse and aggression.'[182]

The age at which drinking starts is decreasing, and the amounts consumed by young people are increasing. Alcohol appears to be readily available to children, despite legal restrictions on sales, and there has been a drop in the 'real' price of alcohol. Alcohol affects children more quickly, because they are lighter than the average adult. The rate of findings of guilt or cautionings for drunkenness reaches its peak at about 18; among 17 year olds the rate is slightly lower but still higher than that for those over 21. A league table of youth drinking in European countries suggests that the UK has an unsatisfactorily high position.[183] Around one in three 15 year old boys and one in five 15 year old girls reportedly have got into arguments or fights after drinking.[184]

Focusing on drug and alcohol abuse would have a greater impact on adolescent suicide rates than any other primary prevention programme, according to the recent Health Advisory Service *Report on Suicide Prevention*.

'It is clear that alcohol and substance abuse are significant risk factors. They affect all areas of functioning, and may act as an immediate precipitant to suicide due to decreased inhibitions. Approximately one in three adolescents who commit suicide is intoxicated at the time of death, and a further number are under the influence of drugs. It has been found that the percentage change in alcohol consumption has the single highest correlation with changes in suicide rates.'[185]

There are well over 100 deaths of teenagers per year related to solvent misuse; some analyses suggest that solvent abuse is the second highest unnatural cause of death after road accidents of young people aged 10-16.[186]

The Commission adds the violence prevention perspective to the strong case for doing more to reduce the serious and apparently growing problem of alcohol abuse by both children and adults. A variety of strategies is required, including taxation increases; stronger enforcement of legislation limiting sales to children; accurate labelling with information on alcohol levels; alcohol education as part of personal, social and health education within the National Curriculum and involving parents; more training for professionals and in particular health professionals; careful local monitoring of alcohol consumption by young people; and co-ordination and evaluation of effective alcohol control programmes at all levels.

As indicated in section 1 (page 68) illegal drugs are related to violence largely through the extent of violent crimes committed in the course of distribution and purchase. The Commission found little hard evidence of the involvement of children in this trade in the UK as yet. The effects of illegal drugs on violence to children in the home, including child abuse is raising serious concern in the USA.

There appears to be evidence of increased illegal drug use by teenagers, but the Commission saw no evidence of any links with increased violence. A self-report survey of drug use among 15-16 year olds at the end of 1992 found that 71 per cent of the representative sample from the North west of England had been in 'offer' situations where drugs were available; nearly half (47 per cent) had tried an illicit drug, most often cannabis, followed by LSD. The rates are substantially higher than those recorded in the 1980s; young women were as likely as young men to have been in 'offer' situations and to have tried illicit drugs. A report of the survey suggested that 'a process of normalisation is underway in respect of adolescent recreational drug use'. Three per cent reported having tried heroin, and four per cent cocaine.

The report also underlines that over 90 per cent of drugs-possession-related cautions and convictions are for the possession of cannabis, followed by amphetamines:

'Basically this is because the routine policing of the street, the overladen car, the pub, the noisy party, or the club almost incidentally enmesh recreational users.'

It perceives a danger of

'criminalising and thus stigmatising large numbers of otherwise relatively law abiding young women and men from all social backgrounds (which) will do little for healthy citizenship and respect for the moral authority of the law.'

The report makes clear that the cohort it is studying has been systematically exposed to primary health education:

'Clearly the "say no to drugs" message has been rejected or at least neutralised by other processes and pressures, for at least half our sample.'[187]

A joint Royal College of Physicians/British Paediatric Association Working Party on Alcohol and the Young is due to publish a major report with detailed recommendations in 1995. The NHS Health Advisory Service is also currently (1995) preparing a report on Adolescent Substance Misuse (Prevalence and Risk Factors).

The Commission on Children and Violence felt unable on the basis of available literature to make more than the following general recommendations from a violence prevention perspective related to alcohol abuse.

Recommendations

Prices of alcohol should be increased through higher taxation to provide a real disincentive for children.

Those involved in alcohol production, distribution, marketing and sales should be encouraged to adopt the commitment to non-violence, and develop clear guidelines and voluntary controls to inhibit alcohol abuse by children and to reduce the potential for violence in and around sales points. The industry should co-operate fully in ensuring that legislation prohibiting sales of alcohol to children is rigorously enforced.

Community-based sources of help for substance addiction should be adequately resourced.

Children and violent conflict: Northern Ireland

Children in Northern Ireland have lived through the longest period of concentrated conflict in the western world in modern times. The current phase began in 1968, but there has been conflict in nearly every decade this century. Its impact on society in Northern Ireland is far-reaching and it is arguable that every child has been either directly or indirectly affected by the conflict. Children's experience of violence arising from that conflict can be either through direct exposure to violent acts – as victim or observer – or indirectly, through living constantly with the perceived threat of violence or intimidation.

Direct experience of violence

During the past 25 years, over 3,000 people have lost their lives as a direct result of the conflict. Information on the number of children killed is not easily available. An answer to a Parliamentary Question indicated that at the end of March 1993, 42 children under the age of 14 had died as a direct result of the conflict.[188] Other sources indicate at least 150 children have been killed.[189] Children have been killed by both paramilitaries and the security forces; eight children have died as a result of the use of plastic bullets by the security forces.

Thousands of children have been seriously and permanently injured as a result of violence arising from the conflict. Injuries include loss of limbs, brain damage, blindness and paralysis. Many others have witnessed violent attacks or have seen parents – mostly fathers – or other relatives violently killed. In the late summer of 1993, in 13 days, 22 children lost a father or mother. The psychological damage of conflict on children is impossible to quantify. International experience suggests that the full psychological extent of the impact is unlikely to manifest itself until long after the conflict has ended. Children have displayed symptoms of being psychologically traumatised by the conflict, including disturbed sleep patterns, phobias, bedwetting, and disturbed and withdrawn behaviour.

A disproportionate number of children also suffer separation from parents who are imprisoned: there are nearly 2,000 prisoners in Northern Ireland, of whom approximately 900 have been imprisoned for offences directly related to the conflict. There is a higher proportion of long term male prisoners than in the rest of the UK. The trauma of separation through imprisonment for children should not be underestimated. Many children exhibit symptoms of distress including running away to look for their father or – knowing their father is in jail – deliberately breaking the law in order to join him. Other children who are unclear about the offence which their father has committed and whose knowledge of prison has been gleaned from television, may become extremely disturbed. They think of their father as having been found guilty of the most serious offences and have fears about how he is being treated in prison or about what he will be like when he returns home. Another effect within families is that large numbers of young people are forced into the role of carers.

Another form of violence directly experienced by young people in Northern Ireland is that of punishment shootings or beatings. There is a substantial number of areas in Northern Ireland which have been extremely difficult, if not impossible, for the RUC (Royal Ulster Constabulary) to police because of the risk of paramilitary attack and the fact that the RUC is not viewed in particular communities as an acceptable police force (the vast majority of security forces personnel come from the Protestant community). In many such areas, paramilitary groups operate an 'informal justice system'. Offenders, usually young people allegedly engaging in 'anti-social behaviour', are often beaten, 'kneecapped' or 'placarded'. All of the main paramilitary groups engage in this kind of activity and it has been estimated that about 1,680 young people in Northern Ireland have been kneecapped. There are no figures for the numbers of young people beaten or placarded. Despite the recent cease-fires, punishment beatings continue to take place and the development of normal community policing in those areas continues to be difficult.

The number of weapons in Northern Ireland is a matter for concern. With many both legally and illegally held guns, there has been and remains a great potential for tragic accidents to occur. Also, for many children, the presence of armed men within communities or on the streets, whether from the security forces or paramilitary groups, is an everyday sight and therefore a continuous reminder of the ever-present threat of violence.

Emergency legislation in Northern Ireland curtails freedoms taken for granted by young people elsewhere in the UK. Its provisions allow children and young people to be stopped and searched in the street, to be subject to arrest and detention in custody without access to a solicitor, parents or others, to spend long periods on remand, and to trial without juries. The upholding of children's rights can be seriously affected by the existence of these powers and their application to children.

Indirect experience of violence

During the past 25 years, images of violence have pervaded Northern Ireland society and children have been confronted by the reality of violence on their streets and with violent images on television. A recent survey of 10 and 11 year old children in Northern Ireland suggested that 20 per cent had been in or near an explosion and 12 per cent felt their area was not safe to live in.[190] In one particular community, a 1990 survey showed that over 90 per cent of children had observed a hijacked vehicle burning, more than 50 per cent had seen people shooting guns and 37 per cent had witnessed a bomb explosion.[191]

While studies have been undertaken with children who have suffered direct violence, there has been little in-depth work on the general psychological impact of simply living in a society with ongoing violent conflict and a risk of violent death. There are differing views on the impact on children of such a scenario. Some suggest that children who have been exposed to conflict over a long period of time exhibit levels of anxiety no higher than those who have never experienced such circumstances; and that this may be due to some extent to the cohesiveness and social support available in some communities, and also to the fact that exposure to violence has become a way of life. Others suggest that those living in situations of ongoing and continuous conflict tend to minimise the implications of their own exposure to violence, or do not recognise the symptoms of psychological stress associated with trauma.

There is a general lack of awareness that children can be adversely affected in the short and long term by exposure to violence or the threat of violence when they are daily occurrences. Children so affected may present emotional and behavioural problems which, because of this lack of awareness, are often attributed to other factors such as lack of discipline, naughtiness or problems at home.

While there is some excellent work being carried out by organisations within the health and educational sectors and by some voluntary and community groups dealing with the impact of the conflict on children, that work tends to be disparate and unco-ordinated.

Although the current (1995) cease-fires and developing peace process have meant a return to a degree of normality within Northern Ireland, violence continues to be a problem, particularly related to organised crime and this includes a dramatic increase in drug-related violence. There needs to be an increasing emphasis on making available to both individuals and communities the resources to address the problems of psychological stress arising from the conflict and from violence in general. Failure to give priority to children's needs in this area will mean that they will continue to remain vulnerable to the adverse affects of violence.

Recommendations

The lack of statistics and more general research makes it extremely difficult to measure both the direct and indirect impact on children of the conflict in Northern Ireland and its associated violence; there is a need to undertake research to fully measure and analyse the effects of the last 25 years before we can fully understand its impact on children. There would be merit in drawing on studies carried out in countries which are now emerging from long periods of armed conflict such as South Africa, El Salvador and the West Bank/Gaza Strip.

In view of the current peace process in Northern Ireland and the likelihood that trauma experienced during the conflict will only now begin to manifest itself, it is essential that Government develops a comprehensive strategy and makes available appropriate resources to enable both individuals and communities to address the effects of the conflict on children.

There needs to be greater co-ordination and co-operation between both statutory and voluntary agencies, including more appropriate referral mechanisms for those children in need of specialist treatment; and the establishment of support structures for various service providers and groups.

There is need for general education and awareness-raising about the effects of violence and the way in which trauma manifests itself.

All training courses directed at those working with children, including teachers, social workers and child care workers, should include a component which deals with the effects of conflict and its consequences for children.

The number and availability of trained counsellors should be increased and it would be beneficial to locate such services in a way that would build on the strengths of self-help groups such as WAVE (Widows Against Violence Empowered).

Additional resources should be made available to build on work already taking place in relation to victim support, prejudice reduction, conflict resolution, mediation and conciliation, and through the schools' 'Education for Mutual Understanding' Programme.

Emergency legislation presently in operation in Northern Ireland should, as a matter of urgency, be reviewed for its consistency with the UN Convention on the Rights of the Child. The use of plastic bullets by security forces should be prohibited, particularly because of the danger they cause to children.

[Northern Ireland Office; local authorities and voluntary organisations in Northern Ireland]

Violent images

We reported in section 1 (page 69) on the extent of debate and disagreement over the significance of the effects of violent media images on children. There is a clear consensus that a heavy or continuous diet of violent images does nothing positive for child development, and may contribute to a potentially serious de-sensitisation of children to violence. It may also contribute to the development of an unrealistic fear of violence, increasing mistrust and negative community attitudes. There is a strong body of psychological opinion, in particular in the US, which, while recognising the impossibility of proving causal connections, believes that viewing violence can increase violence.

The Commission does not subscribe to the view that media violence is a major factor in the development of violent attitudes and actions. A particular focus on violent videos such as we have seen recently in the UK can distract attention from other more potent factors, including in particular children's direct experiences of violence in the home. A useful debate about causes and prevention of violence involving children is hindered by the sort of misinformation about the role of particular videos which followed the Bulger trial and two other brutal murders in 1993. As a Home Office Minister stated unambiguously:

> 'The police reports did not support the theory that those crimes had been influenced by exposure either to any particular video, or to videos in general, and no evidence about the role of videos was presented in any of the prosecutions.'[192]

Nevertheless the Commission does view with concern the gross appetites of many people, including children, for very violent images, seeing it both as a reflection of and contribution to an overall de-sensitisation which can only hinder the development of a non-violent society. This is seen not only in television, film, video and computer-generated images, but in print including comics.

Research commissioned from the Policy Studies Institute to examine links if any between media violence and juvenile crime found that all the 12-17 year olds studied were watching much the same films and programmes. Even those with convictions for violent offences had no particular viewing habits or preferences distinguishable from the group as a whole. There *were* significant identifiable differences in the overall lives of young offenders, and more research is required into their interpretation of violence and violent images.

The Commission's report covers the issues in some detail, not to reflect their relative importance, but rather to promote a more balanced and constructive public debate.

The issue for the Commission was not whether to propose censorship, because from a children's perspective, there are already very considerable attempts at censorship, not only through legislation (increased in the recent Criminal Justice and Public Order Act 1994) and through voluntary controls imposed by the various industries involved, but, much more significantly, through controls imposed by parents and other carers.

Technological advances, the 'digital information super highway', seem likely increasingly to limit the effectiveness of legislative controls and media regulators like the British Board of Film Classification. This gives added support to those who would put most energy into enabling and encouraging parents and children to regulate their own viewing appropriately, into developing media education and into research aimed at identifying what children themselves find disturbing (we welcome, for example, the careful introduction by the British Board of Film Classification of test screenings involving children).

The Commission was glad to find that the public debate and apparent widespread public concern at the portrayal of violence on television and in videos, computer games and so forth has been carefully considered by those responsible for programme-making, scheduling and transmission, and that they are responding practically as well as seeking to ensure that the ongoing debate is based on accurate information. The Commission found no sign of complacency.

Television

Guidelines and codes for BBC and independent television give careful and detailed advice, and in particular emphasise the interests of children and the need to provide parents and others with enough information to enable them to make informed decisions about viewing.

The BBC provides guidelines to its producers on *Violence in television programmes*, which are regularly reviewed. The current (1994) guidelines begin:

'There is much confusing and inconclusive research into whether or not there is a relationship between violence on television and in society. However, it is evident that screen violence does upset some people, and that, in excess, it can be accused of desensitising viewers. The BBC reflects these considerations in its approach to the inclusion of violent materials in programmes.'[193]

In relation to the reporting of real-life violence, it notes that 'there is a balance to be struck between the demands of truth and the danger of desensitising people'.

Producers are also referred to a report of a small committee set up in 1992 to review the advice provided: *Guidelines for the portrayal of violence on BBC television, 1993*. The group concluded that the existing guidelines should be amended to provide:
- a sharper focus on the issues which should be taken into account when considering the inclusion of violent sequences
- a clearer explanation of the significance of the 9pm watershed
- greater sensitivity over scheduling
- enough information to enable viewers to decide whether or not they want a programme to be watched in their households.[194]

Similarly, the Independent Television Commission provides Codes which are drawn up by staff and after public consultation are approved by members. Its powers come from the Broadcasting Act 1990. Failure to comply with the Codes can lead to a range of penalties, including broadcast apologies, fines, and the shortening or revocation of licences to broadcast. Section 1 of the Programme Code covers 'Offence to good taste and decency, portrayal of violence etc.' In relation to scheduling:

> 'Stop printing and showing on television all the violence. Parents who get 18-certificate videos and let their kids watch them and get caught should be sent down.'

> 'Stop violence looking right in some children's programmes.'

> 'Television should show more programmes about bullying, especially about those who have committed suicide.'

'Family viewing policy ... assumes a progressive decline throughout the evening in the proportion of children present in the audience. It requires a similar progression in the successive programmes scheduled from early evening until closedown; the earlier in the evening the more suitable, the later in the evening, the less suitable'. 9pm is "normally" fixed as the point up to which licensees will regard themselves as responsible for ensuring that nothing is shown that is unsuitable for children ... it is assumed that from 9pm until 5.30 am parents may reasonably be expected to share responsibility for what their children are permitted to see.'[195]

The ITC has suggested that where a channel is encrypted, or only available to cable customers through payment of an additional subscription, availability to children will be less restricted, 'and the point at which parents may be expected to share responsibility for what is viewed may be shifted from 9pm to as early as 8pm.' It is hard to see the logic of this flexibility, which looks dangerously like the thin end of a wedge and can only confuse the concept of a clear watershed.

The Code indicates that scenes which may unsettle young children need special care. It also underlines that

'Research evidence shows that the socially or emotionally insecure individual, particularly if adolescent, is specially vulnerable. There is also evidence that such people tend to be more dependent on television than are others. Imagination, creativity or realism on television cannot be constrained to such an extent that the legitimate service of the majority is always subordinated to the limitations of a minority. But a civilised society pays special attention to its weaker members.'

The Code goes on to emphasise the individual responsibilities of programme-makers. Both it and the BBC guidelines emphasise that the portrayal of dangerous behaviour easily imitated by children should be avoided.

Films, videos, games etc – censorship and classification

In Lord Harewood's introduction to the British Board of Film Classification's (BBFC) 1992 annual report he pointed out that it is now one of the few remaining classification bodies anywhere in the world which continues to cut violent material for adult audiences:

'The balance between freedom of expression and the need to protect society from those who might be aroused or encouraged by such material is hard to maintain.'[196]

He noted that classification and consumer advice are replacing censorship as the predominant method of media regulation in most countries.

'Show less violent films, but tell us what has happened to the victims so that people know how serious it is.'

In the report, the Board stated that as the issue of violence gains prominence, it has been forced to consider whether video certificates are so widely disregarded in the consumer market that they no longer provide an appreciable barrier to under-age viewing:

'In the cinema, controls at the box office ensure that age restrictions are widely, if not invariably, enforced. so that "18" imposes significant limits on the available audience. Is that the case on video? Recent evidence confirms that there is far less rigour in some video shops and little at all in many homes. Is that why video distributors now take the "18" uncut, because cynically they know they can reach the younger market anyway?'

During 1993, no film was refused a certificate; cuts were required in 34 feature films, 9.7 per cent of the total, a slight rise over the previous year when the proportion was the lowest since the Board began work in 1913. One video was refused a certificate, and 217 were cut as a condition of certification, a rise in percentage terms from 6.4 to 7.3 per cent

'which reflects a general tightening up on violence. Most of these cuts were in the "18" category, where the Board was no longer prepared to assume that violence at "18" was being safely targeted at an exclusively, or even predominantly, adult audience. If the events of 1993 have given us pause, it is in underlining just how many families in Britain are likely to be seriously dysfunctional, with the result that too many children receive little or no parental guidance and may well be at the mercy of any "18" video which finds its way into the home.'[197]

BBFC examiners visit primary and secondary schools, and for some years, according to the report, they

'have been struck by the concerns of teachers about what pupils are watching and by the evidence that children may not be boasting when they claim to have seen videos classified above their age. If "18" no longer means "18" for teenagers, then it becomes difficult to justify a system which relies on age bars to regulate home viewing. Clearly, better enforcement would make a difference in the shops, but respect for classification begins and ends in the home. It is up to parents to recognise the problem of violence and lay down rules for the children in their care.'

The Video Consultative Council, set up to monitor the progress of the Video Recordings Act and subsequent legislation, has also expressed concern at the problem of children gaining access to '18' videos. The Council supported the Board's policy on violence, but wished that parents would concern themselves more about the issue as it related to their own children. It set up an education sub-committee, which proposed more research , using schools and the pupil body to study how well the classification system is understood, and what effects the media have on young people, as well as to consider how to help parents, teachers and other carers to understand the system.[198]

The Criminal Justice and Public Order Act 1994 amends the Video Recordings Act 1984, to specify criteria on which the BBFC is to base its decisions about classification. Special regard must be paid to any harm which might be caused to potential viewers or (through the viewer's behaviour) to society at large by the way in which the video deals with criminal behaviour, illegal drugs, violent behaviour or incidents, horrific behaviour or incidents or human sexual activity. The change can be applied retrospectively: the Home Secretary can make an order allowing the BBFC to review any previous classification decision.

Another amendment clarifies that the BBFC can issue a 'UC' certificate to indicate a work especially suitable for young children.

The Video Standards Council (VSC) is an independent body set up by the video industry. It has established a registration scheme, whereby members of the video and computer and electronic games industry register and agree to abide by a Code of Practice, and a complaints procedure.

The Council has prepared clear visual material for use in video stores explaining the classification system, and the criminal offence of supplying under-age viewers. A consumer leaflet entitled *A parents' guide to video classification* has recently been published by the Council.[199] The Council told the Commission:

> 'The VSC is very concerned that no opportunity to inform and advise the public (particularly parents) about classification is lost and will progress any practical method of doing this.'

An exploratory study on children and video and computer games, commissioned by the European Leisure Software Publishers' Association (ELSPA), raised some concerns about a lack of parental guidance: the 1993 study surveyed 150 children aged from seven to 16, selected for their particular interest in video games, and quizzed them about their experiences (and those of friends) using questionnaires, interviews and discussion groups. The questionnaire revealed that 74 per cent of children had the games equipment installed in the relative privacy of their bedroom, and in discussion most children suggested that their parents lacked the necessary skills to test out games for themselves.[200]

The Video Recordings Act 1984 introduced a system of classifications designed to indicate the age-group for which a particular video was suitable. All 'video works' (which include computer or video games on floppy disk or compact disk, if the game contains a series of visual images shown as a moving picture) must be submitted to the British Board of Film Classification for classification. But video games are exempt from classification unless they depict such things as human sexual activity or gross violence towards humans or animals or are designed to encourage such things. It is a criminal offence to supply a game which should have been classified but has not been. Indeed the Criminal Justice and Public Order Act 1994 has increased the penalties for supplying a game which should have been classified but has not been to an unlimited fine and/or a jail sentence of up to two years (the penalty for supplying a classified game with an age-restricted rating to a person below the specified age increased to a fine of £5,000 and/or a jail sentence of up to six months).

Beyond the legal obligations for classification of games, there are voluntary controls. The Video Standards Council Code of Practice, adopted by ELSPA members, adds to the list of depictions which may not be permitted in video games 'except when treated with the greatest of caution'. These include 'random and gratuitous violence, aggression towards vulnerable women and children, excessive blood and gore, racial hatred, encouraging criminal acts, etc'. ELSPA has adopted a voluntary proposal for providing age suitability ratings for any games exempt from classification. There are four ratings: suitable for all ages; suitable for persons over 11; suitable for persons over 15; and suitable for persons over 18.

ELSPA has developed a range of shop display and staff training material to explain both the legally required classification system and the voluntary ratings system. It has also published a leaflet for parents – *A parent's guide to computer and video games* – which has a section headed: 'Will video games make my children violent?' The leaflet responds:

'That all computer and video games are based on fighting and shooting is a myth! Many are challenges such as puzzle solving, platform building, sports and action adventure. Furthermore, there has been no conclusive research to establish a link between violence to children and fighting in computer and video games. Take a look at some of the games your children play and you will see why – most "violence" is more like Tom and Jerry than a horror film. If you are still concerned then don't forget that the age suitability system is designed to help – games ticked in the 3-10 box will not have graphic representation of fighting. If you wish to avoid fighting altogether then there is a huge range of alternative games to choose from.'

The leaflet also tells parents how to complain if they believe a game is wrongly classified.[201]

Recommendations
The Commission's recommendations aim:

- *to contribute to the overall denunciation of all forms of inter-personal violence:*

All those involved in media accessible to children should adopt the commitment to work towards a non-violent society, and seek to realise the huge potential of the media for promoting pro-social behaviour and non-violent conflict resolution and discouraging inter-personal violence. In particular there should be recognition of the need to challenge macho male images. 'Soaps', for example, could develop their pro-social role.

All those involved in the production, distribution and sale of media which may include violent images should be aware of the state of current knowledge of the potential effect on children who may have access to them.

We share the concern of the Broadcasting Standards Council that there is insufficient monitoring and regulation of the quantity and quality of children's television, and echo the proposal in the Council's Research Working Paper VIII that either a joint BBC/ITC Children's Television Council, a voluntary body with public support, or a new Broadcasting Consumers' Council, with specific coverage of children's broadcasting, should be established. Children should participate and be consulted.

National and local media and regulatory bodies and their views should be appropriately represented at all levels in the development of community safety strategies to reduce and prevent violence involving children.

[All those involved in the media including regulatory and industrial bodies; local authority community safety strategies]

• *to encourage enforcement of classification schemes, and voluntary controls to limit gratuitous violent images and children's access to them:*

The Commission recommends that careful monitoring by regulatory bodies of the effectiveness of the classification schemes for films, videos etc., including recent changes in the Criminal Justice and Public Order Act 1994, should continue, to inform debate on any further controls.

On television, the evening watershed should be rigorously observed on all channels and clearly explained to viewers in all programme guides.

A code should be developed for the coverage of violent events by news and documentary programmes which emphasises the importance of accurate reporting, avoiding exaggeration, not dwelling on the detail of violence, and providing careful warnings to viewers (see also recommendation on media coverage of sport, page 219).

[Media regulatory bodies]

• *to ensure accurate information and packaging which indicates clearly the content of programmes and materials, to enable children, parents and other carers to exercise informed control over viewing/listening (as proposed in the Checklists for working towards a non-violent society – see Appendix 1, page 250):*

The Commission welcomes the guidance aimed at parents produced by the Video Standards Council and the European Leisure Software Publishers' Association, and encourages the provision of similar guidance by the BBC/ITC and/or the Broadcasting Standards Council (explaining the watershed, encouraging parents to view news programmes which have a violent content together with their children, and to discuss them etc.), and within all publications providing details of television programmes. An understanding of such material should clearly be part of parent education.

Regulatory bodies should ensure that all videos, discs and other materials are packaged in a way which ensures that basic information about classification and violent content is clear and accessible (and printed on the video, disc etc. itself as well as on any removable packaging).

[Regulatory and industry bodies]

- *to encourage appropriate media education:*

All teachers and schools should seek increased critical understanding by pupils of the new communications technologies: the importance of this should be reflected in arrangements for the curriculum throughout the UK. Public education and participation in media policies should be encouraged through public forums organised by the industry and regulators.

[Schools curriculum bodies; teachers; teacher training; schools; media regulators and industry]

Pornography, children and violence

Production, distribution and possession of child pornography are all criminal offences, and the Criminal Justice and Public Order Act 1994 amended the Protection of Children Act 1978 to bring within its scope child pornography produced on computers, including simulated indecent photographs of children; the law covers taking or creating such images, distributing or possessing them.

The Commission received extensive submissions reviewing recent research into the effects of sexually violent pornography. Much recent research, in particular in Canada and the USA, distinguishes three categories of pornography:

1 sexually explicit and violent
2 sexually explicit and non-violent, but subordinating and dehumanising
3 sexually explicit material which is non-violent and non-subordinating, which is based on mutuality and equality (called erotica).

The research consistently showed negative effects on attitudes and behaviour from the first of the two categories, but not the third.

Women's organisations in the UK passed a resolution in 1992 to support legislation enabling people who can prove they are victims of pornography-related harm to take civil action against manufacturers and distributors of pornography.[202] The proposal for a harm-based legal definition of pornography is intended to target sexually explicit material that is violent or subordinating and shown to be harmful.

Article 7 of the *European Convention on Transfrontier Broadcasting* states that :

'All items of programme services ... shall respect the dignity of the human being and the fundamental rights of others. In particular they shall not
(a) be indecent, or in particular contain pornography
(b) give undue prominence to violence or be likely to incite racial hatred.'

The European Forum for Child Welfare (EFCW) published a position paper on *Child pornography and sexual exploitation* in November 1993, making a variety of recommendations including the need to harmonise legal measures to ensure that possession of child pornography is an offence in all countries, appropriate sex education for children, and programmes of public awareness-raising.[203]

Recommendation

The Government should support European and international moves to harmonise legislation and promote measures to reduce the involvement of children in pornography.

[Government; opposition parties]

Aggressive toys

As with violent images, the Commission's concern with the promotion and marketing of 'aggressive toys' (defined as toys whose purpose is to simulate behaviour or stimulate fantasy involving the attempted injury of another person) is that they may reflect and even contribute to the general desensitisation of children to violence, and that they may inhibit more pro-social and non-violent play.

The National Toy Council, which includes representatives of the Child Accident Prevention Trust, British Toy and Hobby Association, National Toy Libraries Association and the Institute of Trading Standards Administration, has published a leaflet for parents on *Aggressive toys and play* which emphasises:

'There is no evidence linking aggressive toys to children's aggression, or their attitudes towards violence. How you behave towards your child has much more influence on them than a toy – however fond of it they may be.'

The leaflet advises:

'Set clear guidelines for the use of toys and be consistent and firm – but not aggressive – in your disapproval of aggression ... Try to remember to participate in your children's rough and tumble play from time to time. Play is one way children have of understanding the world of adults. Be constructive, use it as an opportunity to discuss violence, guns, war and peace.'[204]

The Commission believes that a combination of education and guidance for children and parents, and voluntary controls by the industry, are most likely to achieve useful results. Additional issues are raised by toys which are themselves able to cause significant injury, and by toys which are more or less exact replicas of actual weapons, whose possession by either children or adults may provoke serious violence.

The British Toy and Hobby Association has developed a welcome Code of Practice, acceptance of which is a condition of membership and for exhibiting at the British International Toy and Hobby Fair. In relation to 'realistic' guns, the Code insists that a solid 'blaze orange' plug must be permanently fixed to the muzzle of the barrel as an integral part of any toy gun which 'has the general appearance, shape and/or configuration of a firearm' (this is already a legal requirement in the US and Italy). Other toy water guns and similar toys must have a permanent blaze orange marking. Toy and replica guns may be made entirely of transparent or translucent material, or coloured over their entire surface in bright colours.[205]

In Sweden the production of war toys has been banned; Spain and Germany do not allow war toys to be advertised.

In 1982 the European Parliament adopted a resolution expressing concern at the increasing popularity of war toys and in particular replica weapons. It called on member states to ban visual and verbal advertising of war toys, and also the manufacture and, where possible, sale of replica guns and rifles; the production or sale of war toys should be progressively reduced and replaced with toys which are constructive and develop creativity. The resolution stressed the direct responsibilities of parents and teachers.[206]

Recommendations
As in its recommendations relating to violent images, the Commission believes that in relation to toy manufacture and marketing, a combination of safety regulations, voluntary controls and accessible advice to parents and other carers is required.

Toy manufacturers and distributors and their representative bodies should be encouraged to adopt the commitment to non-violence, and codes which aim to promote pro-social, non-violent play.

Victims of violence

Support for victims of crime, including crimes of violence, began in the voluntary sector in the 1970s. There are now more than 350 local victim support schemes in England and Wales, which received almost £4 million in government grants in 1989/90. Home Office circulars have encouraged the criminal justice system to improve the way victims are dealt with and kept informed, and explained how they can seek compensation through the courts or the Criminal Injuries Compensation Board (now the Criminal Injuries Compensation Authority). Compensation can be imposed as a penalty in its own right, and the Criminal Justice Act 1988 requires courts for the first time to give reasons when they do not make orders for compensation in cases in which they could have done so. The UK recently ratified the Council of Europe Convention on the Compensation of Victims of Violent Crimes.

The Criminal Injuries Compensation Board, which can award compensation for injuries which result from crimes of violence, has increasingly acknowledged the need to compensate children who have suffered abuse. A guide to the scheme indicates that there is no legal definition of 'crime of violence':

> 'Most crimes of violence of course involve force to the person, eg assaults and woundings. Where it is not obvious, the Board will look to the nature of the crime rather than its consequences' (Appendix E of the guide).

The Board's 1993 report stated that the number of applications in respect of children continued to rise, although at a slower rate than in the previous year. The total number increased by 6 per cent to 7,211, within which those for sexual assault rose by 11 per cent to 3,200. The total number of applications in the year was 65,977, and a record total of £152.2 million was paid out in compensation. Applications from those who had been sexually abused within their family or by a relative rose by 2.3 per cent to 1,700. The Board is particularly concerned to ensure that compensation is used for children's own benefit (by March 1993 the Board was holding £24.26 million in interest-bearing accounts for children to be released when they reach 18).

In April 1994 the Board became the Criminal Injuries Compensation

Authority, and a new 'tariff' scheme for compensation was announced. The Home Secretary's powers to introduce the scheme have been successfully challenged in the courts; the Home Secretary is considering an appeal (December 1994).

The new tariff proposes the following awards for sexual and/or physical abuse of children:

Not involving rape or buggery:
• isolated incidents over a period of up to one year: £1,000;
• pattern of abuse over period of 1 to 3 years: £3,000;
• pattern of abuse over period exceeding 3 years: £6,000

Involving rape or buggery
• Rape or buggery (single incident): £7,500;
• Repeated rape or buggery over period up to 3 years: £10,000
• Repeated rape or buggery over period exceeding 3 years: £17,500.[207]

The UN Convention on the Rights of the Child requires that 'all appropriate measures' be taken to promote the physical and psychological recovery and social integration of child victims (article 39). As the Commission has indicated, much violence suffered by children in the UK remains currently lawful, and in relation to it there is no provision for rehabilitation or support. Serious physical and sexual abuse may lead to criminal prosecutions, and in such cases therapy and support are often withheld until after the case, which may be months or years after the event. The scale of government support for schemes designed to help child victims of violence is tiny in relation to the problem.

Recommendations
All child victims of violence should be offered appropriate assessment to determine what measures are needed to promote recovery and social integration. Sufficient resources must be available for necessary rehabilitation.

Appropriate training and support should be offered to local Victim Support Schemes to ensure that services are available to child victims of violence. The work of such schemes should be integrated into local community safety strategies and schemes, and into the work of Area Child Protection Committees.

Compensation should be available to child victims of violence, taking full account of physical and psychological harm. Awards of compensation should not be dependent on prosecution of perpetrators.

[Home Office; Criminal Injuries Compensation Authority; victim support]

Traditional practices

Some communities have traditional practices which can involve physical and/or mental violence to children. The UN Convention, in addition to insisting on protection from all forms of violence, also requires effective and appropriate action to abolish traditional practices prejudicial to the health of children (article 24.3). This was included because of particular concern over the practice of genital mutilation ('female circumcision') of girls and young women. The practice remains common in parts of Africa, Asia and the Middle East, and still occurs within some communities in the UK. The Prohibition of Female Circumcision Act 1985 has not been effective in ending it. Guidance on child protection and private foster-care issued under the Children Act alerts carers and professionals to the issues.

There are other traditional practices which involve violence to children without their informed consent. Some may be related to reinforcing cultural or racial identity, as well as religious ritual. They raise sensitive issues but need to be reviewed in the light of the principles and standards of the Convention.

Recommendation

All communities should review any traditional practices which involve violence to children or may be prejudicial to health, and plan appropriate educational and other action to end them. All those involved in family support and child protection should receive appropriate training.

[Local authorities; family support/child protection]

Sport and violence involving children

Sport is part of our culture, and a dominant part of many children's lives. Chasing, wrestling and trials of strength are part of spontaneous and enjoyable child's play and need not carry any intention to hurt. Organised sport contributes positively to the health and development of many children. Violence in sport, by participants and spectators, has been much discussed over the last few years, and internationally the UK has a poor reputation for violent behaviour of both players and spectators – in almost all cases young and male. In the contact sports, rules seek to make a distinction between aggressive competition and unacceptable violence – high and late tackles for example.

Boxing, and certain martial arts and forms of wrestling in which the intent is to produce bodily harm in opponents, are a special case (see below, page 220). There are other sports such as fencing in which there is an imagery of violence, but the risk of injury is insignificant because of regulation.

The Commission notes that sports bodies have taken the problem seriously, with stiffer penalties for violent players, re-design and improvement of facilities for spectators, training for stewards, limitations on access to alcohol, etc. The new emphasis encouraged in the revised National Curriculum on competitive games in schools should be taken as an opportunity to emphasise the distinction between competition and violence, and to promote non-violent values in sport. There is an international movement to seek ways of reducing violence linked to sport. The Council of Europe Committee of Ministers has adopted a *Code of Sports Ethics*, which emphasises in particular the responsibilities of all involved to work positively with and set a good example to children and young people. In the UK, the National Coaching Federation has run a 'Fair Play for Children in Sport' campaign, in association with MacDonald's Hamburgers.

Professional football is by far the most popular spectator sport in Britain; going to football remains a predominantly male activity (between 10 and 15 per cent of spectators are female). Football hooliganism has a long history. Recent research suggests that those involved tend to be aged between 17 and 27, involved in manual or lower clerical occupations or, to a lesser extent, unemployed. A summary of research published by the Sir Norman Chester Centre for Football Research suggests:

> 'Fighting at football is largely about young working class males testing out their own reputations for manliness against those of other young men from similar communities.'[208]

The tragedies at Heysel and Hillsborough have led to renewed attempts to reduce violence associated with football. The recommendations of the Taylor Report on crowd control and safety are gradually being implemented. [209] The Football Association recently introduced a new coaching initiative for children which involved advice on behaviour for both spectators and players.

There is still insufficient recording of the extent of violence and injuries resulting from sport; the Commission welcomes the decision of the Rugby Football Union to collect data on injuries from all affiliated clubs and schools. This is an essential exercise on which to build acceptable safety standards in contact sports.

As in other areas of national life, there is still not enough consistent denunciation of violence in sport, and this is reflected in media coverage of it. The attitudes and actions of sporting figures may well have considerable influence over children and young people. Television guidelines contain little as yet on violence in sport. There appears to be no central collection of statistics relating to violence by participants or spectators.

The Australian Sports Commission has developed and promoted codes of behaviour for administrators, officials, parents, spectators, coaches, teachers, the media and players. They seek in particular to develop positive, non-violent attitudes in children's sport.[210]

Recommendations

The Department of National Heritage and appropriate sports bodies, and the Schools Curriculum and Assessment Authority should develop and disseminate codes of conduct for participants and spectators of all major sports designed to clearly condemn violence in sport and provide strategies to reduce and prevent it.

[Department of National Heritage; national sports bodies]

Sport violence involving children, and its prevention, should be considered in the development of community safety strategies at central, regional and local levels.

[Local authority community safety committees]

Regulatory bodies for the media, and in particular the BBC and the Independent Television Commission should consider explicit guidance to counter any encouragement of violence in sport – eg avoiding gratuitous replay of violent

incidents, commentators consistently denouncing violence, and promotion of
sporting events avoiding metaphors of violence.

[Media regulatory bodies]

We support the British Medical Association's proposal, first made in 1983, that
there should be a national register of sports injuries and fatalities, and national
collection and publication of statistics on violence in sport. Bodies responsible for
regulation of contact sports should follow the Rugby Football Union in collecting
and monitoring information on injuries.

[National sports bodies]

Boxing

Boxing involves the deliberate infliction of injury, and quite frequently leads
to brain and eye injury in particular, and sometimes death. As the Amateur
Boxing Association states :

> 'Boxing is a contact sport in which points are scored by landing blows with
> force on the opponent. Inevitably, there is a risk of injury to those who
> box.'[211]

Promotion of boxing (and certain other martial arts and forms of wrestling) is
clearly inconsistent with denunciation of all forms of inter-personal violence.
Society has moved gradually away from accepting sporting and other
activities which involve serious violence, even with the consent of the
participants. In 1993 the House of Lords upheld a decision that five
homosexual sado-masochists were not entitled to consent to being assaulted.
Lord Templeman reviewed the circumstances in which violence is not
punishable under the criminal law:

> '... Even when violence is intentionally inflicted and results in actual bodily
> harm, wounding or serious bodily harm, the accused is entitled to be
> acquitted if the injury was a foreseeable incident of a lawful activity in
> which the person injured was participating. Surgery involves intentional
> violence resulting in actual or sometimes serious bodily harm but surgery is
> a lawful activity. Other activities carried on with consent by or on behalf of
> the injured person have been accepted as lawful notwithstanding that they
> involve actual bodily harm or may cause serious bodily harm. Ritual
> circumcision, tattooing, ear-piercing and violent sports including boxing
> are lawful activities.'

Duelling and fighting were once lawful:

> '... The brutality of knuckle fighting however caused the courts to declare

that such fights were unlawful even if the protagonists consented. Rightly or wrongly the courts accepted that boxing is a lawful activity.'[212]

Lord Templeman quotes Lord Lane's review of common law defences to assault, in a previous Appeal Court judgment which referred to

'... the accepted legality of properly conducted games and sports, lawful chastisement or correction, reasonable surgical interference, dangerous exhibitions, etc.'[213]

The health arguments against boxing have been advocated with increasing force, in the UK and internationally. In 1982 the British Medical Association's (BMA's) annual representatives' meeting passed a resolution stating

'in view of the proven ocular and brain damage resulting from professional boxing, the Association should campaign for its abolition.'

The 1992 meeting passed further resolutions calling for a total ban on professional and amateur boxing in the UK, and proposing that as the next stage of the campaign the BMA should seek to ban children below the age of consent from boxing. In a 1993 report, *The boxing debate*, the BMA concludes:

'Notwithstanding strict medical controls and neurological monitoring, there can be no guarantee that boxers will not suffer chronic or indeed acute neurological or eye damage once they enter the boxing ring. The studies carried out over the past 20 years do not provide adequate evidence for there being no risk of cumulative damage attached to participation in amateur boxing and provide substantial evidence for a well defined risk of chronic and debilitating damage in professional boxing,'[214]

A report by HM Inspectorate (of schools) into the National Association of Boys Clubs (NABC) in 1988/89 found that boxing clubs represented the main group of single activity clubs, with a long tradition of boxing in boys' clubs:

'Benefits can come from any activity which requires commitment to training and fitness, but boxing is an inappropriate youth work activity.'

The report proposed that the NABC and affiliated associations and federations should weigh carefully the evidence of the medical effect of boxing on young people against its claimed benefits to particular boys:

'The Association's promotion of boxing serves to legitimise it as an appropriate youth service activity but there are other demanding physical activities which offer the claimed benefits of boxing without its drawbacks.'[215]

The BMA report suggests that the number of children involved in boxing has fallen dramatically in the last 10 years, but there are no clear statistics. In 1992 the Sports Council proposed that a Youth Commission should be set up under the auspices of the Amateur Boxing Association to co-ordinate the participation of children in boxing, but this does not appear to have been followed up.

The World Medical Association recommended in 1983 that boxing should be banned. Similar recommendations have been endorsed by the Commonwealth Medical Association and by many countries' medical associations. The BMA reports that boxing has been banned in Sweden, Iceland and Norway, and that six other European medical associations support a legal ban. Various MPs and Peers have initiated debates on prohibition of boxing. But the Government has rejected calls for a ban, most recently during a House of Commons debate in May 1994, in which the Parliamentary Under-Secretary of State for National Heritage stated:

'... we believe it would be a gross infringement of civil liberties to prevent individuals from participating in a properly constituted sport of their choice.'[216]

A minority recommendation of the Australian National Committee on Violence supported a ban:

'Boxing is a minor sport in Australia but it has medical, social and symbolic significance in the context of an investigation into violence. Brain injury is a major public health problem in young Australians. The Committee has made statements against the condoning of any form of violence and recommends that violence in sport not be glorified. Not to support the eventual banning of boxing is, in our opinion, inconsistent.'[217]

In addition to the convincing medical arguments against boxing, the Commission believes the glorification of deliberate violence that is involved is unacceptable, and its legality now anomalous. Those who support the involvement of children in boxing suggest that it promotes discipline and self-defence and can provide a path for self-improvement of disadvantaged children. The Commission does not accept these arguments. There is an ample range of sporting and other positive activities that do not involve deliberate violence. Many sporting activities involve a risk of accidental injury but that is quite distinct from the deliberate pursuit of injury which is at the heart of boxing.

There is a further argument that legal prohibition will lead to more illegal, unregulated violence. Such arguments can be stated against any legal reforms that seek to control personal violent behaviour, and represent a cynical challenge to the rule of law. Abolition of boxing needs to be seen as a logical part of a move towards a society which rejects violence as a method of conflict resolution, and must be promoted as such.

Recommendation

The Commission supports the international and national campaigns for the eventual abolition of boxing and any other sporting activities in which causing a degree of injury to opponents is an aim. As a matter of urgency and a prelude to abolition, the involvement of children in boxing should be strongly discouraged by the Sports Council, the Department for Education and Employment, the Schools Curriculum and Assessment Authority and appropriate bodies throughout the UK.

[Government; opposition parties; Sports Council; youth organisations; boxing bodies]

Guns and weapons

Guns

There is no evidence of widespread use or misuse of guns by children in the UK. Overall, the use of firearms in crime appears to be increasing steadily but not sharply. In 1992 the police recorded 13,305 offences in which firearms were reported to have been used; the proportion of all notifiable offences in which firearms were used was 0.2 per cent. The proportion of robberies in which firearms have been used has increased from 8.6 per cent of robberies in 1988 to 11 per cent in 1992. If air guns are excluded, then in nearly 90 per cent of offences the weapon was not fired. Of all 13,305 notifiable offences recorded by the police in which firearms were used, almost half, just over 6,000, involved air guns. The number of offences in which firearms caused injury increased by eight per cent between 1991 and 1992, but was still eight per cent lower than in 1982.[218] It appears there has been some increase in young male suicides by firearms, which now exceed suicides by self-poisoning.[219] Analysis of those admitted to accident and emergency departments of hospitals following assaults show a very small proportion of assaults caused by firearms.

In the US in 1987 guns accounted for 60 per cent of all homicides, and for 71 per cent of homicides of 15-19 year olds. For every gun fatality, there were an estimated 7.5 non-fatal injuries.[220] It is not surprising that those seeking to reduce and prevent violence in the US, including violence involving children, invariably focus as one priority on gun control – coming into conflict with a predominant culture which sees gun ownership as a constitutional right, and with a very rich and powerful gun lobby.

Legal controls on possession and use of various classes of firearms by children in the UK, while more rigorous than those in the US, are confused and confusing and need to be rationalised. In England and Wales there is a class of prohibited weapon, including automatic weapons and those for discharging gas, which require both a firearms certificate and the authority of the Home Secretary. The law does not explicitly deny authorisation to children.

In the Firearms Act 1968, section 1 covers rifles and pistols (not shotguns) and certain other signalling equipment. Possession requires a firearms certificate. Under-14 year olds cannot be granted firearms certificates, and can be said to 'possess' such a firearm only when carrying it for another, acting as a member of a rifle club or cadet corps, or when at a shooting gallery. It is an offence to give a firearm or ammunition to an under 14 year-old. Between 14 and 17, a person may be granted a firearms certificate, and may be given a firearm and ammunition, but cannot purchase or hire. Where police issue a certificate to under-17 year olds, they do so subject to very stringent conditions, and mostly to members of rifle clubs.

Shotguns are covered by section 2 of the Act, and the law becomes even more complex and confusing: 14 to 17 year-olds cannot purchase shotguns or ammunition but may receive them as gifts. Under-14 year olds cannot receive them as gifts. Under 15 year-olds must not have assembled shotguns with them unless under the supervision of a person over 21, or the shotgun is in a secured cover. The police can issue a shotgun certificate to an under-14 year old, authorising possession when under supervision; in addition a landowner can lend a shotgun to someone of any age who does not have a certificate.

Airguns remain entirely unlicensed, but under-17 year olds may not buy guns or ammunition. It is an offence to give an airgun or ammunition to an under-14 year old, and such a person commits an offence by having one except as a member of an approved club, at a shooting gallery or when on private property under adult supervision. A person under 17 may not have an air pistol in a public place in any circumstances (contrasting with the right of a 16 year-old to have an uncovered shotgun in a public place), and may have an air rifle or airgun in a public place only if it is in a secured cover. A penalty can be imposed on the supervising adult if a pellet is discharged beyond the private premises. In 1981 an expert involved in firearms research estimated that there were over four million air guns in circulation in the UK; about 1,500,000,000 pellets are sold in the UK each year.

A private body representing the interests of the gun trade and promoting gun sports, the Shooting Sports Trust, acknowledges that there has been some increase in injury and vandalism involving air guns, and believes that misuse could be restricted by increased knowledge of the law by users, the public and the police. The Trust has published a leaflet summarising the law for young people. The Trust also acknowledges that 'in the longer term, rationalisation and simplification of the law would be a positive benefit.'[221]

In 1970 the Home Office completed a study on firearms in crime; there do not appear to have been any major studies since.[222] The Home Office Firearms Consultative Committee is currently reviewing the law on possession and use of firearms, including air guns, by children.

Other weapons

According to the Home Office the weapons most commonly used in crime are everyday items like kitchen and craft knives, whose availability cannot be effectively controlled.

There are various controls on possession and purchase of offensive weapons. The Prevention of Crime Act 1953 made it an offence to carry an offensive weapon in a public place without lawful authority or reasonable excuse. An offensive weapon is defined as any article which is made or adapted for causing injury to the person or intended to cause injury. In addition, the Criminal Justice Act 1988 (section 139) made it an offence to carry bladed or sharply pointed articles, other than a small folded pocket knife, in a public place without good reason. Flick knives and gravity knives and some other offensive weapons which have no legitimate use are banned. The Crossbows Act 1987 prohibits the sale of crossbows to, and the purchase of crossbows by, under-17 year olds. It also makes it an offence for anyone under 17 to have a crossbow in his or her possession, unless under the supervision of someone aged 21 or over.

Recommendation
The law on possession and use of firearms including air guns by children should be reviewed and simplified, with a bar on any possession or unsupervised use below the age of 14, and strict and consistent controls on possession and use under 18. Information about the simplified law should be adequately disseminated to children and parents.

[Home Office; Home Departments for Scotland and Northern Ireland]

Information and statistics

Naively perhaps, the Commission believed that one of the easiest parts of the task it set itself would be to summarise the state of our knowledge on the level of violence to and by children, to provide as accurate as possible a statistical and descriptive analysis.

We quickly discovered there is nothing simple about the task. But it does seem to us extremely important that such information should be available and collected consistently year by year. We need it to ensure that the debate about violence and violence prevention is based as far as possible on facts rather than impressions, to avoid both groundless fears of violence on the one hand, or unjustified complacency on the other. We need it in order to judge whether we are making progress in reducing violence of various kinds. It is also important to encourage some standardisation of collection of statistics on a European and international basis, so that comparisons can be made, which may in turn lead to further understanding of effective preventive strategies. At present, for example, it is not possible to make accurate comparisons of rates of child abuse and other violence to children, because of inconsistent definitions and recording.

There are national criminal statistics, which provide figures and some analyses for prosecutions and convictions for various offences of violence. They also provide some analyses of victims of certain kinds of offence including homicide – demonstrating for example that infants under the age of one are the age group most at risk of homicide in the UK. The Commission heard particular concern expressed about the recording and collection of homicide statistics relating to young victims. There are also concerns about the accuracy of published figures of suicides by young people (see page 189).

The House of Commons Home Affairs Committee in its 1993 report on juvenile offenders recommended that the Home Office should consider how juvenile crime statistics could be improved to enable 'more informed policy decisions to be made', and also proposed further research to provide a more accurate picture of persistent juvenile offending.[223]

Criminal statistics do not of course provide any measure of the real level of violence experienced by the population. Other information covers numbers of violent offences reported to the police (which do not necessarily lead to investigation, let alone prosecution), but there appears to be no consistent collection and analysis of this information across the country. Crime surveys – interview research using representative samples of the population – produce more detailed information and of course much higher estimates of the level of violence. But there has as yet been very little interviewing of children. The latest Crime Survey includes very limited investigation of 12-16 year olds.[224]

Another source of information on the prevalence of more serious forms of violence to (and by) children should come from the health service: doctors' and hospitals' records of injuries should be analysed by the victim's age and other characteristics, as well as by possible causes. In some areas, there has been progress towards this, using the International Codes of Diseases adopted by the World Health Organisation. Computerisation should make the central collection and analysis of figures relatively cheap and easy. There is of course central collection and publication by the Office of Population Censuses and Studies of information on childhood mortality and morbidity. The current *Confidential inquiry into stillbirths and deaths in infancy* set up by the Department of Health may provide further analysis.

In relation to child abuse, information about children placed on child protection registers is now collected and published centrally, but gives no accurate picture of levels of abuse: some children are placed on registers because of concern about rather than evidence of abuse, but it is also clear that much serious physical, sexual and emotional abuse goes unreported. And because of the concept of 'reasonable chastisement', current definitions of physical child abuse condone quite high levels of physical violence to children.

There have been many judicial and other inquiries into child abuse. Most have focused on the death of a child. More recently there have been large-scale inquiries into sexual abuse and institutional abuse of children. These have produced valuable insights and recommendations, and the Department of Health has commissioned two reviews of results of child death and other inquiries. But there is no consistency of investigation into such child deaths and serious abuse. There have been few attempts as yet to gain an accurate picture of the overall level of violence to children. There have been some retrospective studies of prevalence of sexual abuse, interviewing 16 year olds and older young people. John and Elizabeth Newson's interview research into all aspects of child-rearing, including discipline, has provided the most comprehensive information on levels of physical punishment of children. In 1990 the Department of Health commissioned a new and detailed study on physical violence to children in their homes; the first results were published in June 1995 (see page 51). Another new and impressionistic source of information comes from analyses of calls made by children to free helplines and counselling services, including the national helpline ChildLine.

There are obviously special problems in gaining accurate information about the incidence of all kinds of violence to children in their homes, and other settings, and in particular violence to very young children. It is only very recently that there has been any attempt to measure levels of violence, including bullying, towards children in institutions. There is still no systematic collection of such information.

Some studies suggest that particular groups of children, for example disabled children or minority ethnic groups, are particularly at risk of various forms of violence. But there is as yet little detailed information. The University of Oxford Centre for Criminological Research is conducting a research project for the Home Office on people with learning disabilities who are victims of crime. It is important that throughout the recording and collection of information on violence involving children, there should be appropriate monitoring by disability, ethnic background and so on.

Overall, the Commission believes that the lack of any co-ordinated attempt to provide an accurate picture of levels of violence involving children in the UK is a matter of serious concern, and one which blocks an informed public debate and inhibits moves to reduce violence. As the National Committee on Violence in Australia commented:

> 'Knowledge about the extent and distribution of violence in Australia is fragmentary and inadequate. Such knowledge is important not for its own sake, but to inform the rational allocation of scarce and costly criminal justice and social welfare resources in Australia, and to provide members of the public with an objective indication of their own security or vulnerability.'[225]

Recommendations
Appropriate government departments should commission a review of available information on levels of violence to and by children in the UK, undertaking in a more comprehensive way the exercise attempted by the Commission and reported in Appendix 3 (page 256). The review should provide recommendations for the consistent and accurate collection of data on violence involving children which will both inform the public including children and provide information useful for the development of preventive strategies. The review should consider collection of information from various sources including:
- *criminal statistics (age distribution of victims for each offence category)*
- *police statistics of reported offences and investigations*
- *health service injury surveillance*

- coroners' courts
- crime surveys and other interview research with children, parents etc. The review should consider how to use regular interview research with children and parents of young children to provide a wider measure of violence to children, including parents' disciplinary techniques
- child protection registrations (separating out 'actual' from 'likely' cases of abuse), and investigations; (clearer categorisation of sexual abuse is required by age, type and severity of abuse)
- returns from all institutions concerned with children of incidents of violence, including bullying and self-harm
- information from confidential helplines and similar.

The collection and publication of criminal statistics should be reviewed to ensure that they give an accurate picture of trends in the use of firearms, including firearms used in violence involving children.

In making recommendations, the review should bear in mind the usefulness of comparative international studies of prevalence of violence involving children, and consult with appropriate European and international bodies (in particular the World Health Organisation).

[Government departments; OPCS and other agencies; appropriate research bodies]

Detailed statistics should be collected and published annually on all restriction of liberty of children, in the penal, childcare, health and education systems, including statutory, voluntary and private sectors.

[Home Office; Department of Health; Department for Education and Employment]

The national and local collection of statistics relating to suicide and self-harm should be reviewed inter-departmentally to ensure that it provides accurate information in sufficient detail to inform preventive strategies. This should include the collection of detailed information about incidents in residential institutions for children, including in particular secure accommodation and young offender institutions.

[Department of Health; Home Office; OPCS etc]

There should be an attempt to 'cost' the direct and indirect short- and long-term effects of violence involving children.

Research

The level of violence involving children in the USA is clearly very much higher than in the UK, so it is not surprising that there has been more research there attempting to analyse why children become violent, to identify protective factors, and to measure the effectiveness of various strategies of violence prevention. Here, within the overall field of crime prevention, there has been an increasing emphasis on evaluation of interventions. Child abuse has been the subject of a great deal of research, but it has tended to focus most on intervention following abuse rather than on prevention.

The Commission believes that there must be more systematic evaluation of interventions aiming to reduce or prevent violence. It is at present an uphill struggle to convince politicians that money spent on long-term and comprehensive measures rather than narrowly targeted preventive interventions is well-invested. But if impressive results can be demonstrated, and contrasted with the high cost and ineffectiveness of criminal justice responses to violence, there is a greater chance of changes in overall policy.

Recommendations

Relevant research bodies, and in particular the Economic and Social Research Council, Department of Health and Home Office should jointly review current research on the antecedents of violence in children, and how to make the best use of longitudinal studies to give information on risk factors for violence. There is a need for new longitudinal studies to investigate the development of violent behaviour.

[Research-commissioning bodies]

Statutory and voluntary bodies responsible for funding local projects aimed at violence prevention and community safety should insist on arrangements to ensure systematic evaluation, wherever possible both short- and long-term.

[Government; local authorities; voluntary organisations]

In addition there is a need for specific research in the following areas:
- *systematic controlled evaluation of educational materials for parents on non-violent methods of discipline*
- *evaluation of group and individual treatment/training for parents of young children with conduct disorders*
- *follow-up studies of delinquents receiving residential and non-residential (intermediate) treatment*
- *studies of different types of management of children who have been the subject of physical and sexual abuse*
- *case studies or survey-type studies of effects of violent material on TV and videos on vulnerable and non-vulnerable children*
- *further evaluation of effectiveness of anti-bullying strategies in schools*
- *empirical research to build on existing knowledge of the physical and psychological indicators of child sexual abuse*
- *evaluation of therapeutic interventions with sexually abused children and their families*

[Research bodies and relevant agencies]

References

1 *Violence - directions for Australia, National Committee on Violence,* (Australian Institute of Criminology, Canberra, 1990) pp. 118-23.

2 For further details contact the National Association of Local Government Women's Committees (NALGWC), Pankhurst Centre, 60-62 Nelson Street, Manchester M13 9WP.

3 Personal communication from Director of Field Operations, Crime Concern, March 1995.

4 *Taking children seriously: a proposal for a children's rights commissioner,* Martin Rosenbaum and Peter Newell, (Calouste Gulbenkian Foundation, London, 1991).

5 *Safer Communities: the local delivery of crime prevention through the partnership approach*, Standing Conference on Crime Prevention, (Home Office, August 1991) pp. 6-7.

6 *Ibid*, p. 13.

7 *Ibid*, p. 29.

8 *Ibid*, pp. 30-32.

9 *Planning out crime*, joint circular from the Department of the Environment and the Welsh Office, Circular 5/94, Department of Environment *or* Circular 16/94, Welsh Office, (HMSO, 1994) para. 4.

10 Speech to Local Government News Conference on *Vandalism and crime prevention* by Sir Paul Beresford, Environment Minister, Department of the Environment, 10 October 1994.

11 *Out of hours, a study of economic, social and cultural life in twelve town centres in the UK, Summary Report,* (Comedia in association with Calouste Gulbenkian Foundation, February 1991) p. 43.

12 *Non accidental injury to children,* LASSL (74)13, (Department of Health and Social Security, 1974).

13 *Working together: a guide to arrangements for inter-agency co-operation for the protection of children from abuse*, Department of Health and Social Security and Welsh Office, (HMSO, 1988).

14 *Working together under the Children Act 1989: a guide to arrangements for inter-agency co-operation for the protection of children from abuse,* Home Office, Department of Health, Department of Education and Science, Welsh Office, (HMSO, 1991) para. 2.4.

15 *Effective interventions on child abuse: guidance on co-operation in Scotland,* Scottish Office, (HMSO Edinburgh, 1989).

16 *Scotland's children: proposal for child care policies and law,* Scottish Office, (HMSO, Edinburgh, 1993).

17 *Report into the workings of area child protection committees, ACPC Series Report Number 2,* David Campbell, (Department of Health, 1994).

18 *Protecting children in Wales; the role and effectiveness of area child protection committees, a report for the Welsh Office,* Sonia Jackson, Robert Sanders and Nigel Thomas, (Department of Social Policy and Applied Social Studies, University of Wales, Swansea, 1994) p. 12.

19 *Ibid*, p. 148.

20 *Children's Services Plans, LAC(92)18,* (Department of Health, November 1992).

21 *Children in the Public Care, a review of residential childcare,* Department of Health, (HMSO, 1991).

22 See note 20, guidance attached to circular.

23 *Children's Services Plans,* Draft Circular, Social Care Group, (Department of Health, June 1995).

24 *Seen but not heard - Co-ordinating community child health and social services for children in need,* Audit Commission, (HMSO, London, 1994) p. 38.

25 See note 16, paras. 8.13 and 8.14.

26 *Inter-agency co-ordination to tackle domestic violence, Inter-agency circular - draft (2),* (Home Office, September 1994).

27 *Report of an Enquiry into Domestic Violence,* House of Commons Select Committee on Home Affairs, House of Commons paper 245 1992/93, (HMSO, 1993).

28 *Neighbors helping neighbors: a new national strategy for the protection of children,* US Department of Health and Human Services, Administration for Children and Families and US Advisory Board on Child Abuse and Neglect, (US Government Printing Office, 1993) p. xi.

29 See note 1, p. 140; *Introduction to Neighbour-Network,* National Association for the Prevention of Child Abuse and Neglect (NAPCAN), (Australia, 1990); also communication from NAPCAN, September 1994.

30 *One scandal too many...the case for comprehensive protection for children in all settings,* report of a working group convened by the Gulbenkian Foundation, (Calouste Gulbenkian Foundation, London, 1993) pp. 128-31.

31 *America's problems: social issues and public policy,* E Currie and J Skolnick, (Glenview Scott, Foresman, 1988).

32 *Household below average income (HBAI) statistics for 1992/93,* (Department of Social Security, June 1995).

33 *Crime and social policy,* a report of the independent Committee on Crime and Social Policy, (published by NACRO, London, 1995) pp. 29 and 64.

34 *The index of social health: monitoring the social well being of children in industrialized countries, a report from UNICEF,* M Miringoff and S Opdycke, (Fordham Institute for Innovation in Social Policy, 1993).

35 *Within our reach: breaking the cycle of disadvantage,* Lisbeth Schorr, (Doubleday, 1988).

36 *Poverty: the facts,* C Oppenheim, (Child Poverty Action Group, 1993).

37 *Social justice: strategies for national renewal. The report of the Commission on Social Justice,* Institute of Public Policy Research (IPPR), (Vintage, 1994). See also *Social Justice, Children and Families,* Patricia Hewitt and Penelope Leach, (Commission on Social Justice publication, IPPR, December 1993).

38 *Labour force survey, quarterly bulletin, June 1992,* (Department of Employment, 1992).

39 *Working brief,* Issue 45, Youthaid, June 1993.

40 See note 33, p. 44.

41 *Learning in terror: a survey of racial harassment in schools and colleges in England, Scotland and Wales, 1985-1987,* (Commission for Racial Equality, 1988) p. 16.

42 R v Ribbans, Duggan, Ridley, *The Times,* 11 November 1994.

43 Statement from Northern Ireland Information Service, 'Race Relations Legislation announced for Northern Ireland', 27 April 1995.

44 Children Act 1989, section 3.

45 *Report on Family Law,* Scottish Law Commission, (HMSO, Edinburgh, May 1992) para. 2.6, pp. 4 and 5.

46 See note 30, p. 18.

47 *Ibid,* p. 61.

48 *How to make a family covenant: child welcoming ceremonies*, (The Family Covenant Association, 66 High Street, Pershore, Worcestershire, 1994).

49 *Meeting the Needs of Young Children,* Carnegie Corporation Task Force, (Carnegie Corporation of New York, April 1994) p. xiv.

50 *Children First,* Penelope Leach, (Michael Joseph, 1994) provides a detailed critique of current policies and attitudes towards parents and children together with a blueprint for reform.

51 *Seen but not heard: co-ordinating community child health and social services for children in need,* Audit Commission, (HMSO, 1994).

52 *Confident parents, confident children: policy and practice in parent education and support,* Gillian Pugh, Erica De'Ath and Celia Smith, (National Children's Bureau, 1994) p. 207.

53 *Introduction and background to the Henley Safe Children project: interim report,* Norma Baldwin and Lyn Carruthers, (Henley Safe Children Project, May 1993).

54 *Ibid,* pp. 72 and 73.

55 *Summary of a listening ear: an evaluation of Home-Start Charnwood Scheme 1994,* Dr Barbara Bagilhole and Ms Marie Kennedy, (Dept of Social Sciences, University of Loughborough).

56 *Summary of Home-Start statistics for 1993/94,* correspondence from Home-Start.

57 *Helping families grow strong. New directions in public policy,* (Center for Study of Social Policy, USA, 1990) see note 34, p. 91.

58 Now published as *The next step for school age childcare: a costed development strategy for the year 2000 and beyond,* (Kids' Clubs Network, 1995).

59 *Children Act Report 1993, a report by the Secretaries of State for Health and for Wales on the Children Act 1989 in pursuance of their duties under Section 83(6) of the Act,* (HMSO, 1994) pp. 57 and 62.

60 *Promoting social welfare,* First annual report of the Chief Inspector Social Services Inspectorate Northern Ireland, (Department of Health and Social Services Northern Ireland, March 1994) pp. 124-25.

61 'Early childhood services', *Nineteenth Report of the Standing Advisory Commission on Human Rights,* Report for 1993-1994, SACHR, (HMSO, 1994) p. 50.

62 *Policy on early years provision for Northern Ireland,* (The Department of Heath and Social Services and the Department of Education for Northern Ireland, Policy and Planning Research Unit, Belfast, 1994).

63 *Ibid,* p. 8.

64 Early Childhood Education Forum convened by the Early Childhood Unit of the National Children's Bureau (NCB), 8 Wakley Street, London EC1V 7QE.

65 *Parenting Education and Support Forum, Statement of aims* circulated for launch meeting, Parenting Education and Support Forum, c/o National Children's Bureau, 8 Wakley Street, London EC1V 7QE, (June 1995).

66 'Agenda for action', see note 52, p. 225 et seq.

67 See note 52, p. 92.

68 'Preventing Child Abuse and Neglect: programmatic interventions', Deborah Daro and Karen McCurdy, *Child Welfare,* vol. LXXIII, no.5 (Sept/Oct 1994) p. 410.

69 'Training parents to manage difficult children: a comparison of methods', Carole Sutton, *Behavioural Psychotherapy* vol. 20, (1992) pp. 115-39.

70 See note 52, p. 176.

71 *Ibid,* p. 131.

72 List of supporting organisations maintained by EPOCH - End Physical Punishment of Children, 77 Holloway Road, London N7 8JZ.

73 *A community study of physical violence to children in the home, and associated variables,* Marjorie A Smith, Thomas Coram Research Unit, London, Poster presented at International Society

for the Prevention of Child Abuse and neglect, Fifth European Conference on Child Abuse and Neglect, Oslo, 13-16 May 1995.

74 See note 30.

75 London Borough of Sutton *v* Anne Hilary Davis, High Court, 16 March 1994.

76 *Local Authority Circular, LAC(94)23,* (Department of Health, December 1994).

77 Children's Homes Regulations 1991, SI 1991 no. 1506.

78 Recommendations R1985/4 and R 1990/2, Committee of Ministers, Council of Europe.

79 UN Committee on the Rights of the Child, Centre for Human Rights, Geneva, CRC/C/15/Add.34, 15 February 1995, paras. 16 and 31.

80 For example, evaluations of the Perry Pre-School Project in the US: *A summary of significant benefits: The High/Scope Perry Pre-school Study through age 27*, L J Schweinhart and D Weikart, (High/Scope Press, 1993).

81 'Pre-school education has long-term effects, but can they be generalised?', M Woodhead, *Oxford Review of Education*, II, 2, (1985) pp. 133-35.

82 Programme Development Unit established within the Home Office Research and Statistics Department in 1991.

83 See note 62, p. 9.

84 See note 61.

85 *Violence and Youth: psychology's response, vol. 1, Summary Report of the American Psychological Association Commission on Violence and Youth*, (American Psychological Association, Washington DC, 1993) p. 74.

86 See note 1, p. 145.

87 'Prevention of Violence: role of the pediatrician', Frederick P Rivara and David P. Farrington, *Archives of Pediatrics and Adolescent Medicine*, vol. 149, (April 1995) p. 422.

88 *Northern Ireland Travellers Census 1993,* (Department of the Environment, 1993).

89 *Travelling people in West Belfast*, Paul Noonan, (ed. by Bill Rolston), (Save the Children, 1994).

90 *Education and Enmity: the control of schooling in Northern Ireland 1920-50*, D H Akenson, (David and Charles, 1973) referred to in *Caught in Crossfire: children and the Northern Ireland conflict*, Ed Cairns, (Appletree Press, Belfast, 1987) p. 143.

91 *Using ethos indicators in secondary school self-evaluation: taking account of the views of pupils, parents and teachers*, (The Scottish Office Education Department and Her Majesty's Inspectors of Schools, 1992).

92 *Law in Education (11-14) Project,* (eds.) Don Rowe and Tony Thorpe, (The Citizenship Foundation/NCC Enterprises Ltd, 1993).

93 *Cross-curricular themes: review and planning. Guidance materials*, (Northern Ireland Curriculum Council, 1990) pp. 4 and 5.

94 *Who's who in EMU: a guide to organisations which can help teachers to plan and carry out work in education for mutual understanding,* 1993-94 edn, (The Forum on Community Understanding and Schools (FOCUS), Belfast, 1993).

95 'Appendix: The development of an individual potential for violence', in *Understanding and preventing violence*, A J Reiss and J A Roth (eds.), (National Academy Press, Washington DC, 1993) p. 391.

96 *Bullying - don't suffer in silence: an anti-bullying pack for schools*, Department for Education, (HMSO, 1994) p. 10.

97 *The UK's First Report to the UN Committee on the Rights of the Child*, (HMSO, February 1994) para. 7.37, p. 100 and CRC/C/11/Add.1, paras. 333 et seq, 28 March 1994, which is the same report but published by the Secretariat of the United Nations Committee on the Rights of the Child.

98 See for example debate on sport in schools, House of Lords, *Hansard*, 4 May 1994, column 1164 et seq.

99 'Policy update', (National Youth Agency, 1994).

100 *One false move: - a study of children's independent mobility*, M Hillman, J Adams and J Whitelegg, (Policy Studies Institute, 1990).

101 *Review of the play and recreational needs of young people growing up on housing estates,* (National Association for the Care and Re-settlement of Offenders (NACRO), 1988).

102 *Preventative strategy for young people in trouble*, Coopers and Lybrand, (ITV Telethon/Prince's Trust, September 1994) para. 4.

103 *Agenda for play: the way forward. A review of policies and practice in Northern Ireland - recommendations for future developments*, Kathleen Toner, (Playright, Save the Children and Playboard 1994) p. 6.

104 *A charter for children's play for Northern Ireland*, Kathleen Toner, (Playright, Save the Children and Playboard, 1994) pp. 10 and 11.

105 *Play without frontiers: a policy document on community relations in children's play*, (PlayBoard NI, 1990) p. 7.

106 'Assault as a public health problem: discussion paper', J P Shepherd and D P Farrington, *Journal of the Royal Society of Medicine,* vol. 86, (February 1993) p. 89.

107 *Ibid*, p. 91.

108 *Prevention of Violence: back to basics*, Frederick Rivara and David Farrington, (unpublished) but later a revised version published as see ref. 87, pp. 6 and 29.

109 *Ibid*, p. 7.

110 *Poverty and inequality in the UK: the effects on children*, V Kumar, (National Children's Bureau, London, 1993).

111 *The Health of the Nation: a strategy for health in England*, Department of Health, (HMSO, 1992).

112 'Intensive health visiting and the prevention of juvenile crime', David Farrington, *Health Visitor*, vol. 68, no. 3 (March 1995) pp. 100-102.

113 See note 68, p. 409.

114 *Ibid*, p. 409.

115 'Doctors back Prince on smacking children', *BMA News Review*, June 1994.

116 See note 111.

117 *National sexual lifestyles survey*, K Wellings, paper presented to the Sex Education Forum, July 1993.

118 'Teenage pregnancy in industrialised countries', E Jones *et al*, (Yale University Press, 1986) in *Primary health care*, vol. 2, no. 10, (1992) pp. 16-17.

119 See note 108.

120 See note 111, p. 104.

121 See note 30, p. 73 *et seq.*

122 Action for Sick Children, Argyle House, 29-31 Euston Road, London NW1 2SD.

123 *With health in mind: mental healthcare for children and young people*, Zarrina Kurtz (ed.), (Action for Sick Children, 1993).

124 'Conduct disorder: long term outcomes and treatment effectiveness', D Offord and K Bennett, *Journal of the American Academy of Child and Adolescent Psychiatry,* no. 33, (1994) pp. 1069-78.

125 See note 30, p. 33 *et seq.*

126 *The National Prison Survey 1991*, Tricia Dodd and Paul Hunter, OCPS, (HMSO, 1992).

127 *The hidden victims: children and domestic violence*, (NCH Action for Children, London, 1994).

128 'On the relationship between wife beating and child abuse', L H Bowker, M Arbittel and

J R McFerron, in *Feminist perspectives on wife abuse*, K Yllo and M Bograd (eds.), (Sage 1988) pp. 158-74.

129 *Child abuse trends in England and Wales 1988-1990 and an overview from 1973-1990*, Susan J Creighton, (Policy Practice Research Series, NSPCC, 1992).

130 Home Office Circular 60/1990.

131 'Challenging sexual violence against girls: a social awareness approach', Jenny Kitzinger, *Child Abuse Review*, vol. 3, pp. 246-58.

132 See note 26.

133 *Children and Young People on Child Protection Registers, Year Ending 31 March 1993*, England, Department of Health, A/F93/13 Local Authority Statistics, (HMSO, 1994).

134 'Children as Victims of Violence: A National Survey', D Finkelhor and J Dziuba-Leatherman, *Paediatrics*, vol. 94(4), (1994) pp. 413-20.

135 'Impact of Sexual Abuse on Children: A Review and Synthesis of Recent Empirical Studies', K A Kendall-Tackett, L M Williams and D Finkelhor, *Psychological Bulletin*, vol. 113(1), (1993) pp. 164-80.

136 'What's wrong with sex between adults and children? Ethics and the Problem of Sexual Abuse', D Finkelhor, *American Journal of Orthopsychiatry*, 49(4), (1979) pp. 692-97.

137 'The impact of child sexual abuse', A Caffaro-Rouget, R A Lang and V van Santen, *Annals of Sex Research*, vol. 2, (1989) pp. 29-47 and 'Factors associated with an increased impact of child sexual abuse', J Conte and J Shuerman, *Child Abuse and Neglect*, 11, (1987) pp. 201-11.

138 'The Argument for Adult-Child Sexual Contact: A Critical Appraisal and New Data', TGM Sandfort, ch. 3 in *The Sexual Abuse of Children: Theory and Research*, W O'Donohue and J H Geer (eds.), (Lawrence Erlbaum Associates Inc, New Jersey, 1992).

139 'Sexually Abused Children and Young People Speak Out', J Roberts and C Taylor, ch. 1 in *Child Abuse and Child Abusers*, L Waterhouse (ed.), *Research Highlights in Social Work*, 24, (1993).

140 *The evidence of children: the law and psychology*, J R Spencer and R H Flin, (Blackstone Press, London, 1993).

141 'Victims of time', J Plotnikoff and R Woolfson, *Community Care*, (24 March, 1994) pp. 22 and 23; *An Evaluation of the Live Link for Child Witnesses*, G M Davies and E Noon, (Home Office, London, 1991).

142 *Memorandum of Good Practice on Video-Recorded Interviews with Child Witnesses for Criminal Proceedings*, Home Office in conjunction with Department of Health, (HMSO, London, 1992).

143 'Under fire: lawyers questioning children in criminal court', V K Kranat and H L Westcott, *Expert Evidence*, 3(1), 1994, pp. 16-24.

144 *Report of the Advisory Group on Video Evidence*, T Pigot, (Home Office, London, 1989).

145 *Child protection work with children with multiple disabilities*, R Marchant and M Page, (NSPCC, 1993).

146 'Girls abused on streets labelled prostitutes', press notice from Children's Society, London, quoting Home Office figures, August 1994.

147 'Mean streets: the theoretical significance of situational delinquency among homeless youths', J McCarthy and B Hagan, *American Journal of Sociology*, vol. 98, pp. 597-627; *Male prostitution*, Donald J West and Buz De Villiers, (Duckworth, London, 1992).

148 *Setting the record straight: juvenile crime in perspective*, (NCH Action for Children, 1993).

149 *Counting the cost: an alternative strategy to Secure Training Centres*, (NCH Action for Children, 1994) p. 2.

150 *Banged up, Beaten up, Cutting Up*, Report of the Howard League Commission of Inquiry into Violence in Penal Institutions for Teenagers under 18, chaired by Helena Kennedy

QC, (Howard League, London, 1995).

151 *Ibid*, p. 4.

152 *Crime, Justice and Protecting the Public*, Command paper CM963, (HMSO, 6 February 1990).

153 See note 30.

154 *Safe to let out?*, (National Children's Bureau, London, 1995).

155 *Juvenile Offenders, vol. 1, Sixth Report,* Home Affairs Committee, (HMSO, 1993).

156 *Ibid*, paras. 164 et seq.

157 *The nature of adolescence: working with young people in custody*, Juliet Lyon and Dr John Coleman, (Trust for the Study of Adolescence, 1994).

158 *An examination of sentencing trends in the use of custodial sentences and supervision orders in the courts of West Glamorgan 1989-1991*, E Isles, (West Glamorgan Social Services Department, 1992), referred to in note 160.

159 *Car theft: the offenders' perspective*, R Light, C Nee and H Ingham, (HMSO, 1993).

160 *Putting the brakes on car crime: a local study of auto-related crime among young people*, Maureen McGillivray, (Wales Advocacy Unit, Children's Society and Mid Glamorgan Social Services Department, 1993) p. 41.

161 *Ibid*, p. 71.

162 *Ibid*.

163 Personal communication from the Home Office, 1994.

164 *Information briefing No. 5 (1992 Revision) Child Abuse Deaths*, Susan J Creighton, (NSPCC, 1992).

165 See note 14, para. 8.1.

166 *Study of Working together Part 8 reports; discussion report for ACPC conference 1994*, Geoff James, Department of Health ACPC series, Report no. 1, (Department of Health, 1994).

167 South Carolina information from The Alliance for South Carolina's Children, USA.

168 Infanticide Act 1938, section 1.

169 *Suicide and parasuicide,* (The Samaritans, May 1993).

170 'Suicide in children and adolescents in England and Wales 1960-1990', GM McClure, *British Journal of Psychiatry,* vol. 165, (1994) pp.510-14.

171 *The Health of the Nation: Key Area Handbook on Mental Illness,* Department of Health and Social Services Inspectorate, (Department of Health, 1993) pp. 17 and 18.

172 *Suicide prevention the challenge confronted: a manual of guidance for the purchasers and providers of mental health care*, Dr Richard Williams and Professor H Gethin Morgan (eds.), NHS Health Advisory Service Thematic Review, (HMSO, London, 1994) p. 50.

173 See note 170.

174 *Report of a review by Her Majesty's Chief Inspector of Prisons for England and Wales of Suicide and Self-harm in prison service establishments in England and Wales,* (HMSO, 1990) and *Suicides in Feltham: a report by the Howard League for Penal Reform,* (The Howard League, 1993).

175 See note 150, p. 14.

176 See note 111.

177 *Risk factors for adolescent suicide*, D Brent, J Perper, C E Goldstein *et al*, (1988), referred to in note 171, p. 50.

178 'Family therapy and psychotherapy following suicidal behaviour by young adolescents', Michael Kerfoot, in *Suicide in adolescence*, R Diekstra and K Hawton (eds.), (Martinus Nijhoff, Dordrecht, 1987).

179 See note 30, p. 132 et seq.

180 *Inquiry into Community Care for People with Severe Mental Illness - Creating community care,* (Mental Health Foundation, September 1994) pp. 10 and 59.

181 *Ibid*, p. 57.

182 *Understanding child abuse and neglect*, National Research Council, Washington DC, (National Academic Press, 1993) pp. 118 and 119; also summary, p. 8.

183 *Alcohol drinking and family life in Europe: a pilot study*, Report to Alcohol Education and Research Council, London, 1995; *Views and behaviour of 11, 13, and 15 year-olds from 11 countries*, A J C King and B Coles, (Ministry of National Health and Welfare, Ottawa, Canada, 1992).

184 *Adolescent drinking*, OPCS, (HMSO, London, 1986).

185 See note 172, pp. 50 and 99.

186 'Sniffers quit glue for more lethal solvents', *Independent on Sunday*, 13 March 1994, p. 5.

187 'Pick 'n' mix: changing patterns of illicit drug use amongst 1990s adolescents', Howard Parker and Fiona Measham, *Drugs: education, prevention and policy*, vol. 1 no. 1, (1994).

188 *Hansard*, written answers, column 198, 6 May 1993.

189 *Index of deaths*, Malcolm Sutton, (Beyond the Pale Publications, 1994).

190 'Troubles, stress and psychological disorder in Northern Ireland', R Wilson and E Cairns, *The Psychologist*, vol. 15, no. 8, (1992).

191 *Ibid*.

192 Home Office Minister Earl Ferrers, reported in introduction to *British Board of Film Classification Annual Report and accounts for 1993*, (British Board of Film Classification, October 1993).

193 *Violence in television programmes 10*, (BBC, 1993) p. 74.

194 *Guidelines for the portrayal of violence on BBC television 12*, (BBC, 1993).

195 *The ITC programme code*, (Independent Television Commission, 1993).

196 *British Board of Film Classification Annual Report and accounts for 1992*, (British Board of Film Classification, July 1993).

197 *Annual Report 1993, BBFC British Board of Film Classification*, (British Board of Film Classification, October 1994).

198 See note 196, pp. 2 and 22.

199 *Mum can I watch a video: a parent's guide to video classification*, (Video Standards Council and The British Video Association, 1995).

200 *Children and video games: an exploratory study*, Guy Cumberbatch, Andrea Maguire and Samantha Woods, Communications Research Group, (Aston University, October 1993).

201 Information from European Leisure Software Publishers' Association (ELSPA), Suite 1, Haddonsacre, Station Road, Offenham, near Evesham, Worcs. WR11 5LW.

202 *Home Affairs Committee of Enquiry into computer pornography: memorandum of evidence*, Dr Catherine Itzin, (Violence Abuse and Gender Relations Unit, University of Bradford, October 1993).

203 *Child pornography and sexual exploitation*, EFCW Position Statement, (European Forum for Child Welfare, 1993).

204 *Aggressive toys and play*, (National Toy Council, 1 Chelsea Manor Gardens, London SW3 5PN).

205 British Toy and Hobby Manufacturers Association, 80 Camberwell Road, London SE5 OEG.

206 *Resolution on war toys, adopted by European Parliament September 13 1982*; Official Journal of European Communities, no. C267/14, (11 October 1982).

207 *Victims of crimes of violence. A guide to Criminal Injuries Compensation: The tariff scheme, effective from 1 April 1994*, issue no. 2, (CICA, April 1994).

208 *Football and football hooliganism, Factsheet 1*, (Sir Norman Chester Centre for Football Research, 1993) para. 4.2.

209 *The Hillsborough Stadium Disaster: Final Report*, Inquiry by Rt Hon Lord Justice Taylor, (HMSO, London, 1990).

210 See note 1, p. 163.

211 *Medical aspects of Amateur Boxing*, 2nd edn, (The Medical Commission of the Amateur Boxing Association of England, 1989).

212 R *v* Brown and others [1994] AC 212.

213 Attorney General's Reference (no. 6 of 1980 [1981] QB 715).

214 *The boxing debate,* (British Medical Association, 1993) p. 63.

215 *The National Association of Boys' Clubs September 1988-June 1989*, a report by HM Inspectorate, (Department of Education and Science, 1990) p. 16.

216 *Boxing (Brain injuries),* House of Commons, Hansard, 10 May 1994, column 300.

217 See note 1, p. 250.

218 *Criminal statistics England and Wales 1992,* Home Office, (HMSO, December 1993) p. 57.

219 See note 171, p. 23.

220 See note 85.

221 The Shooting Sports Trust Ltd, PO Box 7, Evesham, Worcestershire WR11 6YT.

222 *Firearms in crime,* Home Office, 1970.

223 See note 155.

224 *The 1992 British Crime Survey : Home Office Research Study 132*, P Mayhew, N Aye Maung and C Mirrlees-Black, (HMSO, 1993).

225 See note 1, p. 6.

Checklist for working towards a non-violent society
Draft generic checklist

As indicated in Section 2, page 86, the Gulbenkian Foundation has agreed that it will consider co-ordinating the process of developing this and other Checklists with small working groups of practitioners, involving Commission members.

A commitment to non-violence in parenting, childcare and education involves the application of a few basic principles to many widely different relationships and settings.

The four principles set out below are equally relevant to parents, childcare workers and teachers, and to infants, pre-school and older children. They become doubly relevant in adolescence when young people have parallel roles as 'children' in relation to the adults on whom they depend, and as 'adults' in relation to those younger than themselves. The principles should be taught to, and observed by, anyone who works in any capacity with children of any age, especially parents:

▶ PRINCIPLE ONE
Expectations of, and demands made on children should realistically reflect their maturity and development

▶ PRINCIPLE TWO
All discipline should be positive and children should be taught pro-social values and behaviour including in particular non-violent conflict resolution

▶ PRINCIPLE THREE
Non-violence should be clearly and consistently preferred and promoted

▶ PRINCIPLE FOUR
Adults should take responsibility not only for protecting children from violence done to them, but also for preventing violence done by them

Putting the principles into practice

The ways in which these principles can best be realised, and existing practices brought into line with them, depends on the maturity of the children, the role of the adults and the nature of the interaction between them. Discipline should always be positive and punishment should never be retributive, but what that means in relation to a six month old baby is clearly different from what it means in relation to a 16 year old youth. Non-violent controls are important to toddlers when they are at home as well as when they are in daycare centres, but 'quality control' of the way children are treated at home depends mostly on advance education for parenthood while 'quality control' in centres depends not only on training but also on current supervision.

Generic checklists that can easily be tailored to fit any particular group are a device for explaining the principles of non-violent child care and education in practical terms, and setting out what must, and what must not, be done in order to honour the principles and ensure a positively anti-violent environment for children.

The process of adapting a generic checklist to a particular group can serve to focus members' attention on its often-unrecognised and subtle supports for violence as well as on its potential for purveying positively non-violent messages to children and young people.

The checklist can subsequently be used in training and education; in assessing the performance of groups or individuals and their progress towards, or maintenance of, non-violence, and in identifying unacceptable attitudes and practices.

The draft example that follows is a generic checklist drawn up to be of particular relevance to young children, their parents and early years workers.

Each principle is followed by an explanation of its importance to non-violent child care and a selection of attitudes and practices in the child care environment that will support it.

These positives indicators are shown in **bold**, with explanatory examples in *sanserif*.

Some attitudes and practices that contradict or work against that principle, and therefore against non-violence in general, are also listed, as negative indicators. Their presence in the child care environment suggests that positive practices are not in place or are not working.

▶ PRINCIPLE ONE
Expectations of, and demands made on children should realistically reflect their maturity and development

Children's development is a process, not a race; its sequences are similar for all children but its speed and extent are individual with no short cuts for anyone. Children cannot do, or be, what is developmentally out of their reach. Adults who have unrealistic expectations of children therefore jeopardise the positive relationships on which non-violence depends and lack the basic understanding they need to keep children safe. Uninformed expectations may even evoke violence directly: violence to children whose unrealised needs are neglected or who are punished, physically or otherwise, for failing to meet impossible demands; violence by children who react aggressively to a perpetual sense of failure.

Positive indicators
Everyone who cares for children has background information about normal child development and individual variation. They understand that there is a rough *sequence* or map of development (mental, physical, social and emotional) that all children follow, but that their overall pace, and the speed with which they get from one point to another, is individual.

No baby will walk before she sits alone, but some will walk before other, equally 'normal' babies can sit.

Developmental periods of likely vulnerability and difficulty are recognised. For instance the toddler years as a bridge between infancy and childhood, during which children are liable to experience conflict between growing autonomy and still-powerful dependence, and therefore to be especially liable to frustration.

The toddler does not want to be treated as a baby but cannot manage if treated as a child. She wants to walk and rejects the buggy but her legs get tired; he wants to 'do it self' and demands 'me do it' but cannot manage and feels abandoned and distressed if taken at his word.

The difficulties of predicting later personality from early characteristics, and the dangers of doing so, are recognised.

To label a baby 'nervous' because of newborn jumpiness is to 'give a dog a bad name, and hang him'. A year later he may have to fight for the right to be what he is: a normally-confident toddler.

Likewise only limited predictive weight is given to current advancement or delay in any area of behaviour or performance.

It is vital that children acquire speech, and good for their overall development and relationships to do so comparatively early, but the child who acquires words first is not necessarily the one who is going to have the most interesting things to say later, nor is the child whose speech is delayed necessarily 'backward'.

'Nurture' is recognised as at least as important an influence on individuals as 'nature'. Children's upbringing is therefore recognised as crucial to how they turn out.

Adults hold themselves, individually and collectively, largely responsible for the development, wellbeing and happiness of today's children, but also recognise (and seek to understand) yesterday's children in themselves.

Adults recognise that children cannot be 'born bad' (or 'good') because morals are not natural but social: children are born morally neutral.

The newborn baby who cries and cries may make her parents feel bad but she is not being bad because she is not crying to get at them but to communicate with them. The one year old who keeps fiddling with the TV is not deliberately defying all those cries of 'leave it alone': she may not have understood; she may have forgotten; or she may just need to explore something she can see – and has seen adults doing.

Adults understand that children are born 'naturally' social. The people who care for them are more interesting and important to them than anything else.

Babies pay far more attention to faces than to toys; to voices than to music boxes or TV tunes. Before the end of their first year babies directly copy not just things adults do, but facial expressions and intonations.

It is accepted that children get their ideas of right and wrong, including their attitudes to violence, from important, caring adults, but they get them first and foremost from adult behaviour that they can see; only secondarily from adult words that they may not understand.

Teaching children how to behave depends on 'suiting the action to the words'. You cannot teach a toddler not to bite by biting her (whatever you may say) or teach a five year old not to hit other children by hitting him.

Everyone recognises that almost all small children *want* to behave well (because adult approval is important to them) and that when they do not, it is usually because they have not understood what is wanted of them, or the behaviour demands developments they have not yet achieved.

Young children make the same mistake again and again because they are slow to develop adult memory-competence and therefore cannot 'bear it in mind'.

Young children climb onto and into dangerous places without thinking how to get down or out because they often lack foresight, especially when excited and/or in a peer group.

They cannot even begin to acquire the ability to empathise with other children before the third year – and then only slowly. A child who cries when hit by other children is often amazed that those children cry when hit back; a child who snatches his sister's cake genuinely thinks it unfair when she takes his.

Negative indicators

- Adults believe 'nature' is more important than their own 'nurture': 'Babies are born full of original sin'.

- This child is: 'a monster'/'wicked'/'no better than his father'/'old enough to know better'.

▶ PRINCIPLE TWO
All discipline should be positive and children should be taught pro-social values and behaviour including in particular non-violent conflict resolution

Negative discipline takes violence in the relationships between adults and children for granted by focusing on 'bad behaviour'; expecting it; watching out for, and punishing it. In contrast, positive discipline leaves violence on the sidelines by focusing on 'good behaviour'; expecting it, making sure it is modelled, understood and achievable, and rewarding it.

Positive indicators

All adults who care for children accept the importance of according children the same human rights, courtesy and respect for feelings that they demand for themselves.

You seldom get more from a child than you give: if you do not listen to her, why should she listen to you? If you slap his hand when it goes where it shouldn't, why should he take care not to tread on your foot when it gets in his way?

Adults realise how easily adult power over dependent children can be mis-used in the name of discipline, and the importance of carefully protecting children's dawning sense of self and nurturing their self esteem.

The more a child is made to feel good about herself, the more she will want to be good. The more she is humiliated, made to feel stupid or tiresome, wicked or helpless, the less point she will see in trying to please.

When children's behaviour is unacceptable, adults criticise the behaviour *but not the* child*: 'your noise is giving me a headache', not 'you make me ill'.*

Adults accept that caring for children demands that they themselves behave in a (literally) exemplary fashion. Adults' non-violence, and use of non-violent conflict resolution, between each other as well as towards children, serves as a model of how people should behave towards each other. Being rough and careless with feelings is both a kind of violence in itself and an evoker of violence.

Being bad-tempered and unkind to children matters and so does exposing children to marital strife and, above all, family violence. Children take far more notice of what adults do than of what they say, so 'do as you would be done by' is good practical advice as well as ethical exhortation, whereas 'do as I say, not as I do' is neither.

All caring adults recognise that physical punishment is a direct exercise of physical violence *on* a child liable to provoke violence by the child. Being smacked, spanked or locked up sets an example to the punished child of violence successfully used by a larger person to impose his or her will on somebody smaller, as well as arousing feelings of anger and humiliation that are liable to be released in aggression.

Adults recognise that physical punishments do not evoke remorse but a 'fight or flight reaction' to being hurt.

A smacked child may long to hit back or to run away. He or she is unlikely to long to 'do better next time'.

Adults recognise that children who are hurt and humiliated by adults (against whom they dare not retaliate) may seek to restore their self-esteem and feel powerful and big by bullying smaller children, and perhaps by other forms of disruptive, violent and delinquent activities.

When a 10 year-old gets a spanking and takes it out on his six year old brother, whom does he get to hit? The 'kick the cat' syndrome is as familiar in daycare groups, playgroups and schools as it is in families. And it can be found in adult institutions too.

Even the 'mildest' physical punishments are not regarded as an option, even for the most serious offence or the most recalcitrant child.

Since nobody has the right to smack a child, anyone who loses their temper and slaps a hand, leg or bottom has an obligation to admit that they were wrong and say 'sorry' just as they would if they came to blows in a quarrel with another adult.

Adults do not seek alternative punishments to replace physical ones but to make all formal punishments redundant. Waiting for children to do wrong and then punishing them is ineffective because it is impossible to make children feel like being good by telling them they are bad; to help them control anger, tantrums or aggressive behaviour by being angry; to teach them to be gentle by being rough; or to reform 'attention-seekers' by ignoring them.

If a five year old always spills food down his front, which is more likely to persuade him to take more care when he is eating: being compelled to wear a baby's bib or being offered a nice clean tee-shirt?

Adults believe that rewards make more contribution to discipline than punishments as well as reducing the potential for violence. Motivating children to make the efforts involved in 'good behaviour' depends on making those efforts worth their while.

Rewards do not have to be consumer items. Anything that makes a child feel good serves as a reward. Praise and hugs do as much for self-esteem as the sweets and treats that stand for them.

Adults try to pay even more attention to children who are behaving acceptably than to children who are not. They understand that if most of their attention is devoted to children who are being disruptive, anti-social or violent – leaving better-behaved children ignored – anti-social behaviour and violence is likely to escalate because many children will choose angry attention over none at all.

'Let sleeping dogs lie' may be good advice for canines but it is liable to provoke humans. If a child must clamour, whine, quarrel with other children and pull the dog's tail to get adults to take notice of her, she will. Children should get adult attention most easily by being a pleasure rather than a pain, and if they are ever to be ignored it should be when they are being unco-operative.

Adults believe that it is possible and desirable to teach children pro-social values and behaviour, and take every opportunity to help them empathise with each other and consider the social context of their own actions and wants.

A toddler cannot be forced to put himself in others' shoes until he is mature enough, but once he can do it, he can be helped to do it. A two year old does not know that he and his friend can both play with the playdough if they share, and he doesn't know how to share either. He can learn. Three- and four year olds don't know 'by instinct' that taking turns means that everyone gets a turn: they need to find out and can be shown.

Adults take particular care to demonstrate and teach non-violent social interaction and especially non-violent conflict-resolution.

Learning to be 'nice' or 'good' often means that a child must learn to act against her own best interests: if she does not snatch the last cake, she will not get to eat it. If he does not hit his friend on the head with that toy brick, the friend may snatch it. It is up to adults to balance cakes and toys with praise, hugs, gold stars or whatever constitutes the 'feel-good factor' in their particular group.

Adults take trouble to organise environments and activities to maximise individual choice and minimise interference with others, and thus the risk of aggressive or defensive violence.

Whether it is a family living room or car, or a classroom, available space can and must be organised so that there is room for all the children and all their activities, and so that the more active people and games do not appear to have priority.

Negative indicators

- Children are unhappy.

- Personalities and personal characteristics of children are criticised when they misbehave: children earn labels such as 'troublemaker' more easily than they lose them.; some categories of children (eg girls) are regarded as 'easier' than others (e.g. 'terrible twos').

- Punishment is regarded as a *sine qua non* of discipline.

- Violent and humiliating punishments are used or threatened – smacking, slapping, shaking, naughty chairs; 'wait till your father gets home'.

- Adult attention is scarce overall and most readily attracted by violent, destructive or disruptive behaviour.

- Children are exhorted to be nice to each other but are not taught what that means or how to achieve it.

- Children often lose out by being 'nice' or 'good'.

- Playgrounds and playrooms are overrun by physically active children and games, leaving little space for those who are smaller or quieter.

▶ PRINCIPLE THREE
Non-violence should be clearly and consistently preferred and promoted

This principle goes beyond the obvious because although most individuals and organisations express a preference for non-violence in society as a whole as well as in their own affairs, violent attitudes and behaviour are not always recognised or consistently rejected.

Adults make it clear to children (in their own behaviour as well as in words) that all interpersonal violence is disapproved of on principle. Disapproval of the behaviour is not conditional on its effects. It is recognised, for example, that it is always wrong for one child to assault another.

Violence in the home, even if it is not directed at children, will almost always be reflected in their behaviour to each other; likewise children at school will not respect each others' differences if teachers make certain children butts.

Both men and women take trouble to separate ideas about masculinity from the concepts of personal 'toughness' that often relate to violence.

If boys are taught that they can't cry when their sisters can, it's not surprising if they hit instead. 'Boys will be boys' only if we permit, even encourage, macho attitudes and behaviour.

Enthusiasm for physical sport is balanced by appreciation of non-physical activities, both competitive and otherwise.

Children cannot value the chess team's success as highly as the football team's, unless adults truly regard it as equally creditable.

Children are taught to 'stand up for themselves' only if they can do so without being either aggressor or victim in a violent exchange. The prospect of violence is always a proper reason to seek adult help.

It is important to get the phrase 'telling tales' out of language and folklore. As long as it is current, children know that seeking help is not encouraged, approved or even accepted by all adults. Children cannot feel, let alone be, safe from bullying if they risk scorn for seeking adult help.

Adults make no attempts to stop *conflict* between children; such attempts are useless because conflicts exist. Instead, conflicts are accepted and children are shown how to resolve them *without violence*.

It is useless to tell children not to fight (or snatch and grab, hit or kick) without giving them effective alternative ways of getting what they want or holding on to what they have. All children should be taught to use (and to respond to) verbal requests and protests. If children are to listen to each other, they must be confident that adults will listen to them.

Negative indicators

- Children are unhappy.

- Adults do not consistently model for children the non-violent techniques they try to teach to them.

- Tolerant, even amused attitudes are sometimes taken to physical aggression (especially in boys if both sexes are present), unless one child is hurt enough to be assigned the formal role of victim.

- Some adults strike, admire or tolerate macho attitudes (in children, or between adults).

- Success in competitive sport is given disproportionate importance compared with non-physical kinds of personal achievement.

- Adults admire children who 'stand up for themselves' and therefore implicitly disapprove those who try to avoid violence by seeking help.

- Violent entertainment and other violent and/or discriminatory media images are enjoyed, or at least unquestioningly accepted, by adults.

- Fights between children are stopped (and perhaps formal apologies exacted) without the cause of the problem being explored and resolved.

▶ PRINCIPLE FOUR
Adults should take responsibility not only for protecting children from violence done to them, but also for preventing violence done by them

Although adults perpetrate the extremes of violence in society, adults also represent children's only hope of safety from it, because without adult supervision and control, children's lives can be dominated by each other's violence. Like all mammals, humans are born with weapons – teeth and nails – to defend themselves and their interests, and the aggressive drive to use them. Every individual has to learn to control and direct that vital aggression into channels which his or her society regards as positive and creative. Some people never achieve that, even in adulthood. And even those who abhor personal violence as children need authoritative and powerful adult support if they are to resist the dual pressures of terrifying threat and exciting promise generated by groups of adolescent peers.

Because all the adults who care for children take the possibility of bullying, and their duty to protect children from it, seriously, children who are reluctant to separate from parent-figures to join in a group are never hurried but offered adult support and constant adult protection until they themselves move willingly away.

Adults will not separate children forcibly. Forcible separation does violence to a child's secure dependence and to his dawning sense of competence and control over what happens in his life. His helplessness may lead him to assert himself violently.

While it is true that a small child who separates reluctantly may seem 'fine as soon as you've left', nobody should assume that it will be, or was so. Someone who knows the child well should, ideally, look in after a few minutes, without being seen by him. And however happy he seems, the childcare worker or teacher should stay in close contact and try to ensure that the child's private experience does not belie his public armour.

Adults will never leave children without the protection of adult supervision. Although responsibility for particular children may pass from one adult to the other during the day, the safety of *all* the children is the responsibility of *all* the adults who therefore dovetail their schedules and make emergency cover a priority.

Although children under five are seldom left completely without adult supervision, some 'latchkey children', and children left to 'take care of themselves' during school holidays are only a little older. They are known to be at increased risk of being victims of many kinds of violence, including road and domestic accidents and gang-assaults. They are also known to be at increased risk of gang-membership and delinquency.

Adults are aware that adult supervision becomes inadequate and the risk of bullying and violently aggressive play goes up if there are too few available adults for the numbers of children and the complexity of the environment.

Many children, especially those in inappropriately large groups for their ages, dread 'free play' in school playgrounds, perceiving it as violent, and out of the control of the available adults. Many fear 'wet playtimes' even more because they may be in different rooms from adults and out of sight.

Whether they are with children within a family, an informal group, or a care or education system, the adults are aware that the priority is to provide a space within which each and every child feels comfortable.

Whatever its other qualities, a group within which children are, or feel themselves to be, unpopular or at risk cannot be the right place for them. Rejection easily becomes emotional abuse and in small children in particular, emotional abuse often goes with physical violence towards, as well as from, the victim.

Adults are so aware of the importance to children of being in a setting where they can feel liked and appreciated that they are able to acknowledge the possibility – and support colleagues or friends who acknowledge the fact – of personality clashes between themselves and a child, and the consequent need to re-organise groups or classes.

The assumption that adults 'love children' en masse, or 'like them all the same' means that any trouble between adults and children is blamed on children. However much an adult dislikes or is disturbed by a particular child, it is almost impossible to admit to such feelings and ask for help from colleagues before pressure builds up towards violence.

Adults recognise the power that caretakers or teachers inevitably have over children's lives and the possibilities not only of abuse but also of insensitivity to bullying. They therefore agree to provide every child with an adult outside the group in whom he or she can confide, and an absolute right to confide without offence or risk of being further 'picked on' for doing so.

Such adult confidants can be vitally important to the child who finds herself with the 'wrong' class teacher at day school; almost literally life-saving to the child with the wrong caring adult in boarding school, in residential or foster care, or even at home. It can also be vital when older children rather than adults are put in charge. The notorious abuses of the public school 'fagging' system are now rare, but any 'prefect system' carries the risk of legitimated bullying, while older siblings, foster-, half- and step-siblings sometimes terrorise younger ones when they are left alone at home.

All the adults are concerned about the possible effects on children of exposure to violent material on the media. While not necessarily able, or willing, to control what children see on TV or on video, all make it their business to be familiar with the material to which children have access; to enforce all regulations designed to protect children from 'unsuitable' material; to discuss violent or otherwise disturbing stories and images with children, and to offer non-violent equivalents wherever they can.

There are legitimate arguments against censorship, but there are none for leaving children to cope, unsupported, with whatever material comes their way.

Negative indicators

- Children are unhappy.

- Adults do not acknowledge children's right to be, and to feel, safe, or do not fully accept their own responsibility for guaranteeing it.

- Unpopular or solitary children are regarded as 'misfits' rather than as victims.

- Children have no appeal against adult injustice or incompatibility.

- Children are regularly left without effective adult supervision or companionship.

- Instead of adequate adult supervision being provided, some children are given power and authority over others.

- Supervising adults do not concern themselves with children's exposure to violent entertainment and media images.

Sources of help and advice

Every adult who has charge of children (parent, teacher, caregiver, careworker) should have access to an outside adviser and feel able to consult, without loss of personal or professional dignity, if they feel driven towards emotional and/or physical violence towards a child or feel that a child's aggression is liable to erupt into violence. (*The developed checklists will contain detailed advice on when and where to go for advice and support*).

The UN Convention on the Rights of the Child

Setting an agenda for policy development on violence involving children

The UN Convention on the Rights of the Child is the first detailed international treaty to provide comprehensive minimum standards for treatment of the world's children. By June 1995 175 countries had ratified the Convention. The UK did so in December 1991, thus committing itself to making the rights in the Convention a reality for the UK's 13.2 million children and young people under the age of 18. The Convention provides a valuable framework for policy development and one which the Government is now committed to implementing.

The Commission on Children and Violence agreed that it would base its recommendations not only on research into the antecedents of violence, but also on the principles and standards of the Convention, as has been the case with other recent projects of the Gulbenkian Foundation's Social Welfare programme.

Of course, there are some ways in which UK law and practice already exceeds the demands of the Convention, which was drafted for worldwide application and therefore provides no more than minimum standards. As Article 41 emphasises, the Convention does not affect any other provisions, in domestic law or other international law, which are 'more conducive to the realisation of the rights of the child'.

The Convention upholds clearly children's rights to physical integrity, to protection from 'all forms of physical or mental violence'. The following summary sets out a framework of principles relevant to violence prevention on which recommendations can be built.

Relevant provisions in the Convention

The Convention defines 'child' as every person under the age of 18.

Basic principles

Equal rights, special care
The preamble to the Convention emphasises the 'equal and inalienable rights of all members of the human family', and also children's rights to 'special care and assistance'.

No discrimination
Article 2 insists that all the rights in the Convention must be available

'without discrimination of any kind, irrespective of the child's or his or her parent's or legal guardian's race, colour, sex, language, religion, political or other opinion, national, ethnic or social origin, property, disability, birth or other status'.

In reviewing the implications of other Articles, this principle must be applied throughout.

Best interests
Article 3 insists that

'In all actions concerning children, whether undertaken by public or private social welfare institutions, courts of law, administrative authorities or legislative bodies, the best interests of the child must be a primary consideration'.

Children's views
Article 12 insists on enabling the child to be an active participant:

'1 States Parties shall assure to the child who is capable of forming his or her own views the right to express those views freely in all actions affecting the child, the views of the child being given due weight in accordance with the age and maturity of the child.

'2 For this purpose, the child shall in particular be provided the opportunity to be heard in any judicial and administrative proceedings affecting the child, either directly, or through a representative or an appropriate body, in a manner consistent with the procedural rules of national law'.

Physical and personal integrity
Article 19 goes beyond children's rights to protection from abuse, to assert their right to personal integrity, to protection against 'all forms of physical or mental violence':

'1 States Parties shall take all appropriate legislative, administrative, social and educational measures to protect the child from all forms of physical or mental violence, injury or abuse, neglect or negligent treatment, maltreatment or exploitation including sexual abuse, while in the care of parent(s), legal guardian(s) or any other person who has the care of the child.

'2 Such protective measures should, as appropriate, include effective procedures for the establishment of social programmes to provide necessary support for the child and for those who have the care of the child, as well as for other forms of prevention and for identification, reporting, referral, investigation, treatment and follow-up of instances of child maltreatment described heretofore, and, as appropriate, for judicial involvement'.

In addition, article 37 (a) insists that states parties ensure that

'No child shall be subjected to torture or other cruel, inhuman or degrading treatment or punishment ...'

And article 28(2) emphasises that

'States Parties shall take all appropriate steps to ensure that school discipline is administered in a manner consistent with the child's human dignity and in conformity with the present Convention'.

Also in connection with the right to physical integrity, article 24(3) obliges states

'to take all effective and appropriate measures with a view to abolishing traditional practices prejudicial to the health of children'.

This was drafted with particular reference to the practice of female circumcision, genital mutilation of girls and young women, and other practices which may be based on cultural or religious tradition, but which threaten the physical integrity and/or health of the child.

Other provisions cover sexual exploitation (article 34), sale, trafficking and abduction (article 35), other forms of exploitation (article 36) and armed conflicts (article 38).

Restriction of liberty

Article 37:

'(b) No child shall be deprived of his or her liberty unlawfully or arbitrarily. The arrest, detention or imprisonment of a child shall be in conformity with the law and shall be used only as a measure of last resort and for the shortest appropriate period of time;

'(c) Every child deprived of liberty shall be treated with humanity and respect for the inherent dignity of the human person, and in a manner which takes into account the needs of persons of his or her age. In particular every child deprived of liberty shall be separated from adults unless it is considered in the child's best interest not to do so and shall have the right to maintain contact with his or her family through correspondence and visits, save in exceptional circumstances*...'

(*When it ratified the Convention, the Government made a reservation indicating only qualified acceptance of this article, stating: 'Where at any time there is a lack of suitable accommodation or adequate facilities for a particular individual in any institution in which young offenders are detained, or where the mixing of adults and children is deemed to be mutually beneficial, the United Kingdom reserves the right not to apply Article 37(c) in so far as those provisions require children who are detained to be accommodated separately from adults.')

Article 40:

'1 States Parties recognise the right of every child alleged as, accused of, or recognised as having infringed the penal law to be treated in a manner consistent with the protection of the child's sense of dignity and worth, which reinforces the child's respect for the human rights and fundamental freedoms of others and which takes into account the child's age and the desirability of promoting the child's reintegration and the child's assuming a constructive role in society ...' (Article 40 goes on to provide a detailed framework for the administration of juvenile justice).

Parental care

Article 5 requires states to respect the

'responsibilities, rights and duties of parents or, where applicable, the members of the extended family or community as provided for by local custom, legal guardians or other persons legally responsible for the child, to provide, in a manner consistent with the evolving capacities of the child, appropriate direction and guidance in the exercise by the child of the rights recognised in the present Convention'.

Article 18 also emphasises parental

'responsibilities for the upbringing and development of the child. Parents, or as the case may be, legal guardians, have the primary responsibility for the upbringing and development of the child. The best interests of the child will be their basic concern ...'

It goes on to insist on States Parties providing appropriate assistance to parents and guardians.

Separation from parents

Separation of children from their parents, for protection from abuse or other reasons, is subject to the principles in article 9:

'1 States Parties shall ensure that a child shall not be separated from his or her parents against their will, except when competent authorities subject to judicial review determine, in accordance with applicable law and procedures, that such separation is necessary for the best interests of the child. Such determination may be necessary in a particular case such as one involving abuse or neglect of the child by the parents, or one where the parents are living separately and a decision must be made as to the child's place of residence.

'2 In any proceedings pursuant to paragraph 1 of the present article, all interested parties shall be given an opportunity to participate in the proceedings and make their views known.

'3 States Parties shall respect the right of the child who is separated from one or both parents to maintain personal relations and direct contact with both parents on a regular basis, except if it is contrary to the child's best interests ...'

And under article 20,

'1 A child temporarily or permanently deprived of his or her family environment, or in whose own best interests cannot be allowed to remain in that environment, shall be entitled to special protection and assistance provided by the State:

'2 States Parties shall in accordance with their national laws ensure alternative care for such a child.

'3 Such care could include, *inter alia*, foster placement, *Kafalah* of Islamic law, adoption, or if necessary placement in suitable institutions for the care of children. When considering solutions, due regard shall be paid to the desirability of continuity in a child's upbringing and to the child's ethnic, religious, cultural and linguistic background'.

Standards for institutions, services and facilities
Article 3(3):

> 'States Parties shall ensure that the institutions, services and facilities responsible for the care or protection of children shall conform with the standards established by competent authorities, particularly in the areas of safety, health, in the number and suitability of their staff, as well as competent supervision.'

Read together with articles 2(1) and 3(1), this emphasises the need for consistent and non-discriminatory standards for institutions, services and facilities, in which the best interests of all affected children are a primary consideration.

Other articles and issues

Right to periodic review
Article 25:

> 'States Parties recognise the right of a child who has been placed by the competent authorities for the purposes of care, protection or treatment of his or her physical or mental health, to a periodic review of the treatment provided to the child and all other circumstances relevant to his or her placement'.

Rehabilitation
Under article 39, States Parties must promote the

> 'physical and psychological recovery and social reintegration of a child victim of any form of neglect, exploitation, or abuse; torture or any other form of cruel, inhuman or degrading treatment or punishment, or armed conflicts. Such recovery and reintegration shall take place in an environment which fosters the health, self-respect and dignity of the child'.

The state of our knowledge on prevalence of violence involving children in the UK

PART ONE
Violence to children and young people

Children suffer far more violent victimisations than do adults. Any summary of national statistics on violence to 'children', defined as from birth to 18, blurs the enormous heterogeneity of childhood. A two year old probably has less in common with a 16 year old, other than being a 'child', than with an 82 year old. Their uniquely dependent status renders young children more vulnerable to conventional crimes such as homicide and assault; to family violence including violent punishments, sexual abuse by parents and others, and assaults by siblings; to institutional violence including in particular bullying in schools; and to some forms of violence specific to children, such as family abduction. There are also marked gender differences: boys are more vulnerable than girls to physical abuse and non-family assaults whilst girls are more vulnerable than boys to sexual abuse.[1]

An analysis of violence to children suggested by two American commentators in 1994 defined three broad categories of victimisation: the 'extraordinary', such as homicides, which affects a very small group of children; the 'acute', such as physical abuse, which affects a larger, but still minority group of children; and the 'pandemic', such as physical punishment and sibling assault, which affects most children.[2] They were able to provide national statistics for the USA for the following types of victimisation:

Extraordinary: Homicide
                Abduction homicide
                Non-family abduction

Acute: Psychological maltreatment
                Family abduction
                Sexual abuse
                Neglect
                Physical abuse
                Rape

Pandemic: Robbery
                Vandalism
                Assault
                Theft
                Physical punishment
                Sibling assaults

These were arranged in increasing order of incidence from 0.03 per 1,000 children (child victims of homicide) to 800 per 1,000 children (victims of sibling assaults).

The statistics for the 'extraordinary' and 'acute' categories of victimisation were largely drawn from agency records, as they would be in the UK, whereas the 'pandemic' were drawn from self reports or caretaker reports to large scale surveys such as the US National Crime Survey and the US National Youth Survey.[3] There have been a number of national incidence surveys conducted in the USA in which violent behaviour has been assessed. These include the two *National family violence surveys* in 1975 and 1985, the *National youth survey* and the *National incidence study of missing, abducted, runaway and thrown away children*, 1990.[4] These have provided a unique picture of the pandemic nature of violence within the family and to children, unavailable through statistics of cases which come to official notice.

Few such widespread surveys have been conducted in the UK, but there is an increasing volume of information available from which to begin to draw up a sketchy picture of the overall levels of violence to children. We attempt this in the graphic below, which is based on information from the various sources detailed in the following section (unfortunately we were unable within the Commission's resources to gather together comprehensive figures for the whole of the UK; unless otherwise stated statistics are for England and Wales only).

Incidence of violence to children

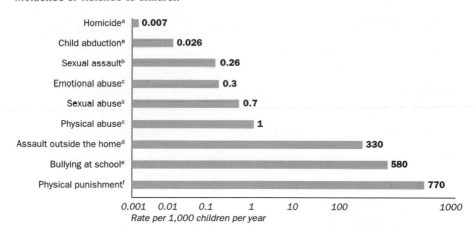

a   Offences currently recorded as homicide, and recorded as child abduction in England and Wales in 1993, from *Criminal Statistics England and Wales 1993*, Home Office, HMSO London 1994.
b   Offences of unlawful sexual intercourse with a girl under 13; unlawful sexual intercourse with a girl under 16 and gross indecency witrh a child recorded by police, England and Wales, 1993, from *Criminal Statistics* – see a.
c   *Children and Young People on Child Protection Registers year ending 31 March 1994*, England, Department of Health 1995; numbers registered in year per 1,000 children.
d   *British Crime Survey 1992*, Home Office, HMSO: 12-15 year olds in England and Wales reporting assaults over six/eightmonth period, 1991/2.
e   *Social Focus on Children*, Central Statistical Office, HMSO 1994: Table 2.41: 11 year olds reported bullying 'once or twice', 'quite often' or 'often' in school year 1992 (National Foundation for Educational Research).
f   *Community Study of Physical Violence to Children in the Home and Associated Variables*, Marjorie Smith, Thomas Coram Research Unit, London, 1995: children hit in the last year.

Physical violence to children in their homes

A recent major *Community study of physical violence to children in the home and associated variables* gives rates for prevalence of physical punishment and other violent treatment of children. This research was carried out between 1991 and 1994, but by June 1995 only two short papers had been published.[5] The study involved very detailed interviews with mothers of one-, four-, seven- and eleven year old children, a smaller sample of fathers and some of the children themselves, in more than 400 randomly selected families (there was a 20 per cent refusal rate among families approached to take part). Like all such interview research, it probably provides an underestimate of the real situation, in that parents are most unlikely to exaggerate violent treatment of their children.

The rates of severe punishment of children by mothers revealed in the study are high (the figures will be even higher when fathers' punishments are taken into account): 15 per cent of children had experienced 'severe' punishment, and a quarter of seven year olds. The vast majority of cases of severe punishment – 88 per cent – involved hitting the child, and children more frequently hit were more likely to have experienced other forms of physical punishment. 'Severe' punishment was defined as punishment involving 'the intention or potential to cause injury or psychological damage, use of implements, repeated actions or over a long period of time'. 'Mild' punishment was defined as involving 'no intention to harm, including psychological harm, no use of implements, no repeated actions, no prolonged effect or action'. 'Moderate' punishment was intermediate between mild and severe.

Severity of hitting (ever)

Severe incidents by punishment type **Frequency of hitting, by age group**

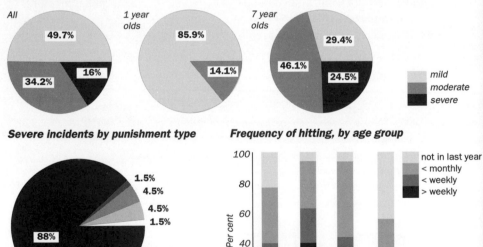

from *Community study of physical violence to children in the home and associated variables*, Marjorie Smith, Thomas Coram Research Unit, London 1995.

Overall, the large majority of children (91 per cent) had already been hit, and three quarters of them in the last year (77 per cent). Physical restraints and punishment by example had been experienced by over 40 per cent of the children, and 12 per cent had experienced an ingestion ('physical restraint' included: 'wipe face with cold flannel, physically restrain child, cold bath/shower, hand/object over mouth, place head under water, choke, shake, push/shove, throw'; 'punishment by example' included: 'pulling hair, scratch, pinch, bite/nip/chew, Chinese burn, burn/scald, put in cold water, use knife/scissors, trap in door, pull nails out'; 'ingestion' included: 'forced to eat food, make eat something nasty (eg mustard sandwiches), force to drink salt water, wash mouth out with soap and water, force to drink poisonous or dangerous substances').

Of the one year old children studied, 75 per cent had already been smacked, and 14 per cent of the punishment incidents involved 'moderate' hitting. Frequency of hitting declined with age: 38 per cent of children aged four, and 27 per cent of children aged seven were hit more than once a week, compared with 3 per cent of 11 year old children (for details of effects of variables on violence to children as revealed in the study, see section 1, page 51).

In addition, a 1994 national survey of 1,034 adults aged 18-45 years in the UK, commissioned by the NSPCC, asked about their childhood experiences of punishment. Around 80 per cent of them had been physically punished in childhood, 16 per cent constantly or frequently.[6]

There appears to be no national data available on assaults by siblings in the home.

Sexual abuse of children

The only sources of information on sexual abuse of children in the home are from prevalence studies involving interviews with adults about childhood experiences, and from statistics of children placed on child protection registers and statistics of convictions for sexual offences.

The 1994 survey of childhood experiences commissioned by the NSPCC found that 11 per cent of the nationally representative group of adult respondents reported sexual abuse involving physical contact during their childhood, and of these one-third experienced abuse by relatives. Abuse involving physical contact usually (that is, in more than two-thirds of reported incidents) occurred either in the child's home or the abuser's home. For one in three of victims, their first experience of sexual abuse occurred before they were 11; for only 15 per cent of them did the first experience occur after they were 15. Girls were three times as likely as boys to have experienced almost all forms of sexual abuse involving physical contact.[7]

Child abduction

There were 275 notifiable offences of abduction recorded by the police in 1993, more than six times the number in 1983.[8]

Children placed on child protection registers

Statistics of children placed on Child Protection Registers provide another indication of levels of violence to children in their home, but of course not a complete picture. The definition of child abuse in policy and practice tends to condone a high level of physical and mental violence to children, much of it justified as 'reasonable chastisement'. The finding (see above) that almost one in six children has been 'severely' physically punished contrasts with the very much smaller proportion placed on registers because of concerns about physical injury. A small number of children are placed on registers because of suspicions of abuse or neglect, which later prove to be groundless. A very small number are placed on registers because of abuse or suspected abuse outside the home. Cases have to be seen to be reported. Once reported they have to be assessed as to whether or not they require registration. If registration is agreed then resources will have to be provided. Each of these steps involves the possibility of bias and the potential for excluding actual cases of abuse. Recent research has helped to clarify the processes involved and enable some attempt at quantification.[9]

There were 36,510 children on child protection registers in England and Wales on March 31 1994, representing 3.1 per 1,000 of all children under 18. The most common reason was physical injury (defined as 'Actual or likely physical injury to a child, or failure to prevent physical injury (or suffering) to a child including deliberate poisoning, suffocation and Munchausen's Syndrome by Proxy'). Girls were more likely than boys to be on the register because of sexual abuse – roughly a third of the girls as compared with a fifth of the boys.[10]

Bullying

There is some national UK data available on bullying in schools, another pandemic problem affecting children. A survey of 11- and 13 year old school children in England and Wales provided data on the incidence of bullying. Nearly 15 per cent of 11 year olds and eight per cent of 13 year olds said they were the victim of bullying at school 'often' or 'quite often' in the last year.[11] Bullying is also endemic in young offender institutions, and found in child care and other institutions.

Assaults and harassment outside the home

The British Crime Surveys have provided more general data on assaults, but have largely concerned themselves with adults. But the 1992 survey also asked a random sample of around 1,000 children aged 12-15 in England and Wales about their experience of crimes and harassment, outside the home, during the previous six to eight months. This is one of the very few national surveys to review some aspects of pandemic violence to children by talking to children themselves about their experiences. A third of the children reported some form of assault, one in five reported harassment by young people, and just under one in five harassment by adults (some of these assaults are presumably school bullying incidents). One in 20 reported sexual harassment by men. The survey of childhood experiences reported above provides some information on sexual abuse outside the home, of which up to a third appears to be by people not known to the child.[12] Only a small proportion of the incidents reported in the Crime Survey were thought to be criminal; about one in 10 had been reported to the police.[13] A national survey of children aged 10-16 years in the USA found a quarter of the completed assaults experienced by the survey children had been by family members.[14] Thus the omission of assaults and harassment within the family from the 1992 British Crime Survey seriously underestimates the overall level of assaults to children.

Offences currently recorded as homicide by age of victim, England and Wales 1993

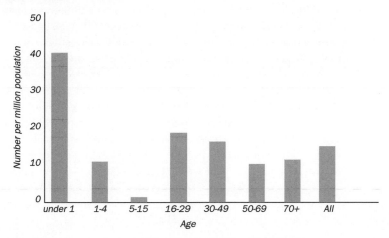

from *Criminal Statistics England and Wales 1993*, Home Office, HMSO, 1994.

Homicide

The younger children are, the more dependent and vulnerable they are. The American Humane Association entitled one of its reports on child abuse *Too Young to Run* in recognition of the dependency of the youngest children on their caretakers, regardless of how abusive they might be. This increased vulnerability of the youngest age groups is shown most dramatically in the figures for child homicides. Children aged less than one year are nearly four times as likely to be a victim of homicide than the national average (the numbers involved are of course small), whereas 5-15 year olds are the least likely to be victims. The overwhelming majority of infant homicide victims are killed by their parents.[15]

Among the infant homicide victims there are more male than female infants.[16]

Official homicide figures represent the most clear-cut and extreme cases of violence to children. It should also be recognised that there are less clear-cut cases, which also lead to the deaths of children but which are not recorded as homicides. These include cases where a child dies from natural causes such as bronchopneumonia, but where persistent violence may have weakened their resistance to the infection. Adelstein et al analysed all the conditions mentioned on the 1975 death certificates of children where the main cause of death was non-violent, and found some 50 deaths where violence had played an underlying contributory part.[17] There are also cases of misdiagnosed deaths. Studies on cot deaths have found between one and nine per cent of cases where there was an unproved suspicion of smothering.[18]

Crimes of violence including sexual assaults against children

What holds for homicide figures is also true of all other criminal statistics of crimes of violence and sexual assaults against children: the recorded figures are an under-representation of the actual crimes. Criminal statistics are seldom analysed by age of victim, so it is not possible to determine accurately what proportion of convictions for violence against the person involved assaults on children. A special data collection exercise by the Home Office in 1988 estimated that 195 offenders had been sentenced for crimes of violence against children aged under 17 in the year.[19] In 1992, 450 people were proceeded against in magistrates' courts for the indictable offence of 'cruelty to, or neglect of children': 148 were cautioned and 212 found guilty. There is some difficulty in extracting accurate figures of prosecutions and convictions for sexual assaults on children because of inadequate recording. The following figures for convictions for child sex offences in England and Wales in 1991 were given in a parliamentary answer: buggery with a boy aged under 16 or with a woman or animal, 168; attempted buggery with a boy aged under 16 or with a woman or animal, 26; indecent assault on a male aged under 16 years, 351; indecent assault on a female aged under 16, 1,469; unlawful sexual intercourse with a girl aged under 13, 105; unlawful sexual intercourse with a girl aged under 16, 223; incest with a girl under 13, 68; gross indecency with children, 219. These figures, together with a small number of convictions for other related sex offences give a total of 2,643.[20]

The Commission on Children and Violence acknowledges with thanks the assistance of Susan J Creighton, Senior Research Officer, NSPCC, with the preparation of the above summary.

PART TWO
Violence by children and young people

Statistics on violence *by* children and young people are more readily available than information on violence *to* them. Official criminal statistics are still the major source of information, and do not of course provide a full picture.

Violent crime by children and young people

Most crime is not violent: for example, of all crime recorded by the police in England and Wales in 1992 (5,592,000 offences) just five per cent was violent. A juvenile is defined as being between the ages of 10 and 17 inclusive (children aged under 10 in England, Wales and Northern Ireland, and under eight in Scotland are below the age of criminal responsibility and not dealt with by criminal courts). The peak age for all offending is 18 for males and 15 for females. Of the 168,000 known juvenile offenders in England and Wales in 1993, 19,700 were found guilty or cautioned for violent offences (violence against the person, sexual offences and robbery), which represents approximately four per thousand of the 10-17 age group. Of all offences (excluding summary motoring offences) committed by young offenders in 1993, for males 9 per cent were offences of violence against the person, and for females 12 per cent.[21] Crime and particularly violent crime is predominantly a male activity: for every known female offender there are around four known male offenders. The differential involvement by males and females is highest for violent and sexual offences, and for burglary.

The overall offending rate per 100,000 of the 10-17 year old population has fallen for males from 7,700 in 1985 to 5,300 in 1993, and for females from 1,700 to 1,400. A Home Office briefing on crime by young offenders comments:

'The fall in the offending rate and a demographic fall in the numbers in the population of 10 to 17 year olds have led to a fall in the number of youth offenders of 39 per cent for males from a peak of 219,100 in 1985 to 134,000 in 1993, and by 25 per cent for females, from 45,100 to 34,000.'

(The briefing also emphasises that relatively few males account for a large proportion of convictions. The one per cent of males born in 1973 who were convicted of six or more convictions before the age of 17, accounted for 60 per cent of all convictions for that age group).

The numbers of 10-17 year old male offenders found guilty or cautioned for offences of violence against the person fell from 12,800 to 12,300 between 1985 and 1993 (although within the 10-13 age group, there was an increase from 1,500 to 2,100); for females aged 10-17 there was an increase from 2,500 to 3,700. Overall the offending rate for offences of violence against the person increased from approximately 267/100,000 in 1985 to 324/100,000 in 1993.[22]

Homicide
According to Home Office statistics the number of juvenile offenders receiving section 53(1) orders for homicide or murder remained relatively constant until 1988 at around 20 a year. It dropped to 11 in 1992.[23]

Sexual offences
Known sexual offences in 1992 represented one per cent of overall offences for the male 10-13 age group, two per cent for 14-16 year-olds and one per cent for 17-20 year-olds. There is no percentage level quoted for female sexual offences. Various surveys have suggested that up to a third of child sexual abuse (much of it not reported to the police) is committed by the under-21 age group.[24] An analysis by the Home Office of all offenders cautioned or found guilty of sexual offences in 1989 found that 32 per cent were under the age of 21, and 17 per cent under the age of 16.[25]

Car crime
The 1992 British Crime Survey found that one in five car owners were the victims of car crime in 1991. By no means all car crime comes within the Commission's definition of violence, but some does. Out of 5,476,000 offences involving cars, 517,000 offences were thefts of cars but there is no indication of the levels of violence involved in or resulting from those thefts. The majority of offenders are male (96 per cent).[26] Under the new (1 April 1992) Aggravated Vehicle Taking Act, out of a total of 1,473 offences (representing just three per cent of overall car crime) 79 per cent were by juvenile offenders.

Robbery
In 1992 a total of 3,440 offences were carried out by juveniles aged 10-16.

Crime surveys
Surveys of self-reported crime show that the great majority of crime goes unreported. They suggest that only about 25 per cent of violent offences against the person are recorded by the police. The first comprehensive, nationally representative study of

self-reported offending by juveniles and young adults aged 14 to 21 in England and Wales was commissioned by the Home Office Research and Planning Unit in 1992, as part of a study of offending patterns and desistance from offending. The survey also provides, for the first time in this country, comparative data on self reported offending among young people from different ethnic groups.

Analysis of the first results of the data indicates that 66 per cent of these 14-21 year-old young people reported that they had offended in some way; about 9 per cent admitted an offence of violence against the person. Less than half (44 per cent) reported offending in the 12 months prior to the survey. Of these, 3 per cent reported offences of violence against the person – that is, 1.3 per cent of all the 14-21 year olds admitted an offence of violence against the person within the last year. Most of those who reported offending said they did so infrequently.[27]

A recent comparative study of self-reported offending by juveniles in five European countries clearly indicates that England and Wales show comparatively low rates of overall delinquency and particularly low rates of violent behaviour – around half the level reported by juveniles in the other four countries.[28]

Prevalence of three categories of self-reported delinquent behaviour by juveniles in five countries (last 12 months) (in %)

	Property	Violence	Drugs
Netherlands	29.5	29.3	15.3
England and Wales	16	15.8	25.9
Portugal	21.4	29.5	11.3
Switzerland	33.5	29.1	20.9
Spain	20.1	34.5	15.4

Prevalence of four violent acts in five countries (last 12 months) (in %)

	Vandalism	Carrying weapon	Group fights esp in riots	Beating up non-family
Netherlands	12.6	15.4	10.1	2.5
England and Wales	3.5	9.4	6.3	1.4
Portugal	16.1	10.8	11.1	2.5
Switzerland	17	11.2	8.8	0.9
Spain	16.3	8.4	17.2	2.3

From *Delinquent behaviour among young people in the western world: first results of the international self-report delinquency study*, ed Josine Junger-Tas and others, Kugler Publications Amsterdam, 1994.

Children's involvement in violence in the home and institutional violence

There have been some small scale studies on the levels of violence by children against other children and adults responsible for them but apart from statistics on bullying in schools (see Part One above, page 260) there appears to be no significant information on prevalence.

Self-destructive violence

Suicide

While overall the suicide rate has dropped slightly over the last decade, and the highest rates of suicide are in the 25-54 and over-85 age groups, there has been a clear increase in deaths from suicide and self-inflicted injury among young men in the UK aged between 15 and 24, from 320 (7 per 100,000) in 1982 to 500 (12 per 100,000) in 1992.[29] For this age group of males, suicide is second only to accidents as a major cause of death. A further analysis published in 1994 found that the particular and only age group to show an increase since the 1970s is males aged 15-19, with no increase in the 10-14 age band.[30] There are very few suicides by children under 15. As with other statistics of violence, there are concerns that official figures may understate the problem, with the causes of a lot of deaths recorded as 'undetermined'. The overall trend is common to almost all European countries and the US. While around 80 per cent of suicides in all age groups are male (in some immigrant populations rates of suicide are higher among women than men) 80-90 per cent of those who attempt suicide (parasuicides) are female; one in every 100 young women aged between 15 and 19 attempts suicide. The vast majority of cases involve intentional overdoses. The incidents of self-injury tend to be acts that draw attention to the person rather than deliberate acts of attempted suicide, but up to 11 per cent of teenagers who take overdoses will commit suicide within a few years.[31]

There has been particular concern over suicides in young offender institutions, with an overall increase in both suicide and self-inflicted injury by prisoners in the last decade. In 1991, according to Home Office figures, there were 2,963 recorded incidents of self-injury, of which 1,208 were by prisoners aged 21 or under. A recent survey found 17 per cent of young offenders had considered suicide. Here again, recording is inconsistent and not detailed enough to be useful in informing preventive strategies.

References

1 *Child Abuse Trends in England and Wales, 1988-1990. And an Overview from 1973-1990,* S J Creighton, (NSPCC, London, 1992).

2 'Children as Victims of Violence: A National Survey', D Finkelhor and J Dziuba-Leatherman, *Pediatrics* 94(4), 1994, pp. 413-20.

3 'Victimization of children', D Finkelhor and J Dziuba-Leatherman, *American Psychologist,* 49(3), 1994, pp. 173-83.

4 'Societal change and change in family violence from 1975 to 1985 as revealed by two national surveys', M A Straus and R J Gelles, *Journal of Marriage and the Family,* 48, (1986) pp. 465-79 and *Missing, abducted, runaway and thrown away children in America: First report,* D Finkelhor, G T Hotaling and A Sedlak, (Juvenile Justice Clearinghouse, Washington DC, 1990).

5 *A community study of physical violence to children in the home, and associated variables,* Marjorie Smith, (Thomas Coram Research Unit, London); Poster presented at International Society for the Prevention of Child Abuse and Neglect Fifth European Conference on Child Abuse and Neglect, Oslo, Norway, 13-16 May 1995; *Children's views on appropriate parental punishment, in relation to their experience of physical punishment,* Marjorie A Smith and Andrea L Heverin, Poster presented at Biennial Meeting of the Society for Research in Child Development, Indianapolis, Indiana, USA, 30 March-2 April 1995.

6 *Public Education Campaign - Adult Survey Findings,* (NSPCC, 1994).

7 *Survey of childhood experiences: sexual abuse: summary*, (NSPCC, June 1995).

8 *Criminal statistics, England and Wales 1993,* Home Office, (HMSO, London, 1994).

9 *Operating the Child Protection System,* J Gibbons, S Conroy and C Bell, (HMSO London, 1995).

10 *Children and Young People on Child Protection Registers Year Ending 31 March 1994, England, A/F94/13 LAS,* (Department of Health, 1995) and *Child Protection Register Statistics for Wales 1994*, (Welsh Office, 1994).

11 *Social Focus on Children*, Central Statistical Office, (HMSO, London, 1994) p. 35.

12 See note 7.

13 See note 11, p. 47.

14 See note 2.

15 Personal communication, T J Leech, Homicide Index, S J Creighton, (Home Office, 1994).

16 See note 8.

17 'Non-accidental injury', A M Adelstein, P O Goldblatt, S C Stracey and J A C Weatherall, ch. 7 in *Studies in sudden infant deaths,* No. 45 of *Studies on Medical and Population Subjects*, (HMSO, London, 1982).

18 *Newsletter No. 27,* (Foundation for the Study of Infant Deaths, 1984).

19 *Home Office Statistical Bulletin,* Issue 42/89, table 4.

20 Parliamentary Written Answer, *Hansard*, 19 April 1993, tables A and B.

21 *Aspects of crime: young offenders 1993,* Statistics 1 Division of Home Office Research and Statistics Department (Home Office 1995).

22 See note 21, pp. 6-7.

23 *Criminal Statistics England and Wales, 1992,* (HMSO, December 1993), Table 7.23.

24 *The report of the Committee of Inquiry into children and young people who sexually abuse other children,* (NCH Action for Children, London, 1992) pp. 7-8.

25 *Criminal statistics*, Home Office, (HMSO, 1989).

26 *Car Crime,* NACRO Briefing, (NACRO, May 1994).

27 'Self-reported offending among young people in England and Wales', Benjamin Bowling, John Graham and Alec Ross, Home Office Research and Planning Unit, in *Delinquent behaviour among young people in the western world: first results of the international self-report delinquency study*, Josine Junger-Tas and others (eds.), (Kugler Publications, Amsterdam, 1994) p. 42 *et seq.*

28 See note 27, p. 371.

29 Suicide statistics, The Samaritans, London.

30 'Suicide in children and adolescents in England and Wales 1960-1990', G M G McClure, *British Journal of Psychiatry*, vol. 165, (1994).

31 *The Health of the Nation: Key Area Handbook on Mental Illness,* Department of Health and Social Services Inspectorate, (Department of Health, 1993) pp. 17 and 18.

Local community safety strategies and the prevention of violence involving children

results of the Commission's survey

The Commission wrote to chief executives of local authorities and to a sample of Area Child Protection Committees (ACPCs) and Safer Cities Projects in July 1994, asking about the development of community safety strategies and their relevance to prevention of violence involving children. The following is a summary of the response and extracts from replies: these indicate the variety of work already in progress or planned which is directed to reducing and preventing violence involving children.

1 Chief Executives

410 letters sent: 152 responses

Question 1
Has your authority adopted a community strategy or other policies relevant to violence prevention? 74 x No : 78 x Yes.

Question 2
If so, does its implementation involve particular activities for reducing/preventing violence involving children (eg early intervention, parent education/support, school programmes, environmental, leisure, youth initiatives etc)? 102 x No : 50 x Yes

Question 3
Does your authority have views on how action to reduce/prevent violence involving children should be co-ordinated locally? If so, please explain and/or send relevant papers. 112 x No : 40 x Yes

Question 4
In your area is there co-ordination between community safety/crime prevention activities and the Area Child Protection Committee? 136 x No : 16 x Yes

Though nearly 50 per cent of the answers to question 1 were negative, a lot of information was supplied about plans and initiatives and a high proportion of the respondents were involved in looking at aspects of community safety. Several authorities are planning or in the process of initiating community safety strategies along the lines of the Morgan Report recommendations.

Many had not previously considered the specific issue of violence against children but were very responsive to the concept and several planned to take the matter up with their committees and wished to receive copies of the Commission's recommendations for consideration.

Extracts from responses

Arun District Council There is an overall county strategy regarding leisure and youth initiatives which is linked to crime prevention.

Avon, County of Community safety policy is one of support for the multi agency approach, and is very much in line with the Morgan Report recommendations and with elements of the 'Practical Guide to Crime Prevention for Local Partnerships' published by Crime Concern for the Home Office in 1993. There is no formal co-ordination between community safety bodies and ACPCs.

Bath City Council Made a number of enquiries but 'unfortunately cannot identify particular instances ... which are aimed at preventing/reducing violence to children'. It is conducting an audit to identify gaps in current crime prevention/community safety with the aim of producing a timetable and action plan. 'Naturally issues such as violence prevention, particularly in regard to young people, should form part of any comprehensive strategy.' The Bath Police Schools Liaison Officer is involved in the prevention of bullying through activities in local schools.

Bolton Metro Community Safety Strategy '... There is a developing link between violence to children and domestic violence and the response to both is increasingly linked ... There is also a trend towards referring men, and sometimes women with a tendency for violence to psychologists for counselling in anger management ... but it is an issue which the Council's Crime Prevention Team and those involved in child protection need to tackle.' (No link as yet with ACPC).

Bournemouth Community Services Regrets that the type of information requested is not set out in the Council Policy in the way described. They do however run a 'Junior Citizens for the 90s' project aimed at teaching junior-aged children personal safety, how to cope with emergencies, and encouraging them to become responsible citizens. Through an annual grant system they have been able to support several voluntary organisations whose clients are either victims or perpetrators of crime, for example establishing a community worker in an area of high unemployment and juvenile crime and a 'Teen Wheels Motor Project'.

Bracknell Forest Borough Council One of the aims of its community safety strategy is to divert young people away from crime (eg a SPLASH scheme for 10-16 year olds during the summer holidays); no specific schemes for reducing/preventing violence to children, and no direct links with the ACPC.

Bradford, City of Metropolitan Council One of the seven key corporate priorities adopted by the council is community safety, which aims to reduce crime, the fear of crime and to encourage initiatives that improve community safety in a wider context. Has played a leading role in establishing Safer City–Bradford and District as an independent multi-agency project, and is focusing on young people by encouraging initiatives that reduce the number of crimes committed by them and supporting projects that provide alternative safe activities. Family centres are used to assist parents and to prevent children being harmed either physically or emotionally as a consequence of violent behaviour by parents. Work is being done with adult males involved in the sexual abuse of women or children. Liaison takes place between hospital casualty units and social services over child protection issues. A Zero Tolerance type campaign is planned for 1995. Bradford Girls' and Young Women's Project was launched in November 1994 to help 'those who are, or are at risk of becoming involved in third-party abuse often referred to as prostitution.'

Braintree District Council Is assessing its approach via a number of joint working parties on various violence-related issues, for example domestic violence and paedophilia, and are fostering crime prevention panels in the district linking with police, schools, youth clubs and other agencies. In 1994 they ran a 'Crucial Crew' initiative targeted at 10 and 11 year olds – 'crucial, practical messages on personal safety, crime prevention, awareness and accident prevention for young children'.

Buckinghamshire County Council (involved in Thames Valley Partnership)
'… The Director of Social Services has commented to me that the issues which the study poses are most interesting, and in her view the reasons why children offend, why they are violent, why they mutilate themselves or indulge in other non-conforming behaviour is that each child is different and the triggers of anti-social behaviour vary very widely. The real task is to diagnose what the individual problem is (it is usually several problems, all of which are inter-related) and apply a personalised programme of diversion, rehabilitation or care. This is certainly the view which I have learnt arising out of the safer communities approach, that there are a whole range of different reasons for criminal activity and until individual problems are tackled and addressed we will never know which solution is most appropriate for which problem. One of the greatest difficulties we appear to face is that we apply global solutions thinking they will bring about an improvement whereas the improvement only actually occurs when a particular problem is tackled properly'.

Burnley Borough Council Is currently embarking on a 'Safer Cities' initiative and is considering participating in a Zero Tolerance Campaign in tandem with the development of an inter-agency Domestic Violence Strategy.

Calderdale Council Has entered into partnership with the police and probation services as well as the business and voluntary sectors and is currently establishing two multi-agency task groups aimed at preventing crime and preventing criminal behaviour. The Preventing Criminal Behaviour Task Group will be considering all the examples given in the Commission's Question two. There is an overlap of representation on the Task Group and the ACPC.

Cambridge City Council Has conducted a youth survey and established a youth crime prevention panel which has identified situations where 13 to 17 year olds are at risk.

Charnwood, Borough of The council is submitting a bid for a Single Regeneration grant for funding research into the problem of harassment (of all kinds), bullying and anti-social behaviour. There is a multi-agency Domestic Violence Panel chaired by the leader of the council, whose activities include reprinting a second revised edition of a domestic violence leaflet; operating a pilot scheme installing domestic violence alarm systems in homes where there is a history of or immediate threat of violence. The

Panel has also made contact with all local state and independent secondary schools some of whom have stated that they will incorporate domestic violence issues in the personal and social education section of the National Curriculum.

Cheltenham Borough Council As a result of a close working relationship with the local constabulary over the past 18 months in order to instigate a proactive approach to tackling crime, a co-funded post of Community Crime Reduction co-ordinator was established in August 1994. The council has adopted a policy document 'A vision for the Town Centre'; one of the objectives is to 'provide a more secure place'.

Colchester Borough Council Stages a variety of activities and publications aimed at young people eg young people's environmental competition, play schemes, a graffiti and vandalism pack and video for schools; would be willing to play a key role in the prevention of violence to and by young people.

Cynon Valley Borough Council Has not adopted any safety strategy or other related policies with regard to community safety. However a number of activities are promoted specifically for children in co-operation with bodies such as the South Wales Police (eg SPLASH initiative).

Daventry District Council – West Northamptonshire Community Safety Group 'A Student Council has been established, holding its first meeting in October 1994. Comprising of student representatives from each of the local senior schools and colleges, its purpose will be to initiate works and projects having community or environmental benefit, to represent the interests of young people and respond to consultations about local services. The creation of the Student Council aims to equip young people with community awareness'.

Dinefwr, Borough of Has launched a Crime Reduction Forum involving various departments of the council, voluntary organisations and representatives of industry and trade. It is particularly addressing drugs and alcohol abuse involving the young.

Doncaster Metropolitan Borough Council Since 1992 the council has been a senior partner in a local multi-agency project – Doncaster Action Against Crime – which has focused upon the experience of young people and women. The project is based upon the belief that local people must be closely involved in the identification of local problems and the implementation of 'solutions'. The Urban Programme Funding ends in 1995 and there are currently no plans for it to continue beyond then. 'Our experience has shown that community safety requires full-time staffing and secure long-term funding to make a significant impact.'

Durham County Council Ran a campaign aimed at raising awareness within the community about issues relating to child abuse: its incidence, symptoms, how to recognise, what to do, local authority responsibilities etc. This involved press releases, a mobile exhibition touring the County and similar public information initiatives over a five-day period.

Easington District Council Has been the main instigator in the area in developing the recommendations of the Morgan Report. 'At the present time the concept of community safety is at an embryonic stage and central government has not really addressed the respective roles of the local authorities in relation to this subject. Recent correspondence has shown that the government clearly expects local authorities to be more involved and to take some form of lead on these matters but this has not been properly reflected through either resourcing or direction through statutory roles and instruments.'

East Cambridgeshire District Council The Safer Ely – Crime Reduction Action Plan 1994 aims to address, amongst other things, the 'disorder and incivilities related to bored young people congregating in the town centre and other parts of Ely. This is known to constitute the fear of crime particularly.' It also aims to support a programme of initiatives aimed at young people at risk and in the longer term develop school safety groups, school watch schemes and policies to keep exclusion and truancy to a minimum. Is also promoting the use of the 'Safer Futures' curriculum pack and Centre for Citizenship teaching aid leaflet in primary schools.

East Sussex County Council Its Community Safety Strategy adopted last year using recommendations of the Morgan Report states that 'As part of consultation for planning applications or at the stage of submitting proposals, community safety implications of design are addressed. Basic land use planning, e.g. layout of town centres, can also aid crime prevention via the Structure and Local Plan policies and proposals.' STEP (School Time Employment Project) is being carried out in partnership with the police and industry providing tailored programmes of school attendance and vocational experience for potentially disaffected pupils who may be at risk of offending.

Essex County Council Has appointed a Crime Prevention Officer based in the Chief Executive's Office and working closely with the police, district and borough councils, the probation service and other agencies on crime prevention measures. Projects include a joint initiative for young offenders, the Essex Motor Project, focusing on motoring and driving offences. The council is involved in the Youth Crime Audit in the South West which will identify gaps in current services and make recommendations, and is also in the process of setting up a multi-agency County Domestic Violence Forum. The social services representative on the Forum is also a local child protection panel member and the two areas of work are closely linked. The County Education Department is involved in anti-bullying projects.

Fenland District Council Has a very active programme which links leisure, education and school programmes to keep children and youths involved in activities, but not part of an overall community safety strategy. Feels that the police should be more involved in schemes, that is, there should be prevention rather than cure.

Forest of Dean District Council Crime Concern is currently undertaking a review of crime problems in Gloucestershire. Part of the purpose is to help develop a community safety strategy. In its Corporate Plan the Authority has identified meeting the needs of young people as being a priority area and therefore many initiatives are focused around young people, some of which will help to prevent violence and crime. It intends to improve the range and quality of information on services to ensure young people take up the opportunities available to them, to actively encourage work experience placements within the Council to give young people a broader understanding and to work closely with colleges and schools regarding training and careers matters. It will continue to support the policies of the Gloucestershire Sports Council set out in 'Sport for Young People' and develop sport and leisure activities that meet the needs of young people, including the possibility of enhancing play facilities, especially on council housing estates.

Gateshead Metropolitan Borough Council Is currently working with Northumbria Police to produce a Community Safety Strategy. The CHAB 8 police referral system includes early notification of violent situations where children were present. The Area Child Protection Committee is also currently looking into the development of a 'no smacking policy'.

Gloucestershire County Council The County Council has adopted the UN Convention on the Rights of the Child as a basis for the provision of services to children in the county. The Gloucestershire Constabulary has adopted a multi-agency approach to all issues relating to crime prevention and community safety. The involvement of young people as victims or offenders is of particular concern and much effort is being devoted to the development of an effective strategy: 'Stranger-Danger' talks for 5-11 year-olds; talks on street safety and bullyingfor 11-13 year-olds; and on personal safety for 15 year olds. A 'Schools Involvement Unit' (5 full-time officers) in accordance with an agreed education service programme, input into all the secondary schools in the county under four broad headings: crime and its consequences; substance abuse; personal issues and general public issues. Other programmes include holiday play schemes with the priority of promoting children's personal safety and welfare; parental seminars on, for instance, drugs and solvent abuse; drugs education (a multi-agency County Drugs and Alcohol Strategy Group has been formed); School Youth Action/Crime Prevention Panels – 12 based in local secondary schools; Operation Gemini 'Schools against Crime' Competition – so far concentrating on burglaries and vehicle crime; diversionary projects for young offenders and improvement to recreational facilities. A Detective Inspector has been appointed as Force Child Protection Co-ordinator, and there is continual liaison between Crime Prevention Officers, Community Involvement and Schools Officers, Drug Squad officers and child protection.

Hammersmith & Fulham Community Safety Unit Is concerned about all violent crime, and in particular has targeted work to prevent violence against vulnerable people in the community, women and children. Domestic violence is a priority and the Domestic Violence Forum published a report in 1994 'Suffering in silence: children and young people who witness domestic violence'; the Forum has also launched a leaflet and resource pack inspired by the International Year of the Family 'Promoting violence free families'.

Hampshire County Council As a result of analysis by Crime Concern, a Youth Crime Co-ordinator has been appointed. Multi agency agreement to promote diversionary projects such as the Meridian Motor project, to address vehicle crime issues with young people and a challenge and adventure project led by the police on the Isle of Wight is now being reproduced in Portsmouth.

Hereford and Worcester County Council Has promoted a Crime Reduction Partnership, with representation ranging from social services to the Crown

Prosecution Service, directly concerned with a community safety strategy, and is currently advertising for a Co-ordinator. Specific initiatives have yet to be developed, but the Education Authority Psychological Service has promoted training in behaviour management and has staged an anti-bullying conference.

Hertfordshire County Council Community Safety Strategy aims to 'reduce crime and particularly amongst the young, to reduce criminality … To assist young people to develop social responsibility and good citizenship' aimed at crime reduction rather than violence. Implementation plans involve children by way of education support, police school programmes and other youth activities.

High Wycombe, Community Safety Partnership Following market research and the publication of the Morgan Report the council established a Community Safety Strategy. It has recently commissioned an audit on youth crime which is in the process of being analysed so that a series of structured initiatives can be developed in partnership with the police, social services, youth service, probation, education and NHS trust. Existing schemes include 'Teen Academy' for legal under-age driving; 'Hazard Alley', a safety centre in Milton Keynes takes 10 year olds through a series of scenarios to help them become aware of safety and what to do in an emergency. They publish a series of crime prevention leaflets including 'victims of domestic violence' and 'protect your child'. 'We feel that action should be co-ordinated locally to prevent/reduce violence involving children … There seem to be quite a few local initiatives at present but it may be useful to everyone involved if they all communicated between each other. We have not been very active in these areas but we hope to develop them in the future. We are not aware of an Area Child Protection Committee being active locally.'

Ipswich Borough Council Has made some progress in setting up mechanisms through which co-ordination can begin. A paper 'Community safety – the Ipswich experience' starts by challenging the statement 'Crime prevention and/or reduction is the responsibility of the police and should be funded by the County Council'. Having considered what activities were already being undertaking which could be considered as having a crime prevention/reduction impact the council members decided that the words 'community safety' more closely represented what the local authority should be striving to achieve for the town. The activities included provision of leisure activities, environmental schemes such as additional lighting and graffiti removal; the use by the police of area housing offices to hold surgeries in encouraging the public to meet the police at a more convenient and 'friendly' location; converting streets into cul de sacs to encourages 'ownership' by residents; referral of all major planning applications to the police architectural liaison officer and the setting up of women's refuges. Initiatives resulting from the new multi agency approach have included grant-aiding the setting up of a Duke of Edinburgh Award Scheme to be run in a 'problem' area of the town. The paper ends with a helpful list of points together with advice for other District Councils not yet undertaking work in the field of community safety.

Kent County Constabulary Employs 17 constables as Schools Liaison Officers. Stranger danger, bullying and drugs are some of the subjects included in their programme the primary aim of which is to heighten children's awareness with a view to keeping them safe and therefore reducing crime.

Kettering Borough Council Has recently adopted a community safety strategy and is still in the process of selecting short-term priorities and identifying performance standards but part of its policy is to provide activities, events, training and educational opportunities which will discourage anti-social behaviour and encourage all local people, particularly young people, to feel they have a role in the community. The Council intends to hold an annual Young Driver Challenge to educate young drivers about safe car handling skills.

Kirklees Metropolitan Council Is moving from the independent model of partnership for community safety matters to a local authority led model on the pattern recommended by the Morgan Committee and is working towards the adoption of a Community Safety Strategy which will involve specific activities and plans for a crime prevention worker and reducing anti-social behaviour involving children. Preliminary discussion amongst various partners of the Working Party for Community Safety indicates an intention to establish a sub-working group from services and community interests who work with children.

Leeds City Council A draft community safety strategy is hopefully being adopted by 1995. Each department of the council will be responsible for developing action plans which meet the aims of the strategy and this will be co-ordinated by the Community Safety Officer Group, senior departmental officers and representatives of other agencies (police, probation, fire services, local transport executive). Multi agency action is already taking place – for example, the Leeds Inter-Agency Project (Women and Violence) addresses the issue of children living in homes where violence occurs, and in the field of child protection, inter-agency forums and support groups have been established. A Children's Services Plan has been drafted and an inter-agency group will be formed to engage in children's service planning, This initiative will be integrated with other work also current in Leeds, eg the Community Safety Strategy and the Children and Young Person's Strategy.

Leicester City Council Funding has been obtained through City Challenge. A Community Safety Shop will be the centre for a number of key projects and support groups and will provide information and advice on community safety including a telephone helpline. There is no specific mention of violence to children. The onus seems to be on juvenile crime prevention: the Mowmacre Estate project, for example, where Crime Concern carried out a youth consultation and strategy, out of which various multi-agency initiatives have been instigated; 'Heartstone' storytelling project addresses the problem of racism and bullying in primary schools; a Parents for Parents Group aims to develop a local network for parents providing information, guidance and support on issues raised by parents, including child safety and behavioural problems; 'Kidstart' is to help develop the skills and strengths of parents of young children.

Lincolnshire County Council Recently adopted a community safety policy. In addition to focusing on the development of out of school provision, and early years' child care there are three projects targeting crime reduction: a befriending project aimed to provide early intervention and diversion into more appropriate activities; a support project for young people aged 16 to 18 who have been in care or are homeless and vulnerable, aimed at assisting transition to independence and an intervention project for vehicle offenders.

Luton Crime Reduction Programme The co-ordinator identified the following problems for youth: 'Lack of care or attention from parents; lack of education in social skills and values; lack of facilities in certain geographical areas; lack of activities which absorb and interest those at risk of offending; transport either too expensive or inadequate. The problem was summed up as "Many young people have nowhere to go and no one to care"'. The strategy that the council has adopted in partnership with others in the field of community safety has used the Morgan Report 'Independent Model' as a structure.

Malvern Hills District Council The Leominster Inter Agency Crime and Liaison Panel ran a Staysafe Campaign, part of which covered stranger danger, bullying, domestic violence and child abuse, producing a series of leaflets – 'Be safe – say no! to strangers'; posters were erected at 20 sites within the district.

Merseyside Police Authority, Safer Merseyside Partnership 'To tackle repeat victimisation on Merseyside': '... the underlying causes of crime and delinquency will be tackled through early years provision for under five's and after-school clubs for the 8 to 14 year olds in priority neighbourhoods.' A pilot project to reduce neighbour disputes is planned.

Mid-Glamorgan Crime Prevention Co-ordinating Committee 'The Chief Officers' Crime Reduction Group is presently considering the issue of a child's experience of violence. This wider perspective has arisen from local data indicating that such experiences are linked to youth crime. The young people who continue in crime and/or commit the most serious offences do appear to have experiences of violence. Whilst the relationship between the direct experience of violence and subsequent behavioural difficulties was known, there was less recognition of links with the indirect experience ie where children are aware of or may unknowingly witness violence by one parent or carer upon another. If, as expected, marital and family violence is targeted as a county wide crime reduction focus from January 1995 the aim would be to develop a wide-ranging multi-agency response at all levels ...' Plans include a joint sub-group of the Child Protection Committee and the Crime Reduction Group.

Milton Keynes Borough Council Established a Violence Against Women and Children Working Party six years ago to provide a discussion forum for the relevant agencies, to promote a multi-agency approach to finding practical solutions and exploring the possibility of asking social services to include prevention of domestic violence in the Community Care Plan. The Working Party is also considering a media campaign to 'Improve relationships by managing family conflict'.

New Forest District Council Has formed a community-based multi-agency crime prevention working party whose current terms of reference include the following: 'To seek to improve the quality of life for citizens of the Council area by reducing both the level of crime and the fear of crime'. It proposes to introduce a pilot scheme of 'mediation' in three local schools to address issues such as bullying; the scheme will be independently monitored.

Newark & Sherwood District Council Participates in two multi-agency forums specifically intended to promote crime prevention and community safety both of which have involvement with regard to the promotion of safety for children in the community.

Norfolk County Council A Safer Cities Programme will commence in November 1994. They recently held a conference 'Community Safety – A proposed local partnership' and work on implementing the conclusions is underway – the conference identified better opportunities for young people relating to employment and training, and affordable leisure and recreational activities. The intention is to consult with young people aged five to 18 from the start, both within their own peer groups as well as within a wider representative forum. Supporting and counselling parents in both the home and school is also important.

North Tyneside Council Feels that a comprehensive youth crime prevention strategy needs to be put in place as part of an overall youth policy mainly aimed at preventing juvenile crime. It has carried out a crime audit and survey (in Northumbria, with the highest incidence of crime in the north east and in the highest band for recorded crime in the country, only 3.5 per cent of all recorded crimes were crimes of violence, with 26 per cent of all known offenders being juveniles under the age of 17 who were responsible mainly for burglary, theft and criminal damage). In addition it has run a Zero Tolerance campaign.

North Wiltshire District Council 'Believes that the Children Act places county councils at the forefront of crime prevention and reduction strategies in local areas, given their roles in overseeing police committees, as well as their responsibility in education and social services. Clearly District Councils would have a role to play in assisting the application of such strategies at local level. It is unfortunate that the Government, in introducing the Children Act, did not do more to enable local authorities to implement appropriate action, especially in relation to the funding problem'.

North Yorkshire County Council There are local 'Partnership Groups for Children and Families' in each division which audit local need and plan service development in a co-ordinated manner. These plans have been published as part of the Community Care Plan. The council believes that services for children in need could be developed on an inter-agency basis as highlighted in the Audit Commission's report *Seen but not heard*. 'The reduction /prevention of violence involving children is an important issue but is not currently specifically targeted by any Committee.' The Bell Farm Estate Project in York was developed on an inter-agency basis, including the police, to create a safer and improved standard of living in this particular area. The police have many school programmes, and youth initiatives have been a feature of their work with children for a number of years.

Northamptonshire Community Safety Strategy 'The corporate strategy identifies ways in which agencies can work together ... This includes support for the early intervention of services through pre-school education, which also includes the involvement of parents in teaching parenting skills, support to schools programmes, the increase of leisure provision and identifies many other areas where community safety and a multi-agency approach is important'.

Northumberland County Council 'Although there is no process in terms of inter-agency co-operation, the social services view on the way forward would be for agencies … to work together to identify children who are subjects of violence and those responsible for violence with a view to addressing the issues via an inter-agency Child Protection Plan. Consideration should be given for referral of the perpetrator(s) to the courts but there is also a responsibility for respective agencies to make people more aware of the effects of violence and measures to combat violence.'

Norwich City Council Is in the early stages of putting together a Community Safety Strategy and will be one of the latest round of areas to benefit from the Safer Cities Scheme. Up to the end of 1993 under the Safer Cities Banner 3,300 initiatives had been funded including help for young people as victims, offenders and potential offenders.

Nottingham, City of Is in the process of developing a community safety strategy/policy but it will not include particular activities or plans for reducing/preventing violence involving children. However, it believes there is potential for initiatives to be developed primarily through the Play and Leisure Services division, and hopefully the Commission research will provide advice on how to respond to the problem.

Nottinghamshire County Council Deplores the fact that the government rejected the Morgan Report recommendation that local authorities be given statutory responsibility for community safety and crime prevention, the result of which is that developments across the country have been patchy. The Council has adopted a number of strategies/policies which are relevant to the prevention of violence to children. The Youth Crime Prevention Strategy adopted by the multi agency Youth Crime Prevention Working Group gives equal weight to young people as victims. Initiatives include: a mentoring scheme for young people leaving care and a touring theatre education programme targeted at 12-14 year olds on crime and attitudes towards it. The Radford Care Project, an early intervention initiative, aims to prevent violence to children but also keep the family unit intact. The County Council has published an Action Checklist for Senior Management Teams on bullying in schools and believes that multi agency partnership is essential.

Oxford City Council Has not yet adopted a Community Safety Strategy but is launching the Zero Tolerance Campaign in the autumn (1994). The Oxford Federation of Community Associations, a multi-agency group for all areas of the City 'does focus on the implementation of the Children Act 1989 thus ensuring a co-ordinated inter-agency approach to child care in the community; this encompasses the issues of violence against children.'

Oxfordshire County Council Is part of the Thames Valley Partnership looking into crime prevention generally. A conference 'Safer Communities in Oxfordshire' was held in 1992 but initiatives stemming from it have not been as numerous as hoped, and have tended to be integrated into partnerships. Relevant activities are a TRAX Motor project, the Oxford Project 'Junior Citizen' (partnership between the Rover Group, Woolwich Building Society and the Thames Valley Police) and Domestic Violence Awareness (similar to the Lothian Project). Though the council is actively involved with their education department in developing a joint youth strategy, the respondent does not think they have ever addressed the issue of how reduction/prevention of violence involving children should be co-ordinated locally.

Peterborough Borough Council Plays an active part on a Countrywide Inter-Agency approach to crime prevention, and funds the Peterborough Crime Prevention Programme. Joint agency work provides some provision for children but the focus is on children as perpetrators of crime.

Portsmouth City Council The Crime Prevention Committee has established the post of Youth Crime Prevention Co-ordinator which is funded in co-ordination with other agencies such as the education, probation and social services. The postholder is currently compiling a strategy to be used in the City to help prevent young people getting involved in crime. There is a multi-agency Domestic Violence Forum whose policy statement included the resolution to work towards preventing violence against women and/or their children and to ensure that everyone is allowed to live free from fear, intimidation and violence.

Powys County Council 'If ... the unacceptable behaviour of children is the result of other and perhaps deeper problems then a more long-term remedy may need to be considered ... It could be argued that many of the mixed messages and double standards that currently abound in society actually confuse communities about acceptable degrees of behaviour.' The ACPC has taken the initiative to link with the education department and a local community theatre group to create greater awareness of child sexual abuse. They are also involved in producing information packs relating to bullying and are constantly seeking avenues to heighten public awareness of the long-term effects of violence to and by children. 'The social services department is interested and willing to participate in further discussions with other agencies about the possibilities of introducing initiatives which will reduce violence to and by children ... but ... because it is a problem of society initiatives should aim to allow the whole community to take some responsibility and be part of the overall scheme.'

Preseli Pembrokeshire District Council States that social deprivation and criminal activity are a recognised problem on certain estates and it is currently providing family centre facilities on these estates in the hope that they will act as focal points for social change. The centres provide a wide range of activities including youth activity supported by the police, social services and probation.

Reading Borough Council Has adopted the general approach as set out in the Morgan report. Neighbourhood crime reduction groups work on various issues such as increased provision for young people and the council is actively supporting improved youth provision, children's playschemes and greater involvement between parents and schools.

Reigate and Banstead Borough Council Community Safety Strategy targets include the protection of vulnerable people – the elderly, victims of racial harassment and/or domestic violence – and diversion of young people from crime through support to parents and provision of activities. A 'Parenthood Initiative' (a Quality in the Community scheme) has published a booklet which aims to reach every parent with a child of five and under, giving sources of information and advice in the Borough. A number of projects are being carried out in local schools including working through junior crime prevention panels to reduce crime, for example dealing with bullying through a mentoring approach and setting up of a young persons' café in an under-served area.

Royal Borough of Windsor and Maidenhead Both the Community Safety Panel (established in 1993) and the Community Development Manager (1994) are developing and implementing a co-ordinated, strategic, multi-agency approach to crime reduction and community safety. One of the key thrusts of this strategy will be to address the social measures required to divert young people from criminal and anti-social behaviour. Long-term objectives will derive from educating young people and where appropriate their parents, in community and environmental awareness and from fostering community-minded attitudes and behaviour.

Runnymede Borough Council Has adopted a positive policy towards the provision of facilities and activities for children and young people. It supports the major new community initiatives that work with young people in a positive way: pump-priming the setting up of two Youth Coffee Drop-ins, promotion and development of sports activities in parks and examination of ways for the young to become involved in the running and organising of the activities. It is working with and where possible supporting the Safer Surrey Partnership initiatives and is currently discussing the development of a Youth Music Project.

Rutland District Council Is starting to address violence through the launching of a Youth Forum in 1994 in partnership with three community colleges, the voluntary sector and local agencies.

Safer Surrey Partnership Team Established by Surrey County Council in conjunction with Surrey Police in 1992, consists of secondees from youth, education and social services, local police, probation and the Metropolitan Police. The Education Psychology Service has been involved in working with parents through parenting skills courses and specifically in the production of the 'ABC of Behaviour' – a booklet for parents of young children designed to help them to manage their children's behaviour. Youthlink is a school-based programme for disaffected youngsters, producing very positive related benefits. 'Our final comment is that I share a concern with others not to engage in a sensationalism of violence, when the reality in Surrey is that violent crime is comparatively low. However I think you can see that we are not content to sit back and allow the present level to become acceptable, but to seek further means of reducing crime or equally removing the fear of crime'.

Salisbury District Council Is part of the recently formed Salisbury District Community Safety Group which has appointed a full time co-ordinator. Part of one project is to hold a Community Safety Week to encourage better relationships and understanding between the statutory agencies, voluntary bodies and the public.

Shropshire 'Ideally the Joint Child Protection Teams should have a role in developing strategies to reduce/prevent violence involving children under the auspices of the Area Child Protection Committee. However, sadly, resources at present have to be directed in the main to investigation and assessment work ... As yet the community safety and crime prevention work has not developed to the point of being co-ordinated with the Area Child Protection Committee'.

Slough Borough Council The council is undertaking a major review of its corporate strategies and will be considering a crime action/community safety strategy as part of that. The Safer Slough Enterprise has an involvement in projects such as 'I'm O.K., you're O.K.' which deals with young people's confidence and self-esteem by aiming to reduce bullying, improve teamwork, reduce vandalism, improve community spirit and teach children to respect other people. 'Not all violence involving children can be identified as criminal activity, and it may be a mistake to criminalise all aspects of children's involvement in violence. Learning to deal with conflict is part of development and it is how society reacts to that which is fundamental to how a child views it. Violence to children from/by adults can never be condoned and is a separate issue from violence between children'. The council believes that play facilities are essential to the development of children and have an impact upon their social skills and feelings of worth in the community. It has a comprehensive play service, 'Slough Play Leadership Scheme' which provides a range of opportunities to school-aged children: 'That alone is a major contributor to reduction in violence. The play service has a role in protecting children and providing a space for them ... The scheme is proactive in helping children deal with violence and conflict amongst their peer group ... Any approach to the co-ordination of reduction and prevention of violence initiatives must draw closely upon inter-agency partnership. It should not be identified as a purely criminal activity and, therefore, vested in crime prevention organisation. It may be appropriately led through a service such as play or closely linked to the voluntary sector.' The Borough Council will consider all the above issues as part of the umbrella strategy it is currently undertaking, and might consider closer links with the ACPC should they become a unitary authority.

South Herefordshire District Hopes that as a result of a 'Healthy Alliance' with other District Councils, the Health Authority and Social Services, officers will be employed to carry out home safety checks, particularly in homes with children under the age of five where the checks will include certain aspects of crime prevention.

South Lakeland District Council Has responded to the recommendations of the Morgan Report by establishing a Crime Prevention Group with a Youth sub-group concentrating on the 11-16 year old group to examine the problems and issues and needs associated with young people and young offenders. It has supported projects initiated by other bodies such as SPLASH schemes, Crimebeat Trust, Junior Citizen Scheme, Black Mime theatre and the Green Bike Scheme.

South Somerset District Council In its annual report 'Promoting Community Safety 1994' the point is made that as 94 per cent of recorded offences in England and Wales involve property and only 5 per cent were violent crimes, 'there is tremendous potential to communicate with the community on allaying fears of assault and, despite the influence of the media, campaigning positively on the facts and the reality not on the hype.' Somerset Domestic Violence Project was opened in 1994.

St. Albans, City and District of Is of the opinion 'that a co-ordinated approach between parents, schools and statutory services is the only way to create an environment and set of values that will contribute to reducing anti-social behaviour and all council policies are designed to minimise rather than aggravate opportunities for anti-social behaviour. The infrastructure of public services is critical to maintaining and developing civilised lifestyles amongst all sections of the community. There are many anxieties that force-feeding market approaches to the provision of public services are beginning to erode some of these core values. Society is a fragile creature. There are many and varied challenges to its basic fabric. There is a major responsibility on public services to maintain a balance, a sense of place and identity, a concern for the other person, a respect for other people's property, and an understanding of our heritage.'

Stafford Borough Council Is intending to devote a section of its proposed community safety strategy to children.

Staffordshire Moorlands District Council Designing out crime would be part of a possible community safety strategy; part of the Council's Environmental Charter to promote environmental works carried out in the local community by the community, particularly aimed at stretching youth. The response from local schools has been excellent and this seems to be the nub of some of the problems in that a high degree of violence is born 'of frustration and underactivity'. The police operate a scheme involving local children in outdoor-related activities during the summer months and this has proved very successful. 'If it has a fault it is most probably that it tends to reach children from the most secure backgrounds and the more disadvantaged ... can miss out on the opportunities.'

Suffolk County Council, Social Services 'Suffolk has identified the significance of violence against children particularly in domestic settings and has plans to develop a strategy for violence prevention. A reduction of violence to children policy does not as yet exist in Suffolk ... Individual and group treatment programmes do exist in the County for those who have been convicted of violence offences particularly sexual offences but it has been recognised that services need to be provided at an earlier stage and it is inappropriate to just rely on criminal justice agencies to deal with heavy-end offenders. Men's groups are therefore being established for those men who recognise that they could potentially seriously harm children and partners ... At present there are no formal links between Suffolk County Crime Reduction Committee and ACPC although some members are the same. Clearly, the prevention of abuse and violent crime is common to both committees and there is clearly a lot to be gained from an agreed joint strategy.'

Swale Borough Council Is awaiting a Crime Audit hopefully leading to a Crime Prevention Strategy. There is a local crime prevention panel whose initiatives include the Sittingbourne Unattached Youth Project, a multi agency approach employing workers to walk the streets and encourage young people with nowhere to socialise to use local youth club facilities; and the Sheppey drugs awareness campaign involving local business people, councillors and agencies in raising money to carry out project work to prevent drug abuse.

Tandridge District Council Runs a programme of police and youth sports/leisure activities organised in conjunction with the Youth Service, giving young people the opportunity to participate side by side with police officers in mutual interest pursuits.

Teignbridge Services, Devon In line with the Morgan Committee Safer Communities recommendations a partnership has been set up between Devon and Teignbridge Local Authorities, Education Department, Social Services, County Engineers' Department, Property Department, Severn and Cornwall Constabulary, Devon Probation Department and lead officers of all lead District Departments: meetings are held twice a year. Their Recreation and Tourism Officer is encouraging affordable or free sports facilities to be offered to young people depending on their circumstances and a recent initiative allows medical practitioners to prescribe a period of physical activity at the Leisure Centres as an alternative to medicines. The respondent '... admits to not being aware of the existence of the ACPC Committee members in the area ...'

Thamesdown, Borough of Welcomes the Commission's aim of encouraging a children's perspective in policy development as it also supports the UN Convention on the Rights of the Child. It has recently begun to focus on community safety but does not have a specific strategy as yet. The Community Development Committee is developing and supporting play activity, which involves a commitment to empowering and promoting the status of all children in society so that they may have positive rights and access to opportunities in order fully to develop their potential, to have greater control over their own circumstances and to be more caring about the circumstances and destinies of others. The council acknowledges the importance of the Morgan Report recommendations.

Uttlesford District Council There is a proposal to set up a working group of the police, social services and the council to look at domestic violence.

Vale of Glamorgan Participates in a School Watch Scheme run by the local police to teach children at an early age (from three to six), the responsibilities of citizenship and is extending the SPLASH programme. A Community Safety Co-ordinator has been appointed and is preparing a report for the establishment of a Community Safety Strategy with the hope that a multi agency forum will be formed.

Waveney District Council Purchases summer holiday play schemes and maintains that since their inception two years ago they have seen a reduction in the amount of violence, vandalism and harassment to the general populace. It believes that preventing violence involving children can be addressed by taking a multi-disciplinary approach to the problem.

Welwyn Hatfield Council Facilitate a specific contact point for young people, the Youth Enquiry Service, which is staffed by the Youth Service and offers premises for youth programmes. The council is concerned about the number of young people who appear to have nothing to do in the evenings and congregate in shopping areas. It established a working group with representatives from all 'appropriate' departments, who approached young people and asked what they needed, and how the council could help them. 'I would consider this a pragmatic approach to real problems. The council made a commitment to talk to young people and consider issues concerning them.' The approach has been judged a successful one and is being widened to include the young throughout the district. There is no community safety strategy as such but a crime reduction panel comprising senior members of the housing, education and health departments, police, community representatives and other agencies such as the Citizens' Advice Bureau meets regularly; however the respondent believes that this reacts to perceived problems rather than being part of a cohesive strategy for the district. The council promotes and supports a well-resourced Women's Refuge, and grant aids a rape crisis service, local youth clubs and youth organisations, under-fives groups and a full programme of events for children during the summer holidays.

West Glamorgan County Council Has a Community Safety Strategy and a Multi-agency Forum for Community Safety; prevention of violence is implicit although not explicit to both. Activities include a programme of family education together with personal counselling and support offered in individual schools and the creation of bullying and behavioural policies within schools etc. 'The authority has no formal view as to how action to reduce/ prevent violence involving children should be co-ordinated locally ... your letter has, however, prompted a number of comments; three areas, the County Children's Forum, the Social Services Transitional Learning Base and Family Centres have been suggested as possible focus for further work ... it may be that we would wish to look at improving co-ordination between the relevant agencies in the light of the Commission's recommendations.'

West Northamptonshire Community Safety Group Believes that it is important to teach children and adults a firm moral code and to educate them to understand right from wrong and to respect other people, property and authority. 'In pursuit of this policy the Group will assist to develop the community and team spirit and loyalty'. Their strategy and action plan for 1994/95 involves the police, the schools liaison officer, local authority and a youth worker. They will liaise with young people and their organisations to give support to the provision of facilities and services to meet the needs of young people. One project, for example, tackles the problem of graffiti on subway walls – the Magic Roundabout Mural Project – encouraging volunteer school pupils between the ages of 13 and 19 to participate in a mural painting in subways and creating a safer subway project. A drop-in centre has been established for young people.

West Wiltshire District Council Community Safety Partnership was set up in 1994 involving a number of voluntary and statutory organisations. The Partnership co-operates with the newly appointed County Council Crime Reduction Co-ordinator and is considering a Youth Strategy – action to help to prevent young people turning to crime by providing them with worthwhile activities to occupy their leisure time – and are considering carrying out a youth survey to collect data on youth experiences and ideas for action. The Junior Good Citizen Scheme and SPLASH are up-and-running schemes and a task group has been set up to look at the problems of violence in the family.

Wigan Metropolitan Council A Domestic Violence Forum is in the embryonic stage and reducing violence to women and to their children is one of the key objectives. The borough wide multi agency group had been successful in reducing crime by improving street lighting, looking at landscaping and introducing CCTV. The group believes it has all the systems in place to ensure that any recommendations arising from the Commission will be debated and could be incorporated into policies and procedure to reduce violence against children.

Woking Borough Council Following a conference held in 1993 'Children's needs in Woking' – covering alcoholism, drug abuse in parents and its effects on children; domestic violence; sexual, physical, mental and ritual abuse; and children suffering from the death of a parent or having a parent who is chronically ill – various strategies are being considered including pre-school and after-school care support and holiday playschemes; education in the recognition of signs of abuse, both physical and psychological, for those who have daily contact with children; preventive education and comprehensive counselling services for both children and parents.

Woodspring The District Crime Targeting Team feels that the Government should implement the Morgan Report by giving statutory power to local authorities to work on crime prevention, and that lack of this currently hampers its work quite considerably.

Wychavon District Council Has just established a community safety working group with the local police divisions. It held a Community Safety Conference in 1994 to open up the initiative to a wider audience.

York City Council: Citizens Services Group Women's Working Group has recently agreed to set up a Domestic Violence Forum, and is hoping to launch a Zero Tolerance Campaign. It has also targeted support for some school youth service initiatives: funding a 'street corner with a roof' drop-in at a community school and provision of a basketball court in response to the wishes of a group of young children.

2 Area Child Protection Committees (ACPCs)

Letters sent to sample of 20 in England only: 8 responses

Question 1
Has the ACPC adopted a strategy for the reduction/prevention of violence to children? If so please send details. 7 x No : 1 x Yes

Question 2
Does the ACPC see itself as having a role in co-ordination of local prevention activities? 4 x No : 4 x Yes

Question 3
Does the Committee have views on how action to reduce/prevent violence involving children should be co-ordinated locally? If so, please explain and/or send relevant papers. 5 x No : 3 x Yes

Question 4
In your area is there co-ordination between your activities and those of any community safety/crime prevention programmes? If so please send details.
5 x No: 3 x Yes

Royal County of Berkshire ACPC Has a strategy on organised abuse, responding to what may have already happened. It held a training day on the process and agreed to improve the sharing of information to prevent further abuse to children. Education is represented on the ACPC and it is regularly updated on training in schools regarding bullying. It is planning a workshop which will take into account the interface between bullying abuse and disciplinary issues which inevitably arise.

Devon County Council ACPC Offers ongoing support for community safety programmes such as Kidscape and supports the activities of a local student theatre group which has produced a specific community safety programme for children in the North Devon area. This programme includes amongst its ambitions the prevention of violence towards children. The Committee continues to view the Multi-agency Handbook as the major information source to alert and educate the public to child protection issues. In this respect the Committee has always seen this document as having the widest possible use, and not merely as a procedural handbook to advise practitioners. All editions of this document have been given the widest possible circulation which has included distribution to the local libraries network and making the document available to a wide variety of voluntary and community based groups.

Dorset ACPC All schools in Dorset have appointed a designated teacher for child protection and they all receive one-day in-service training courses provided by the local education authority, the aims of which are to raise awareness about child abuse and to recognise signs and symptoms, to consider the role of other agencies and to consider the contribution of the curriculum in helping to prevent child abuse. The training includes inputs from local agencies. Dorset continues to encourage a multi-agency approach to training, to indicate a training and development perspective regarding issues of domestic and family violence, race, culture and equal opportunities.

Kent ACPC Does not have a separate strategy but many of the procedures, policies and initiatives have the aim implicit. Current examples include a leaflet and poster campaign designed to alert carers to the dangers of shaking young babies, and a sub-committee examining a county-wide inter-agency strategy for the development of primary prevention services.

Lancashire County Council ACPC Has set itself the task of producing a strategy for the reduction/prevention of violence to children as one of its 1994/95 objectives. The police have recently restructured and formed family protection teams.

Manchester City Council ACPC Sees the committee as having a role in co-ordination of local prevention activities and is hoping to address the issue in the near future. The education and health service reforms have not facilitated an effective or corporate response to issues generally, but the Chair has hopes that the situation is about to change.

Seeking children's and young people's views on how to reduce violence involving children

When organisations and individuals were asked to submit comments and other material to the Commission, we also asked whether they could in addition discuss the issues raised with children and young people themselves. Eighty organisations, mostly schools and youth projects around the UK, expressed interest. We wrote to them as follows:

'... We very much hope that you may be able to discuss the issues with children and young people, and let us have some record of their responses, either direct quotations or summaries. The enclosed brief questionnaire is intended simply to open a discussion. Because of the wide variety of groups that have offered to help, we do not feel it is useful to predict or limit the form of the discussions, but hope that the questions will provide some initial structure. As indicated on the questionnaire, we will assume that any response you send us is quote-able unless you specify that it is only for the eyes of the Commission members. Please indicate in your reply how any quotations used should be attributed.'

Questionnaire

A commission has been set up to find out how much violence there is to and by children and young people (aged up to 18) in the UK, and why some children and young people get involved in violence. The Commission will produce a report proposing ways of trying to reduce violence involving children – violence to them and by them.

The Commission is basing its work on the new United Nations Convention on the Rights of the Child: this charter has been accepted by the UK Government, and sets out detailed rights for children, including the right to protection from 'all forms of physical or mental violence', and a right to a say when decisions which affect them are being made.

The Commission wants to hear the views of children and young people themselves on violence and how to reduce or prevent it.

The following questions aim to get a discussion going. We hope that it will be used to get individual children and groups to consider the questions, and give the Commission their views and experiences. We do not want the questions to limit the discussion. We hope that you, or adults working with you, will send us your comments and ideas in any form. Unless you tell us that we cannot quote your reply, we will assume that we can use it in the Commission's final report.

CHILDREN, YOUNG PEOPLE AND VIOLENCE

Describe an incident of violence involving one or more children or young people which you have been involved in – as victim, as perpetrator or as spectator – at home, on the street, at school, at a club or anywhere else.

Should it have been avoided?

How could it have been avoided?

Why do you think some children and young people are more violent and bullying than others – for example in the school playground, in the street, in sport?

Why do you think boys and men are much more physically violent than girls and women?

Should this change, and if so how?

Do you think it is ever OK to hit animals, babies, toddlers, young children, teenagers, adults?

What do you think are ways of helping young children not to be violent, not to get involved in hurting brothers or sisters or friends, in street fights, in school bullying?

You may think of things that could/should be done by
- parents and the family
- schools
- local councils
- the media – TV and newspapers
- the government
- others

What could be done to stop adults being violent to children – at home, at school, anywhere else?

The response

Of the organisations approached, 35 returned responses. They included youth clubs, schools, a remand centre, semi-independent unit, secure unit, young offender institutions and probation services.

The Commission is very grateful to all the children and young people and those working with them for their responses.

Methods of eliciting responses

The questionnaire, in some cases adapted or extended, was handed out to groups in one or more sessions, and in most cases was filled in following some discussion of the issues. Some groups viewed programmes on bullying, or alternative methods of dealing with aggression. In some but not all cases the age and sex of the respondent was requested and recorded. Some groups used the questionnaire as the basis for discussion in small groups and compiled a resumé of responses; in others workers used the questionnaire as the basis for discussion with individuals and sent tapes and/or a summary. In particular Diana Lamplugh, of the Suzy Lamplugh Trust, encouraged schools to involve pupils in discussions, using an extended version of the questionnaire.

In view of the widely different groups involved and varying methods of discussion, we emphasise that the following summary can only give an impression of the responses. In addition, direct quotes from children and young people have been included in the text of Sections 1 and 2 of the report.

Number of individual responses: 523

Age range of respondents: 11-19 (majority aged between 12 and 16)

Number of males: 203; females: 150; sex undisclosed: 170.

Summary of responses to questionnaires

'Describe an incident of violence ...'

One third of respondents stated they had no incident to describe. Two-thirds of the respondents described incidents of some sort: half of them involved only children, a quarter only adults, and a quarter both adults and children. Sixty per cent described incidents in which they had been spectators, 30 per cent where they had been victims, and 10 per cent where they had been perpetrators. Twenty per cent took place in school, a small number in the home, and the remainder elsewhere.

Reasons for incidents, in descending order of prevalence

- Provoked or unprovoked fights between two people accounted for 40 per cent of incidents (bullying, and verbal harassment were very often the trigger to fighting)
- Groups picking on one person, or fighting each other (20 per cent)
- Alcohol (20 per cent)
- Incidents not described (10 per cent).

Individual incidents included: bullying, verbal harassment, sibling jealousy, siblings fighting, sexual harassment, adult hitting a child, family row/fight between adults. The majority of incidents were between males.

'Should the incident have been avoided, and if so how?'

The majority felt that increased intervention and vigilance from adults would help. It was clear that the respondents did not just mean more policing, but more interest and concern from adults in general. Next came a combination of not losing tempers, more self-control and not allowing oneself to be provoked. Not getting drunk came a clear third. Other responses included: talking about the problem; problem of groups 'egging on' individuals to fight.

Thirty per cent of respondents said the incident could not have been avoided because the perpetrators were 'determined to cause trouble', while a tiny minority clearly felt that the victim deserved all they got.

'Why are some children perceived to be more violent than others?'
Of the 90 per cent who responded to this question:

Thirty-five per cent suggested 'the home', with 'family problems' and 'insecurity' being the most frequently used additional detail; other suggestions were: 'background of violence', upbringing, type of discipline, neglected, unstable environment, parents' uncaring attitude. An additional 6 per cent suggested that the parents were 'hard' and encouraged the children to violent behaviour ('if you don't go and hit him back, I will hit you').

Other suggestions were:
- Wanting to prove themselves: 13 per cent; needing friends; wanting to fit in; males particularly needing to be part of 'a gang', 'macho' ; need to feel important; insecure
- Violence in videos, TV: 7 per cent
- Wanting to be a 'lad': 4 per cent
- Bullied or provoked by others: 4 per cent
- Attention seeking: 4 per cent
- Showing off: 3 per cent
- Alcohol: 3 per cent
- Nowhere to go: 2 per cent
- Retaliation because of comments on personal appearance: 2 per cent (colour of skin, fat, small).

'Why are boys and men much more physically violent than women?'
Ninety per cent confirmed that boys were more violent.

Reasons included: want to rule, impress, look macho (a high level of comments); find it hard to express emotions; no other mechanisms for resolving conflict; drink too much; girls try to talk it through.

Asked whether this should change, two-thirds believed it should, but a minority felt it would never change 'because there will always be violence'. There were a range of suggestions for change, mainly based on mediation, teaching males to talk through their problems, persuading society to stop stressing the 'macho' image; women should stand up for themselves more, but several girls expressed the concern that they should not become as violent as boys.

The small minority who believed girls were as violent or more violent not only stressed their tendency to be more verbally violent, but also as physically violent when fighting.

'Do you think it is ever OK to hit babies, toddlers, young children, teenagers, adults?'
Hit animals A high proportion (90 per cent) 'no', or only in self-defence; some felt 'only if they needed to be taught a lesson'.

Hit babies 90 per cent 'no'; the balance 'to teach them', a distinction was made between the 'light tap' and a 'beating'.

Hit toddlers and young children Over half 'no', but 'to teach them' becomes a more frequent comment, again the emphasis being on a smack not a beating.

Hit teenagers The majority responded 'no' except in self defence; a clear distinction was made between 'play-fighting' and 'hitting'.

Hit adults Again the majority responded 'no', but 30 per cent would in self defence with non-parental adults (the majority would not dream of hitting parents back, whatever the levels of violence to them). However in the summary of responses from the verbal discussions it appears a majority of the males said that if hit (beaten) they would leave home. All the respondents in one young offenders' institution for girls were victims of parental or family violence.

'What can be done to stop adults being violent to children –
at home, at school, anywhere else?'
Twenty per cent did not answer the question. eleven per cent suggested counselling; 11 per cent stricter laws and penalties; 5 per cent felt children should be encouraged to let other people know if they are being abused; 5 per cent suggested teaching adults parenting skills; 3 per cent wanted more adult intervention, protection and support of children.

Other suggestions included: government campaigns and direct involvement; adults shouldn't drink; schools should offer children more support; more helplines for children; supply children with weapons.

Five per cent said nothing could be done, and 6 per cent had no suggestions.

'What do you think are ways of helping young people and children
not to be violent?'
Thirty per cent did not answer the question, and 10 per cent said they could not think of ways.

Proposals included: talk it over with them, offer counselling, give them attention (27 per cent); teach parents to behave in a non violent way, teach parents not to be violent with their children, a secure family background of non violence, courses in non-violence for children and adults (17 per cent); teach them right from wrong, teach them that fighting or bullying is wrong, teach them that hitting people is wrong (14 per cent); adults to be good role models, adults to set good examples, adults to give a non-violent message, not to see adults being violent (11 per cent); less violence on TV, film and computer games (8 per cent); 'it's the way they are, you can't stop them' (7 per cent); show them what violence does to people, show them the consequences of violence, point out that it solves nothing (4 per cent); alter macho imagery for boys, do not give them (toy) guns (3 per cent); provide more leisure facilities (3 per cent).

Things that could be done by various parties/agencies:
parents and the family; schools; local councils;
the media – TV and newspapers; the government; others
45 per cent of respondents did not answer this question.

Of those that did, a significant number felt that all should be involved in promoting non-violence. In particular, parents, schools and local councils should work together to tackle the problem by sharing information and educating themselves as well as children; also, the media should be more actively involved in helping to educate.

Parents and the family (80 per cent) Talk and listen properly to children, be interested in your children, offer role models, ensure that children learn to socialise at an early date, teach them, 'because they (ie parents) are the people you listen to most and respect so they can teach you that violence is wrong.'

Schools (70 per cent) Stricter rules on bullying, listen to and support children.

Local councils (40 per cent) To supply more access to recreational facilities; set up street watch.

Media (30 per cent) Don't endorse violence on TV or films, stop implying that violence is 'hard' or 'cool', alter the watershed to 10 pm, promote anti-violence. There was a general impression that there was too much violence on the media ('makes violence look good'), but that on the whole it affected only those who were predisposed to act violently (one respondent said his younger brother had tried to stab him after watching a stabbing on TV). Parents should be more responsible for their children's viewing ie not allowing them to watch inappropriately age-labelled videos.

Government Was either not marked, or the frequent view was taken that they 'don't care', and are not seen as capable of or interested in doing anything; about 2 per cent suggested that the government should be involved by promoting stricter rules on bullying and child abuse, by supporting organisations and information campaigns in the fields of non-violence; by teaching mediation; by supporting counselling programmes.

Others (5 per cent) Encourage more intervention by adults and children; take children more seriously; 'if children are told that violence is wrong from an early age'; 'they should be taught how to keep safe without violence'; help friends not to resort to violence; voluntary organisations to visit schools.

List of those who provided information to Commission

The following are among those who made submissions, or provided information or advice to the Commission:

Access Committee for England, Margaret Mannion, Administrator

Action Against Abuse, Margaret Arnold, Honorary Secretary

Advancement of Residential Child Care, Tom White, Chair

Advisory Centre for Education

Alliance for South Carolina's Children, The, USA, Betsy Wolff, Executive Director

Amalgamated School Nurses' Association (ASNA), Lynette Thomas, Chairman

Amateur Boxing Association of England Limited, The

American Psychological Association

Archway Intermediate Treatment Centre, Sheffield, T J Galton, Intermediate Treatment Officer

Ashworth Hospital, Liverpool, Janice Miles, General Manager

Association for Jewish Youth, Martin Shaw, Executive Director

Association for Professionals in Services for Adolescents

Association of Chief Officers of Probation, Jill Thomas, Assistant General Secretary

Association of Chief Officers of Probation, Devon Probation Service, Family Court Welfare Committee, Gordon Read, Chair

Association of Chief Officers of Probation, South Yorkshire Probation Service, Jane Geraghty, Assistant Chief Probation Officer

Association of Chief Officers of Probation, South Yorkshire Probation Service, Ms C M Renouf

Association of Chief Police Officers, Assistant Chief Constable Marchant

Association of Chief Police Officers, ACPO Crime Committee, Detective Superintendent Maria Wallis, Staff Officer

Association of Child Psychotherapists, Dr Jill Hodges, Chair

Association of Directors of Social Services, Amanda Fry

Association of Educational Psychologists, Professional Policies Sub-Committee, Adrian Faupel, Chairperson

Association of County Councils, Stephen Campbell

Association of Metropolitan Authorities, Brian Jones

Association for Group and Individual Psychotherapy, Angela Kenny, Chair of the Council

Australian Institute of Criminology, Duncan Chappell, Director

Avon, County of, Social Services Department, Paul Clark, Senior Training Officer Vinney Green

Barlow, Jeanni, Education Consultant

Barnardos, Dr Helen Roberts, Co-ordinator, Research and Development

Barnardos, Roger Singleton, Senior Director

BASW (British Association of Social Workers), Ken Hawker, Assistant General Secretary Practice and Policy

BASW (British Association of Social Workers), Brian Littlechild, Chair, Justice Sub-Committee

Beaumont Leys School, Sue Eley, Deputy Head
Bedfordshire County Council, Social Services Department, T J Hulbert
Bedfordshire Police, A Stephenson, Force Child Protection Officer
Belfairs Community College, Leigh-on-Sea, Ms M E Younie, Principal, T C R Davies and
    M J Imms, Assistant Headteachers
Berkshire Probation, Berkshire Family Courts Welfare Service, Brian Harrington,
    Probation/Court Welfare Officer
Berkshire, Royal County of, Social Services Department, Christopher Brown, Children's
    Rights Officer
Berkshire, Royal County of, Social Services Department, Pauline Poynton, Child Protection
    Adviser
Berkshire, Royal County of, Woodley Social Services Centre, Janet Rose, Senior Care Manager
Berkshire, Royal County of, Maidenhead Social Services Centre, Ann Cole
Birmingham, University of, Department of Social Policy and Social Work, Professor
    Nicholas Deakin
Birmingham City Council, Social Services Department, Paul Sutton, General Manager
Birmingham City Council, Social Services Department, Children and Families Policy Unit,
    Neil Grant, Planning Officer
Blunkett, David, MP
Boarding Schools Association, Frank Bickerstaff, Secretary
Community Healthcare Bolton – NHS Trust, Bolton General Hospital, Department of Clinical
    Psychology, Helen Carlton-Smith, Clinical Psychologist and Joint Head of Specialism
Both Parents Forever, John Bell, Co-Director
Bourton, Annie, Guardian ad Litem
Bristol Mediation, Val Major, Co-ordinator
British Association for Community Child Health, Dr Tony Waterston, Convenor
British Association for Early Childhood Education (BAECE), Cynthia James, National Chair
British Association for the Study and Prevention of Child Abuse and Neglect, (BASPCAN),
    Judy Sanderson, National Office Administrator
British Association of Paediatric Surgeons
British Board of Boxing, Simon Block
British Board of Film Classification
British Broadcasting Corporation
British Deaf Association, Laraine Callow, Consultant to the Education and Training
    Department
British Medical Association, Dr E Armstrong, Secretary
British Medical Association, Scottish Office, Dr V H Nathanson, Scottish Secretary
British Paediatric Association, Paul Dunn, Secretary
British Paediatric Association, Professor Roy Meadows
British Psychological Society, The Division of Clinical Psychology, Pat Frankish, Chair
British Toys and Hobbies Manufacturers' Association, The
British Transport Police, Inspector Halton
Broadcasting Standards Council, Colin Shaw, Director
Broadcasting Standards Council, Andrea Millwood Hargrave, Research Director
Bryson House, Northern Ireland

Calderdale, Metropolitan Borough of, Social Services Department, Mrs M M E Denton,
    Director
Cambridgeshire Constabulary, Headquarters, Training Department, WDC 8 Julie Solley
Cambridgeshire County Council, Social Services Department, Tad Kubrisa, Director

Campaign against Violence, Stewart Willis
Cantonian High School, Cardiff, Mrs G Williams, Year 7 Tutor
Carers National Association, Sylvia Heal
Catholic Housing Aid Society, The, Robina Rafferty, Director
Center on Children, Families and the Law, University of Nebraska, Lincoln, USA,
    Brian L Wilcox, Director and Professor of Psychology
Central Council for Education and Training in Social Work
Central Lancashire, University of, Department of Psychology, Professor John Archer
Cheshire Probation Service, Andrew Taylor, Chief Probation Officer
Child Abuse Review, Dr Kevin Browne, Editor
Child Abuse Studies Unit, University of North London, Dr Liz Kelly, Research Officer
Child Accident Prevention Trust, Louise Pankhurst, Director
ChildLine, Hereward Harrison, Director of Counselling
Children in Scotland, Kay Tisdall, Policy Officer
Children in Wales
Children's Defense Fund, USA, James D Weill, General Counsel
Children's Family Trust, Alun Edwards, Parent
Children's Rights Development Unit, Gerison Lansdown, Director
Children's Rights Officers' Association, David Hodgson, Press and Information Officer
Children's Society, The, Ian Sparks, Director
Children's Society, The, Social Policy Unit, Roger Smith
Children's Society, The, Midlands Group Office, Celia Winter, Project Leader
Childwatch, Dianne Core, Founder and Director
Chinese Welfare Association, Northern Ireland, Deborah Gadd Martin, Co-ordinator
Chinese Welfare Association, Northern Ireland, Tony Chan, Secretary
'Choices for Children', Coventry, Barbara Plumb, Principal Worker
Churches' Commission for Racial Justice, Rev David Haslam, Associate Secretary
Citizenship Foundation, Jan Newton
City General Hospital, Stoke-on-Trent, Clinical Psychology Department, Olwyn McCubbin
Cleveland County Council, Development Unit, Julian Bird, Child Protection Co-ordinator
Cleveland Probation Service, Dr Philip Whitehead, Information Manager
Clwyd County Council, Social Services Department, Jackie Thomas, Principal Officer,
    Children and Family Services
Coleg Menai, Gwynedd, School of Business, GNVQ Advanced and Intermediate Business
    Groups
Commission for Racial Equality, Jean Coussins, Director Social Policy Division
Committee on the Administration of Justice, The Northern Ireland Civil Liberties Council,
    Liz Martin
Commonwork Land Trust, Jenifer Wates, Trustee
Community Development Centre, North Belfast, Northern Ireland, Marion de Frinse, Child
    Care Development Worker
Community Development Foundation, Paul Henderson, Director North of England
    and Scotland
Community Development Foundation, Gabriel Chanan
Community Service Volunteers (CSV), Elisabeth Hoodless, Executive Director
Conyngham High School, Kent, Year 8 pupils
Cornwall County Council, Social Services Department, D Richards, Assistant Director
Cotswold Community, The, John Whitewell, Principal
Coventry, City of, Education Department, Raymond Evans, Educational Psychologist
Craigavon and Banbridge Community Trust (Shadow), Louis Boyle, Director of Social
    Work/Children and Families

Crime Concern, Jon Bright, Director of Field Operations
Criminal Injuries Compensation Board
Crown Prosecution Service, Criminal Justice Policy Division Policy Group, Nicola Reasbeck
Croydon, London Borough of, Social Services Department, Fergus Smith, Project Manager
Croydon Playcare Company, The, Sue Dzendzera, Director
Crusaders, Olaf Fogwill, PR Support Manager
Cull, Mrs A P, Voluntary Worker in Mental Health
Cumbria Social Services, Child and Family Care South Division, Tony Bishop,
    Placement Manger,
Cumbria Probation Service, Ian White, Chief Probation Officer

Dalston Youth Project, June Jarrett, Director
Dartington Social Research Unit, Dr Michael Little
David Lewis Centre, The, H N M Thompson, Chief Executive
De Montfort University, Leicester, Dr Carole Sutton, Senior Lecturer in Psychology
Department of Education, Northern Ireland, Mrs W Montgomery, Co-ordination Branch
Department of Environment
Department of Health, Carolyn Davies, Senior Principal Research Liaison Officer
Department of Health, Research and Development Division, Angela Williams
Department of Health and Social Services, Northern Ireland, Child Care and Family Branch,
    Dr Bill Smith
Department of Health and Social Services, Northern Ireland, Social Services Inspectorate,
    R Orr, Social Services Inspector
Derby Junior Attendance Centre
Derbyshire County Council, Educational Psychology Service, Simon Priest, Educational
    Psychologist
Devon and Cornwall Constabulary, Community Involvement, Inspector A Bibey
Devon County Council, Social Services Department, J Randall, Policy Manager (Child Care)
Devon Youth Council, Richard Jennings, Co-ordinator
Diocese of Worcester Board for Social Responsibility, Youth Support Services, Roger Marshall,
    Manager
Divorce Conciliation and Advisory Service, Hilary Halpin, Director
Druglink North Staffs, Jane Christian
Durham County Council, Social Services Department, Michael Balmer, Acting Strategic
    Planning Officer - Children
Durham County Probation Service, John Howard, Assistant Chief Probation Officer
Durham Family Mediation, NCH Action for Children, Rick Bowler, Project Leader

Eating Disorders Association, Joanna Vincent, Director
Edinburgh Women's Aid
Equal Opportunities Commission
Erne Hospital, Enniskillen, David Bolton, Director of Community Care
Essex County Council, Education Department/North East Area Office, Mrs Molekamp,
    Educational Psychologist
European Union, General Direction 10
European Leisure Software Publishers' Association Limited
Evangelical Alliance, John Earwicker, Church Life Director and Chair of EA Children's
    Committee
Exploring Parenthood, Carolyn Douglas, Director

Family Covenant Association
Family Law Bar Association, The, Paul Coleridge QC, Secretary
Family Mediation Scotland, Maureen Lynch, Education Liaison Officer
Family Service Units, Adah Kay, Director
Farrington, David P, Professor of Psychological Criminology
Firearms Research and Advisory Service, Colin Greenwood
Foot, Anne
Football Association, The, David Davies, Director of Public Affairs
Foresight, The Association for the Promotion of Preconceptual Care, Belinda Barnes,
Frant Court, David Thirlaway, Principal and Director Frant Care Services
Friends United Network, Francesca Weinberg, Co-ordinator

General Registrar Office
General Synod of the Church of England, The, Board of Education, Rev Jonathan Roberts,
    National Youth Officer
General Teaching Council for Scotland, David Sutherland, Registrar
Glapton Primary School, Nottingham, Mrs C M Elkins, Headteacher
Glasgow University, Centre for Housing Research, Professor David Donnison
Godolphin and Latymer School, The, London, Year UIV
Grandparents' Federation, Noreen Tingle, National Secretary
Gray, Professor Peter, Professor Emeritus of Child Health, University of Wales
Greater Manchester Police, Divisional Police Headquarters, Chief Inspector Peter Sloan
Greenwich, London Borough of, Chief Executive's Department, Judy Wolfram, Head of
    Women's Equality Unit
Greenwich, London Borough of, Social Services Department, Gary Robinson, Adolescent
    Resource Manager
Greenwich, London Borough of, Youth and Community Section
Greenwood School, Essex
Guild of Psychotherapists
Gwent Constabulary, Superintendent J J Sanderson
Gwent County Council, Social Services Department, T S Bowen, Principal Officer
    (Social Work)
Gwynedd County Council, Social Services Department, Gethin Evans, Assistant Director of
    Social Services (Children)
Gwynedd County Council, Social Services Department, Group of Young People

Hammersmith and Fulham, London Borough of, Domestic Violence Forum, Kalpana Thakar
Hammersmith and Fulham, London Borough of, Social Services Department, Pam Mansell
HAPA (Handicapped Adventure Playgrounds Association), Mary Januarius, Information
    Officer
Haringey Council, Housing and Social Services, Andrew Turnbull, Youth Justice and Family
    Support
Havering, London Borough of, Social Services, Ben Brown, Head of Service, Children and
    Families
Health Education Board for Scotland, Ian Young, Programme Manager: Schools
Health Promotion Wales, Peter Farley, Director of Education and Training
Health Visitors' Association
Henley Safe Children Project, Lyn Carruthers, Community Development Worker
Hereford and Worcester Probation Service, Barry Johnson, Assistant Chief Probation Officer
Hertfordshire Constabulary

Hillingdon, London Borough of, Social Services Department, Middlesex Lodge, Brian Feldman, Centre Manager
HM Inspectorate of Prisons, His Honour Judge Stephen Tumim, HM Chief Inspector of Prisons
HM Prison Blakenhurst, Jim Farebrother, Senior Probation Officer
HM Prison Service, Headquarters, Suicide Awareness Support Unit, David Neal
HM YOC Glen Parva, Psychological Services, Jennifer Stepney, Higher Psychologist
HM Young Offender Institution and Remand Centre, Feltham, J Whitty, Governor
HM Young Offender Institution, Onley, D R George, GV Residential
HM Young Offender Institution, Rugby
Holmewood, Sunderland Social Services
Home and School Council, Mrs B Bullivant, Hon. Secretary
Home Office, CI Division, Rob Allen, Neil Bradley
Home Office, Crime Prevention Unit, Diana Greene
Home Office, D Division, Jennifer Flaschner
Home Office F8 Division, Mr Drummond and Chris Potter
Home Office, Research and Statistics Department, Croydon, Patrick Collier
Home Office, Research and Statistics Department, London, S1 Division, JP Batt, Paul Taylor
Home Office, Research and Statistics Department,Programme and Development Unit,
Home Office, Research and Planning Unit, Natalie Aye Maung, Research Officer
Home-Start UK, Sue Pope, Assistant Director
Howard League for Penal Reform, Frances Crook, Director
Humberside County Council, Education Department, A B Branwhite, Senior Educational Psychologist
Hyperactive Children's Support Group, Mrs I D Colquhoun, Honorary Chairman

Independent Schools Information Service
Inner London Probation Service, A E Leach, Deputy Chief Probation Officer
Institute for Public Policy Research, Anna Coote
Institute for Self-Analysis, The, Kate White, Secretary
Institute of Child Health
Institute of Criminology, Cambridge, University of, Professor David Farrington, Acting Director
Institute of Leisure and Amenity Management, Alan Smith, Director
Institute of Psychiatry, Department of Psychology, Professor William Yule, Professor of Applied Child Psychology, Head of Psychology Services
Institute of Race Relations, The, A Sivanandan, Director
Institute of United States Studies, University of London, Anna Brooke, Programme Officer
Islington Play Training Unit, Bridget Handscomb, Training Co-ordinator

Jenner Park County Primary School, G W Goode, Headteacher
Joint Council for the Welfare of Immigrants, Claude Moraes, Director
Juniper Green Primary School, Edinburgh, C Bennett, Headteacher

Kahan, Barbara
Keele, University of, Department of Politics, Dr Bob Franklin
Keele, University of, Department of Psychology, Michael Boulton, Lecturer in Psychology
Kent County Constabulary, Police Headquarters, Detective Chief Superintendent Blackburn
Kent County Constabulary, Specialist Crime, Detective Inspector Greg Barry, Vulnerable Victim Co-ordinator
Kent County Constabulary, Duke of Edinburgh , Students

Kent County Council, Social Services, Mary Gordon, Head of Service Standards - Children and
    Families
Kent County Council, Social Services Department, Peter Thomason, County Child Protection
    Co-ordinator
Kids' Clubs Network, Colette Kelleher, Head of Policy and Campaigns
Kids Moving On, NCH Newcastle, Dory Dickson, Co-ordinator KMO
Kidscape, Michele Elliott, Director
Kirkby Youth Club, David Matthews, Chairman
Kirklees Metropolitan Council, Social Services, Carole Smith, Service Manager Children
    and Families
Kirklees Metropolitan Council, Child Protection and Support Unit
Kurtz, Dr Zarrina

Lakeside Primary School, Cardiff, J A Williams, Headteacher
Lambeth, London Borough of, Social Services, David Pope, Director
Lancashire County Council, Social Services Department, Mrs M Hartley, County Child
    Care Manager
Law Commission, Brenda Hoggett
Law Society, The, Legal Practice Directorate, Jane Leigh, Secretary to the Family Law
    Committee
Law Society of Scotland, The, Micheal Clancy, Deputy Secretary
Lead Scotland, Elaine Burns, Administrative Officer
Leeds, University of, Division of Psychiatry and Behavioural Sciences Department, Professor A
    Sims, Professor of Psychiatry
Leeds City Council, Social Services Department, Anthony Mallinder, Principal
Leeds City Council, Corporate Projects Group
Leicestershire Constabulary, Support Services
Leicestershire Constabulary, PC Steve Parker, School/Youth Liaison Officer
Leicestershire County Council, Social Services Department, R C Parker, Divisional Manager
Leicestershire Probation Service, Roger McGarva, Assistant Chief Probation Officer
Lestor, Joan, MP
Liberty
London Boroughs Children's Regional Planning Committee, John Ogden, Principal Adviser
London Connection, The, Colin Glover, Director
London School of Economics and Political Science, Department of Sociology,
    Professor Paul Rock

Manchester, University of, Department of Social Policy and Social Work, Fiona Measham,
    Research Fellow
Mencap, E B McGinnis
Mental Health Foundation, Dr John Henderson, Director
Merseyside Youth Association Limited, young people
Metropolitan Police Service, Neil Fisher, Executive Officer
Metropolitan Police Service, Youth and Community Section, Southgate Police Station,
    Paul Gee, Community Involvement Officer - Haringey
Metropolitan Police Service, Solicitor's Department
Metropolitan Police Service, Child Protection Team
Mid Glamorgan Education Committee, Ysgol Gyfun Llanhari, Ann Taylor and Peter Griffiths
Middlesbrough Junior Mixed Attendance Centre, Cleveland, Inspector M P L Grey, Officer
    in Charge

MIND, National Association for Mental Health, Judi Clements, National Director

Minsthorpe High School and Community College, Mrs B A Mawtus, Deputy Head Year 11 and young people

Mothers Against Murder And Aggression (MAMAA), Celestina Schofield, Director

Murray, Christine, Principal Solicitor Child Care, Lancashire County Council and Vice Chairman Child Concern

NACRO, National Association for the Care and Resettlement of Offenders, Kimmett Edjan

NAFSIYAT Inter-Cultural Therapy Centre, L K Thomas, Clinical Director/Principal Psychotherapist

National Alliance of Women's Organisations, Joan Woodward, Psychotherapist

National Association for the Prevention of Child Abuse and Neglect (NAPCAN), Australia

National Autistic Society, The, Phil Druce, Director, Development and Outreach

National Childminding Association (NCMA), Gill Haynes, Director

National Children's Bureau

National Children's and Youth Law Centre, Australia, Robert Ludbrook, Director

National Coalition Building Institute, Val Carpenter, Director

National Consumer Council

National Council of Voluntary Child Care Organisations (NCVCCO), Virginia Burton

National Family Mediation, Thelma Fisher, Director

National Foster Care Association, Scottish Office, Susan Clark, Scottish Officer

National Foundation for Educational Research in England and Wales

National Institute for Social Work, Daphne Statham, Director

National Institute for Social Work, Research Unit, Dr Jan Pahl, Director of Research

National Society for the Prevention of Cruelty to Children, The (NSPCC), headquarters staff and regional offices

National Youth Agency, Janet Paraskeva, Director

NCH Action for Children, Sandy Ruxton

Nexus Institute Northern Ireland (Northern Ireland Rape Crisis Association), Dominica McGowan, Director

NHS Cymru Wales, Gwynedd Community Health Unit, Dr R H Davies, Consultant Community Paediatrician

Norfolk Constabulary, Inspector Bealey, Staff Officer

North Yorkshire Probation Service, M B Murphy, Assistant Chief Probation Officer

Northamptonshire Probation Service, R Kay

Northern Ireland Council for the Curriculum Examinations and Assessment, Belfast

Northern Ireland Council for Travelling People, Maria Farry, Co-ordinator

Northern Ireland Intermediate Treatment Association, The Northside Project, David Weir, Senior Social Worker

Northern Ireland Office, Criminal Justice Services Division, Paul Skitt

Northern Ireland Women's Aid Federation, Karen McMinn, Regional Management Co-ordinator

Northumberland County Council, Social Services, Gordon Nicholson, Juvenile Justice Team Manager

Northumbria Police, Detective Chief Superintendent Stewart

Northumbria Probation Service, Paddy J Doyle, Senior Probation Officer

Northumbria Probation Service, young people

Norwood Child Care, Ruth Fasht, Director of Social Services

Nottinghamshire County Council, Social Services Department

Nuffield Foundation, The, Patricia Thomas, Deputy Director

Nugent Care Society, The, John Kennedy, Director
Nugent Care Society, The, St. Catherine's Centre for Girls

Office of the Commissioner for Children, New Zealand
Oliver, Dr J E
OPCS, Office of Population Censuses and Surveys
Optimum Health Services, Newcomen Centre, Guy's Hospital, Dr Margaret Lynch, Senior
    Lecturer in Community Paediatrics
Ormiston Trust, The, 92 Stretten Avenue, Olga Foottit
Oxfordshire County Council, Social Services, Health Division, Jenny Lee,
    Team Manager
Oxfordshire County Council, Social Services, Independent Inspection Unit, Roger Morgan,
    Chief Inspector
Oxfordshire Probation Service, Susan Toner, Assistant Chief Probation Officer
Oxfordshire Probation Service, Eddie Procter, Research Officer

Parent to Parent Information on Adoption Services, Mrs P M E Morrall
Parents Advice Centre, Londonderry, Pip Jaffa, Director
Parkside Health, Dr Marion Miles, Consultant Community Paediatrician
Pathway-to-Recovery Trust, The, Ken Grigor, Director
PCCA Child Care (Promoting Christian Care and Action), David Pearson, Director
PLANET (Play Leisure Advice Network), Judy Denziloe, Project Manager
Play Link, Sandra Melville, Director
Play Matters (The National Association of Toy Libraries Association), Phillipa Barton,
    Hon Fundraising Administrator
Play Wales, Beverly Noon, Director
Playtech, Stephen Rennie, Company Secretary
Plymouth Attendance Centre, Devonport High School for Girls, J M Pengelly,
    Officer-in-Charge
Poets' Corner Family Centre, Colin Hooker, Project Leader
Portman Clinic, Dr Judith Freedman, Consultant Psychotherapist
Powys Health Authority, Brecon Hospital, Dr C B Vulliamy, Consultant Paediatrician
Primarolo, Dawn, MP
Prison Officers' Association
Prison Reform Trust, Adam Sampson, Deputy Director
Probation in Cornwall, Mrs G C Kendall, Assistant Chief Probation Officer
Professional Association of Teachers, Jackie M Miller, Deputy General Secretary
Professional Association of Teachers, Geoffrey Carver, Professional Officer (Education)

Quaker Peace Education Project, Londonderry, John Lampen

Ravenswood Primary School, Newcastle upon Tyne
Refugee Council, The, Ros Finlay, National Adviser Health and Social Services
Re-Solv, Jonathan McVey
Regional Forensic Adolescent Psychiatry Service, Manchester
Religious Society of Friends, Quaker Peace and Service, Marigold Bentley, Education Adviser
Right from the Start, Sarah Woodhouse, Executive Director
Robertson, Dr P D, Consultant Physician, Children's Panel Advisory Group
Rosenbaum, Martin
Royal College of General Practitioners, Dr Mollie McBride, Honorary Secretary of Council

Royal College of Midwives Trust, Joan McDowall

Royal College of Nursing, Jane Naish, Community Health Adviser

Royal College of Physicians, June Lloyd, Paediatric Vice-President

Royal College of Psychiatrists, The, Dr F Caldicott, President

Royal College of Psychiatrists, The, Andrea Woolf, Committees Officer

Royal Free Hospital, Department of Child and Adolescent Psychiatry, Dr Dora Black,
Consultant Child and Adolescent Psychiatrist and Director of Child Psychological
Trauma Clinic

Royal Hull Hospitals, Hull Royal Infirmary, Dr John Gosnold, Clinical Director, Accident
and Emergency

Royal National Institute for Deaf People, The

Royal National Institute for the Blind, The, Lillian Lawson, Service Director

Royal Ulster Constabulary, The, Belfast, Dr D R Jones, Force Statistician

Royal Ulster Constabulary, Londonderry, Child Abuse and Sexual Offences Unit,
Inspector Andrew Bailey

Rural Development Commission, Rural Services Branch, Toby Johns

Ryton Comprehensive School, Tyne and Wear, Year 9 Communications

Salford Health Authority, Regional Forensic Adolescent Psychiatry Service, Dr Susan Bailey,
Consultant Adolescent Forensic Psychiatrist

Samaritans, The, Su Ray, Information Officer

Child and Family Psychiatrist

Sandwell Metropolitan Borough Council, Department of Social Services, Child Protection
Unit, Karen Stone, Manager

Saunders, Margaret E, Head of CPR and M Service Sunderland

Save the Children, Bill Bell, Assistant Director (Policy and Research) UK and European
Programmes

Save the Children, Michael Taylor, Director UK and European Programmes

Save the Children, Care and Justice Yorkshire, Deirdre Quill

Save the Children, Northern Ireland Division, Diarmuid Kearney, Assistant Divisional Director

Save the Children, Northern Ireland Division, Margaret Kelly, Social Policy Worker

Save the Children, Scotland

School Library Association, Valerie Fea, Executive Secretary

Scottish Child Law Centre, Deirdre Watson, Director

Scottish Council for Civil Liberties

Scottish Council for Spastics, M Martin, Social Services Manager

Scottish Health Visitors' Association, David Forbes, General Secretary

Scottish Law Commission, Dr E M Clive

Scottish Office, The, Social Work Services Group, J W Sinclair

Scottish Office, The, N G Campbell

Scottish Secondary Teachers' Association, Alan Lamont, Acting General Secretary

Scottish Traveller Education Project, Elizabeth Jordan, Co-ordinator and Lecturer in Special
Educational Needs

Scottish Women's Aid, Shirley Cusack and Claire Houghton, National Workers -
Children's Rights

Sefton Social Services Department, Dennis Charlton, Child Protection Consultant

Selly Oak Hospital, Dr L M Winkley, Consultant Child Psychiatrist

Serota, Baroness, of Hampstead

Shooting Sports Trust Ltd., The

Shoreditch and Hackney Police, Chief Inspector Robert Anthony

Sims, Roger, MP

Society for Public Health, The, Dr P A Gardner, Hon Secretary

Solihull Metropolitan Borough Council, Social Services Department, Michael Hake

South Glamorgan County Council, Child Protection Training, Sylvia Banks, Training
Co-ordinator

South Glamorgan County Council, Phil Harris, Assistant Director, Adolescent Services/
Youth Justice

South Somerset Petty Sessional Division, Youth Court Panel Committee, Mrs E A Melvin,
Chairman

South Yorkshire Probation Service, Darrell Fisher, Probation Officer

Southampton, University of, Department of Social Work Studies, Dr Ann Buchanan,
Lecturer in Social Work Studies

Southwark Diocese Social Responsibility Department, Wel-Care Service for Parents and
Children, Denise Mumford, Director

Spicer, Dr Faith

Sport for all Clearing House, Sports Information Service, Albert Remans, Executive Director

Sports Council, The, Young People and Sport Development Unit, Roger Davis

Spurgeon's Child Care, H R Minty, Director - Operations

St. Helens Family Centres, Patsy Southwell, Project Leader

St. James' University Hospital, Department of Community Paediatrics, Dr C J Hobbs,
Consultant Community Paediatrician

St. Luke's Hospital, Department of Child Clinical Psychology, Linda Walker

St. Piers, Lingfield, Surrey, Gerald Loney, Principal Care Officer

Staffordshire County Council, Social Services Department, Ms C Walby, Director

Staffordshire Police, Chief Constable's Office, Community Services, Chief Superintendent
K S Perrin

Standing Conference on Public Health, Miriam Knight

Standish, Elizabeth, Member of the Severnside Institute for Psychotherapy

Stepping Stones in Scotland, Isobel Lawson, Director

Strathclyde, University of, Division of Education and Psychology, Dr Gerry Finn,
Senior Lecturer

Strathclyde Regional Council, Department of Reporter to the Children's Panel,
Frederick Kennedy, Regional Reporter, Headquarters Level

Strathclyde Regional Council, Social Work Department, Mark Wilson, Community
Psychologist

Strathclyde Resource Unit

Stutz, Elizabeth, Founder and President for Life of Play for Life

Suffolk Constabulary, Administration Department

Suffolk Probation Service, A J Barrow, Chief Probation Officer

Sunderland Social Services, young people

Surrey County Council, Education Services, David Saunders, Curriculum Development
Manager

Surrey County Council, Social Services Department, Graham Gatehouse, County Director

Surrey County Council, Social Services Department, Children and Family Services,
Dr John Beer, Head

Surrey Police, Youth Affairs, Inspector Peter Nightingale

Sussex Police, R J N Childs, T/Assistant Chief Constable

Suzy Lamplugh Trust, The, Diana Lamplugh, Director

Sutton, London Borough of, Housing and Social Services, Annie Shepperd, Assistant Director

Swadlincote Police Station, PC 1607 Sund, Officer-in-Charge

TACADE (The Advisory Council on Alcohol and Drug Education), Jeffrey Lee, Chief Executive

Thames Valley Police, Slough Attendance Centre, Graham Widdows, Officer-in-Charge

Tavistock Clinic, The, Child and Family Department, Professor I Kolvin

Tavistock Clinic, The, Child and Family Department, Gill Gorell Barnes, Clinical Lecturer in Social Work

Tavistock Clinic, The, Child and Family Department, Juliet Hopkins, Consultant Child Psychotherapist

Tavistock Clinic, The, Child and Family Department, Dr Judith Trowell

Tavistock Clinic, The, Tavistock and Portman Clincs Special Committee, Dr Sebastian Kraemer, Consultant Child and Family Psychiatrist

Thomas Coram Research Unit, Professor Harry McGurk, Director

Thomas, David

Tomlinson, T, Personal Development, Counselling and Training Consultant

Toynbee Hall, Children and Families with Special Needs Department, Bob Le Vaillant, Director, and young people

Trafford Metropolitan Borough Council, Social Services, Glen Mason, Service Manager (Child and Family)

Trent College, Nottingham, J S Lee, Headmaster

Trust for the Study of Adolescence, Dr John Coleman, Director

Tuormaa, Tuula, Researcher and Writer on Clinical Ecology and Nutritional Medicine

Ulster, University of, Centre for the Study of Conflict, Ed Cairns, Professor of Pychology

UNICEF UK, Robert D Smith, Executive Director

UNISON, Local Government Service Group, John Findlay, Assistant National Officer

United Kingdom Sports Association, Roger Briggs, Director

Unityne Health

University College London, Faculty of Laws, Professor Michael Freeman

Van der Eyken, Willem

Victim Support, Jane Cooper, Development Officer

Violence, Abuse, and Gender Relations Research Unit, University of Bradford, Dr Catherine Itzin, Honorary Research Fellow

Violence, Abuse, and Gender Relations Research Unit, University of Bradford, Jalna Hanmer and Dr Jeff Hearn, Co-Convenors

Violence Research Unit, University of Wales, School of Social and Administrative Studies, Professor Rebecca Dobash and Dr Russell Dobash

Voluntary Service Belfast, Northern Ireland

Volunteer Centre UK, Andrea Kelmanson, Director

Warwick, University of, Department of Applied Social Studies, Norma Baldwin, Senior Lecturer

Wales Advocacy Unit, Principal Advocacy Officer

Wales, University of, College of Medicine, Professor J R Sibert

Wales, University of, School of Education, Professor Edward Melhuish, Professor of Human Development

Waltham Forest, Social Services Children and Family Division, Liz Tunnicliffe, Planning and Service Development Manager

Weitzman, Anne

Welsh Office, Social Services Inspectorate Wales, J F Mooney, Deputy Chief Inspector

Welsh Women's Aid, Sarah Williams, National Child Work Co-ordinator

West Sussex County Council, Social Services Department, Roger Mortimore, Director
West Sussex Probation Service, Youth Court Services Team, Terry Bishop, Manager
West Yorkshire Probation Service, Paul Wilson, Deputy Chief Probation Officer
West Yorkshire Police, Superintendent C P Bennett
Western, Mrs R
White and Sherwin, Solicitors, Richard White
Who Cares? Trust, Tory Laughland, Director
Winchester Health Authority, Community Unit, Dr Tony Saunders, Consultant in Child and
    Adolescent Psychiatry
Wisconsin, University of, USA, School of Social Welfare, Professor Adrienne Haeuser
Women's Aid Federation England Ltd, Thangam Singh, National Children's Officer
World Health Organisation, Division of Mental Health, Dr J Orley, Senior Medical Officer

Yorkhill NHS Trust, Community Child Health Services, Dr June Ross, Consultant
    Paediatrician in Community Child Health
Young Abusers Project, Child and Family Department of The Tavistock Clinic, Martin
    Williams, Project Manager and Dr Eileen Vizard, Clinical Director and Consultant Child
    Psychiatrist

Index

abduction of children 257, 259
abuse *see* child abuse; sexual abuse of children
accidents
    prevention 23, 155-6, 157
    road accidents 156, 180
ACPCs *see* Area Child Protection Committees
Action for Sick Children 156
adults
    preventing violent behaviour 84, 248-50
    protecting children from violence 84, 248-50
    violent behaviour by 40, 64-5
        and youthful violence 11, 35-6
    see also parents
aggression, positive forms of 81
aggressive toys 26, 213-14
air guns 22, 224, 225, 226
alcohol
    abuse 12, 17, 25, 67-8, 195-7
        and suicide 190, 192, 195-6
    consumption 67
    pre-natal exposure to 45
antisocial behaviour 33, 39, 91
APA (American Psychological Association)
        Commission on Violence and Youth
        (1993) 33-4
    on availability of firearms 55
    on biological factors 44
    on family influence 35, 46
    on inequality 57
    on schools 139
    on society's attitude to violence 54
    on television violence 71
    on temperament 39
    on delinquent gangs 62
Area Child Protection Committees (ACPCs)
        97, 98, 101, 102-3, 104, 105, 185,
        216, 267
    letters sent to 284-5

assaults on children 260
    sexual 261-2
Australian National Committee on Violence
        33, 229
    on biological factors 43
    on boxing 222
    on drug use 67-8
    on family break-up 47
    on mental illness 63
    on personality traits 40
    and promotion of non-violent attitudes 87
    on school influences 59-60, 139
    on society's attitude to violence 54
    on television violence 70-1

babies
    and health visiting 152-3
    infanticide 187
    risk of homicide for 10, 31, 184, 261
benefit levels 23
Beresford, Sir Paul 100
biological factors 41-3
    environmental or acquired 44-5
'birthrights contract' 119
boxing 22, 54, 218, 220-3
brain function
    conditions affecting 42-3
    and violence behaviour 11
brain injury
    and accidents 155, 157
    and boxing 54
    and violent behaviour 44-5
Bulger, James, murder of 31, 107, 109, 172,
        202
bullying 10, 12, 22, 35, 59, 140
    anti-bullying strategies 83, 91, 143-5, 153
    and conduct disorders 66
    Elton Inquiry on 61-2
    and head teachers 60, 61